# Breaking Twitter

Ben Mezrich is the *New York Times* bestselling author of *The Accidental Billionaires* (adapted by Aaron Sorkin into the David Fincher film *The Social Network*), *Bringing Down the House* (adapted into the number one box office hit film *21*), *The Antisocial Network*, and many other bestselling books. His books have sold over six million copies worldwide, and he is one of the world's leading business narrative writers.

# Breaking Twitter

**ELON MUSK and the
MOST CONTROVERSIAL
CORPORATE TAKEOVER
in HISTORY**

# Ben Mezrich

MACMILLAN
BUSINESS

First published 2023 by Grand Central Publishing,
a division of Hachette Book Group, Inc.

First published in the UK 2023 by Macmillan Business
an imprint of Pan Macmillan
The Smithson, 6 Briset Street, London EC1M 5NR
*EU representative:* Macmillan Publishers Ireland Ltd, 1st Floor,
The Liffey Trust Centre, 117–126 Sheriff Street Upper,
Dublin 1, D01 YC43
Associated companies throughout the world
www.panmacmillan.com

ISBN 978-1-0350-3246-4 HB
ISBN 978-1-0350-3247-1 TPB

1 3 5 7 9 8 6 4 2

A CIP catalogue record for this book is available from the British Library.

Interior book design by Timothy Shaner, NightandDayDesign.biz

Printed and bound by CPI Group (UK) Ltd, Croydon, CR0 4YY

Visit **www.panmacmillan.com** to read more about all our books
and to buy them. You will also find features, author interviews and
news of any author events, and you can sign up for e-newsletters
so that you're always first to hear about our new releases.

*For Tonya, proof that this is all one wonderful simulation. I'm the luckiest NPC in the game.*

# A Note from Bestselling Author Ben Mezrich

**Breaking Twitter** is a dramatic narrative account of one of the most unique and fascinating corporate takeovers in history, based on dozens of interviews, multiple first-person sources, and thousands of pages of documents. Though there are different and often contentious opinions about some of the events in the story, to the best of my ability, I re-created the scenes in the book based on the information I uncovered. Some dialogue has been reimagined, and the dates of some of the events have been adjusted or compressed. Also, at some points in the story I employ elements of satire. In some instances, composite characters have been created or descriptions and character names have been altered at the request of my sources to protect privacy.

This is not an authorized narrative of the events surrounding Elon Musk's takeover of Twitter—as was his wont, Elon chose not to respond to requests for his participation. I can only imagine that this is not a version of the story Elon would be eager to see told: a narrative that isn't just about the ends, but about the means used to get there, and the consequences of those actions. Scenes and comments from Elon's perspective are triangulated from various inside sources, and are based on my own speculation as well as deep reporting.

I've been an avid Twitter user since November 2008. I've watched the site grow from a scrappy start-up to one of the most important social media sites online, with an outsized imprint on culture, journalism, and politics. When the news of Elon Musk's interest in the site first broke—on Twitter, of course—I was instantly intrigued. To me, Elon is one of the most complex characters I've ever encountered: one of the richest men on Earth, the brilliant entrepreneur behind Tesla and SpaceX, and at the same time, the most outspoken "troll" on the internet, a man who seemed as comfortable baiting the Securities and Exchange Commission with humorous memes as he did running a trillion-dollar company.

Even so, I never could have predicted the wild, and sometimes absurd, dramatic turns that ensued as he set his sights on Twitter. From the serpentine road that led up to Elon's takeover of the platform, to insiders' accounts from within the San Francisco headquarters as the billionaire took control and began his chaotic first few weeks, to the much wider political and cultural implications of the privatization of our global town hall, *Breaking Twitter* is populated by outsized personalities with polarizing ideologies.

I believe it is one of the most important and thrilling stories I've ever told, the incredibly public, sometimes darkly comic battle between one of the most influential men of our time and the platform that sits at the center of our shared conversation.

# Breaking
# Twitter

# November 29, 2022

**Ten minutes past midnight** on a Monday in late November, one of those crisp San Francisco evenings where the breeze sweeping up from the bay hit with the subtlety of a fist bristling with razor blades, Esther Crawford found herself in a dimly lit conference room, desperately trying to talk the richest man in the world out of starting the Silicon Valley equivalent of World War III.

It was just the two of them, alone and next to one another at a ridiculously long, rectangular table that sliced through the center of the tenth floor of Twitter's main headquarters. Esther had her laptop open in front of her, the screen casting a cone of light across her porcelain skin. Elon Musk, hovering over her right shoulder, was in shadow, his wide, square face, impish eyes, and ever-present smirk barely lit by the fluorescent ceiling panels high above. Beyond the table stood a wall of glass that had once looked out onto the bustle of the rest of the floor, an open design that encourages a collaborative culture that the company had once been known for. After choosing the space as one of his preferred roosts, one of the first things Elon had done was to frost the glass—unintentionally transforming the once-lively room into a dark, cavelike bunker. During the day, the change was subtle, a muted glow from the office beyond; but at night, ominous shadows crept over the ergonomic furniture and lacquered wood fixtures.

Esther had been in the bunker since noon. Though colleagues had filed in and out during the day, she had been mostly on her own since sundown, when the view from the windows on the other side of the room had shifted from a vibrant cityscape of marble, glass, and steel, and the San Francisco State House offset by a pincushion of office buildings, to little more than a sea of flickering lights struggling against an ink-black sky.

She was hungry and tired, and hadn't slept more than a few hours over the past forty-eight; she had just been contemplating heading home to her husband and three kids when Elon had wandered in, ten minutes before, flanked by his two hulking bodyguards, who were now positioned just outside the conference room door, like oversized gargoyles.

It wasn't out of character for Elon to stop by the conference room without notice, even at odd hours of the evening. For weeks now, he'd been living in Twitter's headquarters, sleeping on a couch in the library on the eighth floor until someone had carted a handful of beds up the service elevators for the billionaire and his team. Nor was it abnormal for him to meet one-on-one with Esther, even though she wasn't officially upper management, and before the takeover she had been low enough on the chain of command that she'd have more likely found herself with the gargoyles on the other side of the frosted glass.

Her life had taken some dramatic turns in the past four weeks, since Elon had famously walked through Twitter's front doors carrying a kitchen sink—"let that sink in"—and Esther was now, arguably, one of the most important people at the company. She might not have officially been in Elon's "inner circle," which was comprised almost entirely of middle-aged men, friends from outside Twitter; but she was one of the few people left at the company who had a direct line of communication with the mercurial, self-described "Chief Twit." That put her in the privileged, and often terrifying, position of being the person in the room tasked with steering Elon away from the edges of cliffs he seemed so particularly fond of racing toward.

Tonight, it seemed, was going to be another one of those moments.

He'd burst into the room, crossing the conference area in three determined steps. The nearest chair to Esther had happened to be a miniature design piece that someone had wheeled over from a privacy alcove by the windows, and it took Elon an extra beat to stuff his boxy, six-foot-two frame into the confining apparatus. With arms and legs tucked awkwardly in front of him like a praying mantis, he'd launched right into it, continuing a conversation that had begun almost two days earlier. His tone had remained controlled, his volume low, but Esther had been able to tell from the start that he was already headed toward that cliff. If she didn't act quickly, there was a real chance he was going to barrel right over the edge.

It didn't help that the issue that had him so worked up at midnight on a Monday had begun as a simple misunderstanding. During the weeks she'd worked with the billionaire, she'd learned that at his core, he wasn't driven by facts or expertise, but by instincts and intuition. Neither did it matter that in her heart, Esther actually agreed with Elon's take on the situation, and shared his frustration: the system he had run up against was clearly unfair, and possibly even legally untenable.

But she was also certain that the decision Elon was heading toward, at breakneck speed, publicly declaring war on *Apple*, the world's biggest tech company—and barely a month into his tenure at the helm of Twitter—would end in disaster.

To be fair, Elon wasn't the first CEO to balk at Apple's weighty fee structure, which took a 30 percent tithe on any in-app purchases made by customers; nor was he the first entrepreneur to have been under the illusion that he'd be able to work around this seemingly usurious fee by sending subscribers through a custom system of his own design. But when it had been made clear to him, in a meeting two days before in this very room—the long table sparsely attended by what remained of Twitter's upper-level marketing and sales department—just how binding Apple's payment structure was, Elon's face had blanched, and his eyes had begun to blaze. Clearly, he didn't see Apple's fees as a simple, heavy-handed, profit-driven business strategy; to Elon, Apple's behavior was a direct affront to his belief system of innovation, freedom, and competition.

At first, Esther had done her best to just listen to Elon's concerns, acting as a sounding board. Maybe, despite his dismay at Apple's policies, the rational portion of his brain would take over and he'd come to the conclusion that it was simply a noxious pill Twitter would have to continue to swallow. But very quickly, it had become clear that Elon wasn't interested in accepting the status quo. By their third conversation on the subject, he'd told her that he intended to fight Apple, make it a legal battle, bring it all the way to the Supreme Court if necessary. Sensing that he was beginning to spiral, Esther had offered a potential solution; what they really wanted to do was divert Twitter's paying customers to the web, and away from Apple's platform—but Elon had immediately shut that idea down. The web, he had exclaimed, was an insecure place for payments; pushing paying subscribers toward the web would open Twitter up to bot attacks, a fear so antiquated that it had caught Esther by surprise. She'd tried, gently, to explain the safety of modern web payments. Esther herself had been on the team that had integrated Stripe as Twitter's payment provider—to which Elon had icily replied, "I know more about payments than any of you."

To better make the point, he'd demanded that Twitter immediately turn off all web subscription. Meaning, from that moment on, the only way anyone could make a payment to Twitter was via the app—primarily, via Apple. To Esther, this had been a bad business decision, stemming from paranoia. But she'd also realized that she herself had misstepped; rather than attempting to steer Elon away from that ephemeral edge, she'd confronted him—which had only sent him hurtling further forward.

There was a *right* way to handle Elon, and more important, a decidedly *wrong* way to handle Elon. And it wasn't simply experience that had taught Esther this maxim; the day after she'd first met the billionaire, she'd been taken aside by a member of his entourage—the impressive young COO of his Boring Company, Jehn Balajadia, who in recent weeks had become Elon's main operational liaison.

"You should know some things," Jehn had told her, after sitting her down in a quiet corner of the headquarters. "Elon is a very special guy, and as someone who is going to be close to him, your job is to help take care of him, protect him, to make things go well for him. The world is going to want to get in through you, and you need to be really careful from now on. . . ."

In the previous few weeks, Esther had experimented with different ways to communicate with the billionaire, and had found that what worked best was a combination of humor and appeal to ego. What Elon seemed to love the most were memes, emailed to him at night (never in the morning), the edgier the better; what he feared most was anything that might damage his public reputation. For years, he had been known to most of the world as a genius, one of the greatest entrepreneurs in history. Since his takeover of Twitter, though, the conversation surrounding him had shifted in a decidedly negative direction, and he was extremely sensitive as to how people viewed him.

Over the past few days, as Elon had become more entrenched in seeing Twitter's battle with Apple in ideological terms, Esther had attempted to use humor to placate the billionaire—sending him meme after meme poking fun at Apple, their fee structure, whatever she could think of that might defuse his growing vitriol. But just glancing at his Twitter account from the past twenty-four hours, she could see that her strategy was failing.

Calling Apple politically "biased" in a tweet to his one hundred million-plus followers, Elon had further expounded that *"Apple has mostly stopped advertising on Twitter. Do they hate free speech in America?"* He'd accused Apple of threatening to *"withhold Twitter from its App Store."* Worse yet, at seven a.m. that very morning, he'd tweeted an image of a highway dominated by an exit sign offering two choices: *"Pay 30%"* accompanied by an arrow pointing straight ahead, and a left turn signal aiming toward *"Go To War."* Though he'd since deleted the *"Go To War"* tweet, it was clear the idea had lodged itself in his mind.

Rocking slightly in the minuscule chair next to Esther, he was almost rambling now, deep in a monologue about Apple's authoritarian behavior. How their in-app fees were a form of robbery, proof of their monopoly over the tech sector; how they needed to be broken up, fought legally. Then he began to go further, testing what she perceived to be another potential tweetstorm, setting off alarm bells within Esther that had her sitting straight up in her chair. He began talking about rallying his followers to go after Apple, not just online, but IRL, some sort of loosely defined protest at Apple's headquarters. She could hardly believe she was hearing him right—he was essentially talking about sending people with pitchforks over to Cupertino.

Now she knew she had to act quickly. This path would not only have serious repercussions for Twitter's future, but also wider implications that might destabilize the entire tech sector. A war between Twitter and Apple wasn't an act of genius; it would be more akin to madness, and would surely tarnish the reputations of both companies.

She put her hands down on the table and rose out of her seat, all four foot eleven inches of her, now eye to eye with the mantislike entrepreneur. Then she laid it out in a way that Elon would understand. Twitter 1.0, as Elon had been calling the past regime, had left skeletons in Twitter's closets that made a war with Apple unwinnable. So through no fault of his own, Apple had the billionaire by the balls.

Specifically, Twitter 1.0 had done a very poor job of monitoring adult content on the platform. In fact, pornography was a much bigger driver of engagement than anyone in former management would have cared to admit. It was a "don't ask, don't tell" side of the business. Even worse, it was no secret that over the years, there had been an even darker, and continuous infiltration of the platform: child porn, which had proliferated despite the best efforts of Twitter's security and moderation teams to snuff it out.

Not only did Apple know about Twitter's adult content and its troubles with child porn; since the Twitter app ran primarily through them, *they must have the receipts.* If Elon went to war with Apple, they might use these receipts against him. Apple could remove Twitter from their platform, as Elon had tweeted—but not for violating a payment issue. They could go after Elon with real dirt, adult content and *child porn,* sullying him in a way that would resonate on the world stage.

For the first time since he'd sat down at the conference table, Elon went silent as she finished speaking, staring at her as she stood next to him. Then he finally shook his head.

"That was before I was in charge. None of that was my fault."

"But you're in charge now," Esther responded.

She realized she was trembling. Another beat passed, and then, thankfully, he nodded. He was obviously contemplating how it would look to the outside world, if Apple began to lob accusations involving child porn at Twitter, while he was CEO. He knew what that would mean: another hit to his reputation, which was already being dragged through the mud daily by the mainstream media.

Esther felt relief move through her. She lowered herself back into her seat, as Elon began dialing back the vitriol, suggesting that instead of sending lawyers—or a pitchfork-waving mob—it would make more sense for Elon himself to head to Cupertino. *Talk it out, find a middle ground, a peaceful way forward.*

As Esther listened to him talk, she noticed she was still trembling. She knew how easily things could have gone differently. What a tightrope she had walked, getting through to Elon before the idea of war became imbedded. Because once it became imbedded, once it became about winning and losing:

*Elon didn't lose.*

But he did have the capacity to change course, if someone got to him in time. Lately, it was becoming more and more difficult to know when that moment had passed. Worse, Elon's paranoia seemed to be growing—and not just about bots attacking payment platforms. He now seemed to barely trust anyone outside of his inner circle. His fears weren't entirely unwarranted; just a few days ago, Esther had been secretly contacted by a handful of the second-level managers who were still employed by the company, informing her that they were planning a "mass quitting event," asking if she'd add to their number.

She had turned them down, but not turned them in. She still believed she could do more good having Elon's ear than by walking out the door. But every day, she felt her ability to redirect him away from those edges and cliffs was deteriorating; sooner or later, it seemed likely, his paranoia, his genius, maybe even his madness would get the better of him.

Once that happened, no amount of memes, threats of lost approbation, or frosted glass would keep him from plummeting down the other side—and taking Twitter, or what remained of it, along with him.

# PART ONE

"I say something, and then it usually happens. Maybe not on schedule, but it usually happens." —ELON MUSK

## CHAPTER ONE

# More Than Two Years Earlier, January 15, 2020

**The George R. Brown** Convention Center, downtown Houston, Texas.

Spotlights danced over a packed auditorium, in sync with a hyperkinetic throb of music spilling out of speakers on either side of an immense stage. Five flat-screen video monitors hung from the ceiling above, casting a neon blue haze over the crowd. The atmosphere was more rave than corporate conference; even now, minutes before the CEO would take his place before the monitors, the electricity in the air was palpable. This was a moment, a *happening*.

Mark Ramsey, a boyish and fit thirty-two, with a shock of brown hair and shoulders that betrayed his brief military past, navigated through the throng of his fellow Tweeps. He'd always found the term, *Tweeps*—adopted by his colleagues to refer to anyone who worked at Twitter—mildly nauseating. But after a decade with the company, it had wormed its way into his vocabulary. Picking his way through the crowd to one of the rows of cushioned seats closest to the stage, he could feel the deep bass from the speakers vibrating in his chest and couldn't deny a tingle of anticipation spreading down his spine.

This was the near-orgiastic keynote at the center of a three-day off-site studded with team-building exercises, lavish cocktail parties, and overtly ambitious public works excursions. Four thousand colleagues with a shared sense of purpose, many of them lifers, who together had built and maintained one of the most powerful, talked-about, far-reaching—if not profitable—social media companies on Earth.

Mark didn't consider himself an emotional guy; his friends, workmates, and fiancé might have even described him as stoic. But even he had to admit that the excitement in the room was contagious. Or perhaps it was simply a lack of sleep. The events of the past seventy-two hours had been nonstop, veering from the inspiring—handing out bottled water at a homeless kitchen—to the ridiculous—attending an astronaut-themed cocktail party at the Johnson Space Center.

And yet, as Mark took his seat in the third row, he felt more energized than he had in months. Next to him was a young woman he recognized from the National Diversity Outreach Committee, and on the other side, an engineer from the San Francisco head-quarters who couldn't have been older than twenty-four. So many young, passionate faces.

Mark's own Creative Strategy Team was spread out farther back throughout the auditorium. A decade ago, he'd started out lean, a dozen new hires who'd joined him in his satellite office in Charlotte, North Carolina, mostly advertising and marketing refugees who'd jumped at the chance of being part of something artistic and imag-inative. His CST was something special, described in internal com-pany memos as a "secret weapon" aimed at pitching large advertisers on unique social media campaigns. Now Mark had a hundred talented creatives beneath him, living in a half-dozen cities all over the world. Not that physical location meant much anymore. Twitter had veered toward a "work-from-home" model since its inception, and had gone totally remote since Jack Dorsey—the goateed guru who had started it all—had resumed his role as CEO in 2015.

Mark was proud of what he'd accomplished at Twitter, which was why his sudden burst of energy and enthusiasm was bittersweet. In all likelihood, this was his last OneTeam Conference, and it was amazing. What had begun years ago as a small off-site gathering of a bootstrapped, tech start-up—just a few hundred employees—had grown into a full-sized convention, thousands of his fellow Tweeps filling hotels all over the city. And the venue, Houston itself, seemed a fitting exclamation point to how far the company had come.

Three years before, Hurricane Harvey had barreled through Texas, flooding the streets of Houston and turning this very convention center into an emergency shelter. This same setting had shown the world the importance and power of Twitter, how the app could, overnight, become a force for good. Even as power across the city had turned spotty, Twitter users had been able to share information with each other in real time. Likewise, emergency personnel had been able to tweet resources out to the public, guiding people to shelters, along evacuation routes, to first aid stations.

Mark had grown up in North Carolina, but he'd gotten his MBA in Austin, so the events of that day had hit him particularly hard. As the storm had raged, he'd watched friends and distant family connecting with one another on Twitter from his glass-walled office eight hundred miles away. It was the best that Twitter, the app, could be; Mark only wished that Twitter, the company, could have remained anywhere near as effective in maintaining its internal sense of shared purpose.

He felt his body tense, even as the auditorium darkened and the music rose in volume. For months now, his frustration had been building, and just two days before he had told his immediate supervisor of his plans to leave at the end of the year.

For Mark, it was hard to imagine what life would be like outside of Twitter. He'd joined in 2008, shortly after Dorsey had been removed as CEO for the first time, something most outsiders had seen as a natural progression. The growing needs of a company graduating from guerrilla-style infancy to corporate adolescence were seen to be at odds with Dorsey's laid-back, philosophical personality.

Two years before that, Dorsey had cofounded the company under the name "Twttr," along with entrepreneurs Noah Glass, Biz Stone, and Evan Williams, sending the very first tweet on March 21 of that year: "*just setting up my twttr.*" Though there were differing narratives about the origins of what was originally a simple way to send status updates, it was generally accepted that Dorsey had come up with the idea. He'd pitched it first to Glass, then to Stone and Williams, who had been partners in a podcasting startup called Odeon, a company that had just been doomed to irrelevancy by Apple's announcement that they'd be including podcasting in their iTunes application.

Dorsey, a self-described hacker, had dropped out of New York University after a stint at Missouri University of Science and Technology. He had been a licensed masseur working at a coffee shop in 2006 when he'd randomly met Williams, who hired him to work at Odeon. Dorsey had built the prototype of his messaging—or "status" service, as he'd originally called it—during a hackathon competition between Odeon employees, set up to generate ideas in order to save the company. Four months later, on July 15 of that year,

Twitter had gone live to the public, generating around 20,000 tweets in its first few days.

A year later, after winning "best start-up" at South by Southwest, Twitter's usage had skyrocketed to 60,000 tweets a day—a number that would grow to nearly 50 million by 2010. Mark had enjoyed a front-row seat to the meteoric rise, as well as the quick succession of CEOs. Dorsey had been replaced in 2008 by Williams—also a college dropout, and the serial tech entrepreneur who'd invented the term *blogging* before founding Odeon. Williams had only lasted a couple of years as CEO, replaced by Dick Costolo, with Dorsey remaining as a powerful member of the board. Despite this instability, Twitter had risen to prominence, with an assist from celebrity "tweeters" such as Oprah Winfrey and Ashton Kutcher. By the end of 2012, the social media start-up had gone mainstream, accruing more than 200 million active users. Barack Obama had used Twitter to announce his victory in the presidential election—and the following year, the company had gone public with an initial valuation of $31 billion.

Twitter continued to gain ground over the next few years, as Mark had worked his own way up through the marketing wing of the company. Even so, as Mark launched his Creative Strategy Team and began building a stable of high-profile advertisers—advertising made up nearly 90 percent of Twitter's revenue—Twitter's growth had still lagged behind other social media behemoths like Facebook, Instagram, Snapchat, and Google. It was obvious that Twitter had a vastly outsized impact on the public consciousness, as the focal medium for conversation, especially in the fields of journalism, politics, and entertainment. But it was also a messy playground that seemed to lurch from one controversy to the next.

Keeping the site clear of online harassment, abuse, and hate speech had become a full-time occupation, eventually involving thousands of employees, numerous algorithms, regulations, councils, and loosely controlled gatekeepers. When daily use eventually plateaued in 2015—followed by numerous dips in advertising revenue, the lifeblood of the company—Dorsey had returned as CEO to try to right the ship. The next twelve months had proven to be the most tumultuous in the company's history. The 2016 presidential race divided the country, as the national conversation turned contentious—a barrage of demagogic voices, viral misinformation, competing messaging, and, perhaps, foreign intrusion pitching the medium toward madness.

By 2017, Donald Trump had become the biggest show on Twitter, with an influence far outreaching his 30.7 million followers. Advertisers, already skittish pitching campaigns into the maelstrom of a cultural and political landscape that seemed continuously on the verge of civil war, tightened their purse strings. But as destructive as the growing conflict could be, it was undeniably entertaining; despite advertisers' concerns, engagement had risen nearly every month of the following year, reaching a height of over 321 million monthly users.

In September 2018, Dorsey and Sheryl Sandberg, the COO of Facebook, had gone in front of the Senate Intelligence Committee to discuss alleged Russian interference—by way of social media—in Trump's victory over Hillary Clinton in the 2016 election. Rumors of potential acquisition offers escalated, with megacompanies including the Walt Disney Company, Google, and Verizon all floated as possible buyers.

For Mark, the tail end of 2018 had seemed a turning point in his journey at Twitter. Although the sailing had never been smooth in his early years with the company when it was in a continuous race against bankruptcy, he'd always felt a sense of purpose at Twitter.

He and his fellow Tweeps had been trying to do something *good* and *important*. Representing the medium where the public conversation took place had been a responsibility Mark and his colleagues had taken seriously. His team hadn't just been pitching creative advertising campaigns to reluctant soda companies, software behemoths, and auto manufacturers. They had been propping up a platform where anyone, anywhere, could have a voice, be heard, and yes, shout at a rival, or into the void. That had been Dorsey's vision, and Mark had bought in entirely.

Settling back into his seat in the auditorium, which had suddenly gone quiet, he glanced at the woman to his left, who had her phone out in front of her so she could snap a selfie with a smiling PR rep seated directly behind her. Then he looked to his right, at a pair of engineers turning to the stage from discussing their plans for the next morning—something about a golfing excursion. They all looked so young to him, even though he was probably only a few years their senior. It wasn't their actual physical age that bothered him, nor was it their enthusiasm for the off-site in Houston; in the past, the OneTeam Conference was indeed a chance for Tweeps from all over the country—all over the world—to celebrate, face-to-face, the part they were playing in building something positive. But today, looking at these happy, smiling faces, everything felt wrong.

In Mark's eyes, what was lacking in those smiling faces, for lack of a better word, was gravitas. Somewhere along the way, the lean, bootstrapped, purposeful company he had joined a decade ago had gone soft.

He'd always hated the term *snowflake*—even more than he'd been disturbed by the word *Tweep*—but it seemed apt. Over the past couple of years, he'd seen his colleagues at the company swept up into a veritable snowdrift, putting creature comforts, personal conflicts, and extracurriculars ahead of company work at every turn. Maybe it was part of a larger, cultural shift, maybe it was in conjunction with a wave of excess and decadence sweeping through Silicon Valley itself, or perhaps it was just a symptom of the company's own success, but in any case Twitter's mission had become secondary to employees' lifestyles. Two-hour lunch breaks morphed into two-month leaves of absence. New committees on every possible imagined cause were formed almost daily, eating up hours of productivity and usually collapsing over petty disagreements without ever accomplishing a thing. When people did, eventually, show up to work, there was a noticeable lack of focus. The most passionate movement Mark had witnessed as of late had occurred when management had removed the main headquarters' smoothie bar as part of the latest round of cost-cutting measures.

Mark had insulated his own team from the cultural drift as best he could, even as his group had grown to over a hundred members—in part because chasing advertising dollars had always been fundamental to the survival of the company. Revenue kept the lights on and the smoothies churning: for Twitter, advertising equaled revenue. But Mark yearned for the days when his colleagues showed up at the office—or for a Zoom call—ten minutes early, not because they were lining up for perks like a cereal dispensary or a video game room, but because they wanted to grow the core business.

Mark's attention shifted back to the stage, and he realized that the audience around him was on its feet. He could see why; even in silhouette, Jack Dorsey cast a striking figure. Five eleven, a hundred and sixty-five pounds of lithe, laid-back charisma; a soft-spoken guru who, with his long beard, oversized hoody sweatshirt, pierced nose, and perpetual slouch, looked like a cross between some sort of

Jedi warrior and an antique marionette whose strings had just been cut. If Jack had pulled a lightsaber out from under his sweatshirt, nobody would have batted an eye.

The fact that Jack was CEO again thrilled Mark's colleagues, but Mark himself was ambivalent. He didn't entirely blame Jack for the shift in culture at Twitter, but he suspected Jack himself would have accepted some of the responsibility. Jack was a philosopher at heart, and though Twitter had made him a billionaire multiple times over, and he'd gone on to found the payment processor Square in 2009, he didn't seem particularly fond of capitalism. Putting him in charge was, to Mark, like voting the popular stoner as president of the class. Everyone loved him and would happily follow, as he floated by in a cloud of marijuana smoke, toward the nearest abyss.

Maybe Mark knew he was being harsh; Jack was odd and untraditional, but he was clearly a genius. So what if he ate only one meal a day, took regular ice baths, went on weeklong yogi retreats, and walked five miles to work every morning? He had the Tweeps eating out of his hands, and if he'd wanted to shake the company back toward a culture that worked as hard as they used to, he certainly could have. Sadly, Jack's aspirations seemed more ethereal, as far as Mark could tell: a general sense of oneness with the universe, along with a decentralization of commerce—great if you were running a Jedi temple, but not so useful when you were managing the day-to-day operations of a multibillion-dollar social media site.

As much as Mark wanted to remain a Tweep, as much as he enjoyed his good salary and stock options, he knew the clock was ticking, the snowdrift was rising, and sooner or later, the company he had dedicated himself to for the past ten years would become so weak from the inside as to be unrecognizable.

He intended to get out before that happened.

Somewhere during Mark's bittersweet musings on his future, the audience had gone quiet again. Jack had his back to the crowd and was facing one of the huge monitors hanging from the ceiling. In the center of the screen a glowing rectangle had taken form, and it took Mark a moment to realize it was a video call coming in; he saw an office appear, sleek, framed by a massive wall of windows and a lot of modern-looking furniture. Another wall was taken up by a large poster showing what appeared to be a satellite of some sort, or maybe part of the International Space Station. Which made more sense, as Mark's focus shifted to the man in the center of the video call.

The audience recognized the man, instantly identifiable, at the same moment, and an excited murmur moved through the auditorium. Elon Musk was one of Twitter's biggest users, with over 30 million followers, and his tweets were a constant source of entertainment and controversy; at times, he'd wax philosophical, at other times, he'd shoot for humor—and once in a while, he'd play the character of an internet troll, tossing off memes and comments that seemed purposefully designed to piss people off. But he was mostly beloved by the Tweeps, as much as he was revered by the general public as one of the most successful men on Earth, the genius who had revolutionized the auto industry with Tesla and was changing the face of space exploration with SpaceX—where he was presumably calling in from, by the looks of the office behind him.

Mark gazed at the billionaire's vaguely cubic features, his slightly slouched shoulders, his fidgeting hands, his small, bright eyes. Elon's outfit fit his personality; a hip leather jacket, left open over a T-shirt emblazoned with the phrase "Occupy Mars." Face-to-face with an enormous digital Elon, Jack began the conversation, obviously as thrilled by the entrepreneur's presence at the conference as the audience was. The two men seemed to have an easy rapport, and it was clear they shared a lot of respect for one another.

"Give us some direct feedback," Jack began. "Critique: What are we doing poorly, what could we be doing better, and what's your hope for our potential as a service? If you were running Twitter—by the way, do you want to run Twitter?"

At this Jack paused, giving the audience time to laugh, then continued:

"What would you do?"

Elon's answer began as a trickle, off the cuff, growing into a stream.

"I think it would be helpful to differentiate between real and— to differentiate between real and, you know, like is this a real person—not just like a verified person—but like is this a real person, or is this a botnet or a sort of troll army or something like that . . . basically, how do you tell if the feedback is real or someone tries to manipulate the system? Or probably real or probably trying to manipulate the system?"

Elon went on from there, and as he spoke, it was evident that he'd given a lot of thought to these concerns. His main critique seemed to be that it had become harder and harder to know what was real on the site and what wasn't. Not just accounts, which were largely anonymous, but the tweets themselves, people's thoughts, opinions, arguments. Had the playing field been overrun by inconspicuous interests trying to manipulate users—to guide the public conversation toward certain outcomes?

Mark was intrigued by this line of criticism; as someone who constructed advertising campaigns on Twitter for paying clients, he understood that the market of ideas was, indeed, a *market*. But he'd always done his best to draw a clear line between posts and comments that had been paid for, to try to sell something, and posts and comments that were supposed to be "real." Elon was making a very important point: bots, which were automated, fake accounts, and trolls, which were human, and often collaborating to operate primarily fake accounts, could muddy the medium to the point where it was impossible to know where those lines were, or if they even existed.

As the conversation continued, Elon pushed toward an even bigger point. If Twitter was supposed to be the medium where the public conversation took place, a sort of Global Town Hall, they had to do more to make sure the playing field remained free of manipulation. The more Elon spoke, the more passionate he became. This was something he believed, deep in his soul.

It was exactly the sort of devotion that Mark had felt had gone missing in many of his colleagues at Twitter. Although the audience around him was clearly enraptured by the wealthy, charismatic entrepreneur, Mark had only recently seen that level of intensity from any of them when a free smoothie was being taken away, or a vaguely defined personal leave was being cut short by the drudgery of actual work.

By the time the tele-conversation with the entrepreneur came to a close (and after Jack asked Elon when the first tweet from Mars might come: "five years from now, probably not more than nine years from now"), the deafening applause seemed to suggest that some of the entrepreneur's optimism had caught the Tweeps' attention. It was an even bigger ovation than the other act of the evening: a video call from *actual* astronauts, aboard the International Space Station. When Jack finally left the stage and the music throbbed back to life, Mark definitely felt something new in the air.

Before Mark's MBA at the University of Texas, before his four-year stint in the army to pay off his college loans, Mark had grown up in an extremely rural area, outside Huntersville, North Carolina. Not on a farm, but farm adjacent. The feeling he had now reminded him of what he'd often felt, back in the country, during the hours before a storm came through.

A sense, intuition, maybe. Clouds gathering, humidity rising, a tightness in the air. Deep down, in his molecules, he had the sudden feeling that something was heading his way.

## CHAPTER TWO

# March 25, 2022

## A little after 1:30 a.m.

Elon Musk, CEO and techno-king of Tesla, CEO and chief engineer of SpaceX, founder of Neuralink and the Boring Company, soon to be the richest man in the world, lay on his back in an alcove tucked into the labyrinthine, glass-and-steel entrails of a ten-million-square-foot alien spaceship, crash landed on a scar of sand and brush twelve miles outside the city of Austin, Texas. Twenty-foot ceilings, glistening catwalks, Plexiglas safety windows, polished floors; endless corridors of white on white snaking past workstations occupied by bright red, giant, dystopic metal creatures, things with treads and claws and swiveling electronic eyes. An awe-inspiring glimpse forward toward a technologically advanced future ruled by silicon networks and interlocking gears.

Elon's thumbs hovered over the glowing screen of his cell phone, which rested on his chest. His shoulders ached against the hardness of the floor beneath him. Somewhere between the hours of midnight and one a.m., someone had loaned him a yoga mat to separate his body from the unforgiving surface, but it was little more than window dressing, like a scarf against an arctic wind. Three straight weeks sleeping on a floor took its toll, no matter how futuristic your spaceship.

It wasn't really a spaceship, of course, but a factory—although that, too, was inaccurate. The massive building, filled with tech straight out of a science fiction movie, was as similar to the grimy assembly lines and mechanical sweatshops of its forebears as a supercomputer was to an abacus.

Gigafactory Texas was a great leap forward in both engineering and ambition, the largest production facility in the Tesla portfolio. The factory was also the second-largest building in the world, the size of fifteen city blocks, utilizing more steel than the Empire State Building, and still expanding as the company continued filing plans to grow. Although construction of Giga Texas had only begun less than two years earlier, in July 2020, the first Model Ys of the company's popular electric car would be delivered within days, at a planned "Cyber Rodeo." The event would draw thousands of attendees and highlight upcoming products such as the Cybertruck, a robotaxi, and a humanoid robot called Optimist. Musk would take the stage in a black cowboy hat after a drone show in which the sky would explode with images including physicist Nikola Tesla, the Model Y, and the canine mascot of the cryptocurrency Dogecoin.

The theatrics, and Giga Texas itself, were signature Elon: dramatic, bold, satiric, and tending a little bit toward madness. But beneath the spectacle lay something serious—another step forward in the entrepreneur's goal to revolutionize the auto industry. Not only would Giga Texas produce sustainable electric vehicles—with a goal of a *million* cars a year, and a finished car every forty-five seconds—the facility itself was equipped with a solar panel system and Powerpack batteries, making it a showcase for the company's clean energy vision. It was Elon's latest masterpiece, a monument to his quest to save the world, one electric vehicle at a time.

Elon lifted his head from the yoga mat, just high enough to see around the edges of his alcove. The scene around him was beautiful chaos: the huge, futuristic machines interacting in a tightly choreographed dance, while engineers in Tesla uniforms flitted in and out between them. To Elon, the humans looked like ancient people tending to great mechanical gods.

At the core of the complex were the most powerful of those gods, a pair of Giga Press manufacturing rigs: massive six-thousand-ton aluminum die-casting machines, each approximately the size of a train car, painted in bright swaths of white and red. The Giga Presses, sprouting hydraulic tubes and snakelike metal cylinders, had a clamping force of over sixty thousand kilonewtons and could turn a superheated mix of molten aluminum and silicon into the rear end of a Model Y in mere moments. Five such machines, spread out between Giga Shanghai, California, and Berlin, were already pumping out Teslas to feed the growing international demand for what was inarguably the most advanced electric car on the market; but at Giga Texas, foundations had already been laid for a number of even more massive versions—a nine-thousand-ton iteration that would construct more Ys as well as the coming Cybertruck's body in a single piece—spitting out full-sized cars and trucks in much the same way toy cars were made by Mattel.

The Giga Press, built specifically for Tesla's Giga factories, represented a key component in Elon's mission. He hadn't set out to build an electric car, but rather to change the face of transportation. To Elon, sustainable energy was not just a trend or a buzzword that college kids might spray-paint on a picket sign; it was a carefully crafted business strategy, and part of a much larger vision.

Awake now, he rose to a sitting position, stretching his aching shoulders. Of course, he could have found a bed somewhere in the giant building, or made the short trip to a luxury hotel in nearby

Austin. He didn't have an actual home at the moment, because he was in the process of selling most of his possessions. He'd never really cared much about creature comforts, and in a world of vast inequalities, he'd noticed that things like mansions and yachts made easy targets for the many critics looking for ways to puncture his image. But sleeping on the floor of his newest factory for nights on end wasn't a PR stunt, nor was it purely performative.

The aching in his body reminded him of a period of time he'd often called the most painful in his life. During late 2017, the run-up to the launch of the Model 3, the company's first attempt at a high-volume product with an affordable base price had turned into a nightmare of delays and manufacturing problems. Elon had taken over the production line himself. He'd spent many nights on the floor of the Fremont, California, factory, often under his desk, later telling Bloomberg, "I wanted my circumstances to be worse than anyone else at the company. Whenever they felt pain, I wanted mine to be worse." Unbeknownst to the outside world, the company had been a month from bankruptcy, dangerously close to joining the crowded graveyard of automotive start-ups.

The current moment was worlds apart from those difficult times; Tesla was humming forward at an insane pace, and just that week, the stock had crossed three hundred dollars a share. Its total valuation was well over a trillion dollars, one of only six companies in the world to cross such a benchmark. But Elon knew that what he'd accomplished so far with Tesla was just the beginning. The success of the Model S, and now Giga Texas, were part of a mission that kept him awake most nights, whether he was on the floor of a factory or on his jet traveling between his businesses.

Elon had first hinted at that mission two years after he'd helped launch the company. Shortly after the debut of the Tesla Roadster, Tesla's first hundred-thousand-dollar electric sports car, Elon had published a blog post explaining himself, titled "The Secret Tesla Motors Master Plan (just between you and me)."

"The overarching purpose of Tesla Motors (and the reason I am funding the company)," the blog post had announced, "is to help expedite the move from a mine-and-burn hydrocarbon economy towards a solar electric economy. . . ." To that end, the plan for Tesla was simple: "1) Build a sports car. 2) Use that money to build an affordable car. 3) Use that money to build an even more affordable car. 4) While doing above, also provide zero emission electric power generation options."

"Don't tell anyone," Elon had signed off, and over the next decade and a half he had followed that game plan surprisingly well. After barely surviving the 2008 financial crisis, firing a quarter of the company's staff, and attaining financing on Christmas Eve of that year, in the last hour of the last day possible to save the company, Tesla had followed up the Roadster with the more affordable Model S sedan in 2012, then an SUV called the Model X in 2015, then the Model 3 in 2017–18. Along the way, Tesla had reached profitability by July 2009, and in June 2010 had become the first automaker to go public in the US since Ford, back in 1956. Tesla's initial IPO valuation of 2.22 billion had grown as the company debuted more models, like the Model Y crossover, and more innovations, such as rapid charging stations in 2012 and an automotive holy grail: a sophisticated autopilot system in 2014.

Although the company itself was no longer facing any sort of existential moment—quite the opposite, Tesla was flying higher than it ever had—to Elon, the stakes were much too high to take his foot off the gas, even for a moment.

Now, in the spring of 2022, Elon had set his sights on new problems to solve. The country—the world—had just survived a second pandemic winter, but Elon was eager to put Covid in the rearview mirror. Economies across the globe seemed poised for turbulence, which only made Elon's instinctual need to press forward more urgent. Pushing sustainable energy and helping humanity to escape dependence on fossil fuels might have been the company's initial mission statement, but it was only one part of a much bigger vision.

Rising from the yoga mat, Elon lifted his phone from his chest and glanced down at the glowing screen. He read the words he had just typed, only moments ago:

> Free speech is essential to a functioning democracy.
> Do you believe Twitter rigorously adheres to this
> principle?
> 1) Yes
> 2) No

Not a text, or an email, or a blog post—a tweet. A Twitter poll, offering anyone on the social media site a chance to choose between the two answers to his question, which Elon had blasted out to his nearly seventy-nine million followers. Already, hundreds of thousands of people had responded, with votes, likes, and comments. By the time the poll would close, twenty-four hours later, over two million people would have voted, with 70 percent choosing "No."
To Elon, the results of the poll weren't surprising; in the past year, the social media site had become particularly tumultuous, in tune with a society that had been reeling from multiple traumas: vicious political battles, numerous media scandals, a once-in-a-century pandemic that had already killed over six million people worldwide. But it wasn't the general sense of hostility, of argumentation, that had inspired Elon's tweet. He had been aiming at something bigger—something that had been bothering him for some time.

He headed out of the alcove, skirting around a self-guided smart cart moving along a predetermined track, then by a group of engineers huddled around an automatic multipoint welding machine. The welding machine was one of the more complex pieces of equipment in this part of the factory; from Elon's vantage, it looked like some sort of bright red robotic spider flipped on its back, articulate arms sprouting upward, each tipped with a glowing, superheated point. The engineers were in the process of training the machine, using a handheld digital deck; though they didn't pause as he walked by, he could sense the excited tension in their posture. He could be a demanding boss, but he was there with them, well beyond midnight. In his own mind, and perhaps in the minds of his engineers:

*Hardcore.*

In an auto factory, even one as futuristic and automated as Giga Texas, there was no room for anything less. Mistakes, strategic or operational, could be dangerous, even fatal. Engineers, as a breed, were methodological, detail oriented, results focused, and careful. Elon was an engineer; but there was a whimsical side to his personality, which often came out late at night, or when something was aggravating him.

Often, during those moments, he turned to Twitter.

Elon had a special and complicated relationship with the social media app that went back almost thirteen years. Not only did he have one of the biggest followings on the site, but he was one of its more prolific tweeters, having posted nearly twenty thousand times—as often as six times a day in recent months. It was common for him to whip off a thought, retweet a meme, or make a philosophical statement while in transit, late at night, or when he woke up in the morning, sometimes while sitting on the toilet. Famously, he'd gotten himself into trouble with the SEC because of a tweet in 2018, when he'd announced "funding secured" to take Tesla private at $420 a share—resulting in a trading frenzy, driving up Tesla's stock price by 10 percent. He'd had to settle with the government agency for $20 million, making it the most expensive tweet in history.

If Twitter was the greatest show you could access with your thumbs, Elon was one of its biggest draws. Over the years, he'd developed a personal friendship with Jack Dorsey; the two billionaires shared libertarian philosophies, especially around decentralized money and the importance of freedom of speech. Jack was once again no longer the company's CEO—likely forced out by Elliott Management, a hedge fund with a major financial interest in Twitter. He had handed the reins off to the company's chief technology officer, a previously obscure engineer named Parag Agrawal. Still, Dorsey remained an outsized influence on the sensibility of the site, the blueprint for which he'd been the primary architect.

Something that Elon understood, better than most, was that even the most brilliantly drawn blueprint was only as good as the engineers who developed and maintained the product that came from it. Jack's blueprint—a global town hall of ideas—had been revolutionary; but Elon was beginning to believe that the product had frayed, and was coming dangerously close to disintegrating.

When he'd crafted his Twitter poll, moments before, he hadn't been trolling, or simply posting a thought to garner a response. He'd been as intent as an engineer watching a product he loved beginning to go off the rails.

His poll had been triggered by something that was arguably quite foolish. A site that Elon often followed, calling itself the Babylon Bee, had just been suspended for posting an off-color joke. The Bee—a conservative parody site—had posted a picture of the US assistant health secretary Rachel Levine with the caption "The Babylon Bee's Man of the Year Is Rachel Levine"—purposefully misgendering the transgender official, in response to *USA Today* naming Levine as one of its Women of the Year.

The banning of the account had struck a nerve with Elon. Not necessarily because he agreed with the Babylon Bee's politics—although he would, many months later tweet that his pronouns were *"Prosecute/Fauci"* and follow that up by explaining, *"Forcing your pronouns upon others when they didn't ask, and implicitly ostracizing those who don't, is neither good nor kind to anyone"*—but because he saw the suspension as the latest in a cascade of over-reaching moves by the site, to stifle what he believed should be protected free speech.

Elon understood that his views were not always in line with the mainstream; he described himself as being along the Asperger's spectrum, which made it difficult for him to read social cues and often caused him to interpret things literally. Despite a difficult childhood, spent isolated, bookish, and bullied, he'd become fascinated with the idea of fundamental truths, which had led him to study physics and computer science. Understanding the universe was a central part of Elon's philosophy—but he believed that this could only be achieved through asking questions and expanding the scale of human consciousness.

Because of this, to Elon, freedom of speech was crucial: if you couldn't ask questions, if you were silenced, you could never find your way to fundamental truths. Without fundamental truths, you had no chance of truly understanding the universe.

In the same way Elon hadn't built Tesla to make cars, he didn't engage with Twitter simply to amuse himself and others, or to promote his various companies. He believed that a global town hall—a place of unfettered free speech, as Jack had first envisioned it—could be a powerful component of his mission, of which Tesla was just one piece. But conversely, a global town hall that had been co-opted by moderating forces could be the opposite—*an existential threat to everything he was trying to achieve.*

In recent months, he had begun to see evidence that something horrible was happening on Twitter, something that he'd started to think of as a sort of virus. A rapidly spreading, silencing force that was stifling comments that didn't agree with the mainstream, and vanishing accounts—by suspensions, shadow bans, and outright purges—that didn't bow to majority opinions. If Elon was right, this virus would undermine the very conditions necessary for a global town hall—and by extension, threaten the potential of his overarching mission—which went well beyond electric cars and sustainable energy.

A mission that involved, at its core, the very survival of the human race.

His pace quickened as he moved through his spaceship of a factory, passing more insectlike machines of silicon and steel. In his head, he was already crafting a follow-up to his Twitter poll, which he would post in just a matter of hours:

> Given that Twitter serves as the de facto public town
> square, failing to adhere to free speech principles
> fundamentally undermines democracy. What should
> be done?

And shortly after that:

> Is a new platform needed?

He was wide awake now, once again consumed by thoughts of this new, potential threat. For some time, Elon had grown to believe that the world was balancing on a knife's edge; perhaps it was time for him to take another step, to try to set it right.

## CHAPTER THREE

# April 4, 2022

**Seven a.m.,** and Parag Agrawal had made it two steps out of his modest, Spanish-style home situated on a quiet, tree-lined stretch of Palo Alto, California, when his phone started to go off. Text after frantic text ricocheting across cell towers all over Silicon Valley, tiny packets of excited electrified molecules streaming through the air of his sleepy neighborhood and plunging into the sophisticated hunk of Apple engineering nestled in a fold of pocket by his chest.

By the time Parag had reached his Mercedes SUV parked at the curb, the damn phone was spitting like a rattlesnake, vibrating so hard against his jacket that he thought it might tear its way out. Still, he didn't reach for the phone right away. Instead, he slipped behind the steering wheel and shut the door behind him, taking a moment to just breathe in the solitude.

As usual, the interior of the car was impeccably clean, the leather seats soft and supple beneath him. *Christ, he was exhausted.* He reached for the dashboard, adjusting the temperature and ventilation, his fingers running over the smooth surfaces as he tried to collect his thoughts. It had been a hectic morning, as usual, and he was still feeling the effects. Two kids under the age of four, one of them just born—hell, just getting out of the house felt like a military operation. His wife was a brilliant, beautiful force of nature: an MD-PhD who'd trained at Harvard and the Massachusetts Institute of Technology and was now a general partner specializing in biotech at the mega VC firm Andreessen Horowitz. Yet the two of them, combined, were barely a match for the energy of a toddler and the decibels of a newborn. More than once over the past few weeks, Parag had escaped to the solace of the Mercedes, or, more often on weekends, behind the wheel of one of three other vehicles, his Range Rover, his Land Rover Defender, or his Cadillac Escalade.

Despite the car collection—and Parag had always been a car guy, though never before in his thirty-seven years had he been in the financial situation to own so many—he wasn't a naturally ostentatious person. Quite the opposite: most of his friends would have described him as unassuming and quiet. He didn't dress flashy— jeans and a white button-down shirt, thick, square-framed glasses, and a zippered jacket that was more athletic gear than business wear. Nor did his tastes, other than the cars, run expensive. Sure, his home hadn't come cheap, but nothing in Palo Alto went for less than $3.5 million, and that was before the pandemic had kicked in, rocketing prices toward the stratosphere.

In fact, looking at Parag, settled behind the steering wheel of his Mercedes in front of his relatively ordinary home, studiously avoiding the screaming chunk of metal dancing in his jacket pocket, an onlooker might have been shocked to learn that he was the newly minted CEO of one of the most-talked-about social media companies in the world.

Certainly the pundits, tech journalists, and entrepreneurs scattered across the Valley had been surprised when Parag had ascended to the throne of Twitter, just six months earlier, in November 2021. In his darker moments, Parag himself might have admitted that he too was stunned by the turn of events. Although he'd been elevated to CTO of the company back in 2017, he didn't fit the mold of a CEO, and certainly not a *tech* CEO. He didn't look or act like a cult leader, hadn't dropped out of college, and had never eaten koala, dated a supermodel, or traveled across an ocean by balloon.

Parag had first joined Twitter back in 2011, when the company had consisted of just under a thousand employees. An engineer by personality and training, he'd spent his formative years at Microsoft, Yahoo, and AT&T, after a stint at Stanford. Even before that, he'd been on track with a thorough education at the Indian Institute of Technology in Bombay. At IIT Bombay he had been one of the top students in the school, and had made his name by placing second in an exam given to every freshman. Math and science had always come easy to him, probably due to his upbringing; his father had retired from the refueling-tech division of the Bhabha Atomic Research Center, and his mother was a professor of economics and management at the University of Bombay.

At Twitter, Parag had focused on machine learning and consumer engineering; even as he'd ascended to CTO, he'd had little first-person experience with the more social and political aspects of the company, and had primarily learned to manage such a huge, multitiered business on the job. He was likable, and didn't ruffle many feathers. The only time in his entire career at Twitter he'd garnered any sort of attention in the press—negative or positive—was when an old tweet of his from 2010 had surfaced shortly after he'd been made CTO, in which he'd been quoting a piece from *The Daily Show*: *"If they are not going to make a distinction between Muslims and extremists, then why should I distinguish between white people and racists."* The miniature scandal surrounding his admittedly poorly construed tweet, which he'd tweeted before he'd been with the company, had taught him to be even more careful and subdued in public than he already was, and over the past five years he'd been one of the more invisible upper-management faces in the entire industry.

Which, when he thought about it, was probably the point *and* the reason he'd been pegged to be the new CEO when Jack Dorsey had stepped down—or been forced out, depending on how you looked at it. Rumor was, Jack had handpicked Parag himself, precisely because he was unassuming, an engineer, and if not a Jack acolyte, unlikely to be any sort of threat to Jack's potential plans going forward, or to his reputation.

Parag was the opposite of the celebrity CEOs you saw on CNBC and Fox Business, usually white men in slick suits with even slicker hair who looked like they could either sell you a vision of the future that would change the world, or a vacuum cleaner, or even some bizarre combination of the two.

The few times Parag had appeared in public as CEO of Twitter, he was boyish and soft-spoken, with dark hair, thick glasses, and an affable Indian accent. It was clear to everyone that he wasn't an entrepreneur, and it was equally clear he wasn't trying to sell anyone anything. He had goals and aspirations: in particular, to add a hundred million daily active users to Twitter's base, which would have been a 45 percent increase over 2021, and to grow revenue from $5 billion annually to $7.5 billion. But at the moment, neither of those goals had him reaching for the gas pedal of the Mercedes, or took his mind off the buzzing phone in his pocket—or, for that matter, the small yet growing kidney-shaped stain he suddenly noticed in the center of his button-down shirt—spit-up, applesauce, or coffee, not that it really made much of a difference.

He took a deep breath and finally reached past the stain on his shirt toward the inside pocket of his jacket. He withdrew the phone, still vibrating with another hail of new texts, and stared down at the screen.

Then his eyes went wide.

Most of the texts were from Twitter's chairman, Bret Taylor, who had joined the board at Twitter in 2016 and matriculated to chairman in 2021, after stints at Facebook, where he'd been CTO, and Google, where he had famously co-created Google Maps. A few were from other members of Parag's management team. The rest were from coworkers, colleagues across Silicon Valley, friends, and even one from his wife, who must have just seen the news as she finished feeding their newborn.

Parag's face went numb as he read through the texts, then scrolled through various links to news sites—then of course, to Twitter itself. It didn't take him long to get the gist of what had just happened, though it would take more time to digest the ramifications. He closed his eyes for a moment, then removed his glasses and wiped at the smudges of humidity that had just formed across the lenses.

According to the texts, news sites, and tweets, Elon Musk, currently the world's richest man, had just filed with the SEC, effectively announcing that he had acquired a 9.5 percent stake in Twitter. The shares he'd quietly accumulated were valued around $3 billion.

Parag shook his head, then put the glasses back on. Then he blinked, as if willing the texts, news, and tweets to vanish from his phone's screen, and from the timeline he was obviously about to live through. Not because he had anything personal against Elon; quite the opposite, he considered Elon one of the most brilliant entrepreneurs in history, an engineer—like Parag—who obviously loved Twitter as much as anyone.

But here was Parag, six months into his new role of CEO, and he had a deep suspicion that his entire world was about to be turned upside down.

The manner in which Elon had acquired—and announced—the stake was one big, glaring, unavoidable warning sign. In the SEC filing, Elon had called the accumulative shares "passive," but he had bought them in secret, backdoor fashion. According to the filing, he'd actually acquired the stake back on March 14: twenty-one days before, indicating the filing was in violation of SEC regulations, which mandated that any purchase of shares beyond 5 percent of a company had to be declared within twenty days. The extra day seemed purposeful, especially considering Elon's notoriously public battles with the SEC, and his vocal dislike of the organization.

By breaking regulations with the Twitter shares filing, Elon would subject himself to a penalty—usually in the range of a hundred thousand dollars—though, to a man worth $300 billion, a hundred grand was like pennies an average person might lose behind a couch cushion. What concerned Parag were the possible ramifications of Elon's current focus on the site, which had made headlines both within and outside the company.

Elon's Twitter poll of March 25, around Twitter's actions concerning free speech, had garnered enormous attention. In retrospect, one of his follow-up tweets—"*The consequences of this poll will be important. Please vote carefully*"—wasn't some throwaway remark. According to the SEC filing, Elon had already acquired nearly 10 percent of the company *before* he'd posted his poll.

Parag sunk deeper into the leather of his Mercedes' front seat. Now he realized that none of the events of his past week had occurred in a vacuum; likewise, after seeing this filing, he had a suspicion he knew exactly how and why this was happening. The real thorn digging into his side, causing his glasses to fog and his blood pressure to rise, wasn't Elon, or his "passive" shares. It went back further—not six days, to Elon's Twitter poll and its aftermath, but six months.

Parag owed his job to Jack Dorsey—but Jack hadn't stepped aside quietly, whether it had really been his own decision or someone else's. It was public knowledge that he had been feuding with Twitter's board for some time; primarily, he had been in a battle with Elliott Management, the activist hedge fund managing over $50 billion, who owned around 4 percent of Twitter's shares. It was no secret that Elliott had been searching for a replacement for Jack from the moment they had bought into the company—and apparently, Jack had finally reached his breaking point.

Jack's conflict with Elliott and the Twitter board hadn't revolved around the financial future of the company, which might have been Elliott's main focus, but the philosophical direction Jack believed the company was heading. As a manager, Jack had been notoriously hands-off when it came to issues like content moderation and the banning of problematic accounts; he'd always been a free speech advocate, and especially during the tumult of the recent elections, he'd become uncomfortable with the lengths Twitter had gone to try to police its platform.

Parag couldn't be sure when Jack had first reached out to Elon Musk regarding his concerns about Twitter, but at least as far back as a year ago, Jack had been pushing the Twitter board to reach out to the entrepreneur. Though the board had resisted the idea of giving Elon a seat, it was clear Jack saw Elon as a potential savior for Twitter; a fellow free-speech near-absolutist with the money and power to effect real change at the company.

Parag was aware that in just the past week, there had been multiple conversations between Jack and Elon, precipitated in part by Elon's poll concerning the free speech issue. Though Parag had not yet seen the texts that had flown between the two "tech bros" during those days, he would not have been surprised by their content:

The text conversation had begun in abrupt fashion, when, on March 26, the day after the Twitter poll, Jack had texted to Elon:

"Yes, a new platform is needed. It can't be a company. That's why I left."

Elon had responded: "Ok."

Then: "What should it look like?"

Jack: "I believe it must be an open source protocol, funded by a foundation of sorts that doesn't own the protocol, only advances it. A bit like what Signal has done. It can't have an advertising model. Otherwise you have surface area that governments and advertisers will try to influence and control. If it has a centralized entity behind it, it will be attacked. This isn't complicated work, it just has to be done right so it's resilient to what has happened to twitter."

Elon had seemed to agree: "Super interesting idea."

"I'm off the twitter board mid-May and then completely out of the company," Jack had texted back. "I intend to do this work and fix our mistakes. Twitter started as a protocol. It should have never been a company. That was the original sin."

Elon had obviously been intrigued by the call to action:

"I'd like to help if I am able to."

"I wanted to talk with you about it after I was all clear," Jack had responded. "Because you care so much, get its importance, and could def help in immeasurable ways. Back when we had the activist come in, I tried my hardest to get you on our board, and our board said no. That's about the time I decided I needed to work to leave, as hard as it was for me."

It appeared the two entrepreneurs were now on the same page.

"I think it's worth both trying to move Twitter in a better direction," Elon had finished, "and doing something new that's decentralized."

Jack's plan, to push Elon into a bigger role with the social media company, now appeared to be coming to some sort of fruition. After their back-and-forth and at least one phone conversation, Jack had reached out to Parag, Bret, and members of the Twitter board, introducing them to Elon and pushing for a face-to-face. After another series of texts—Parag had been dutiful but brief in his messages, wanting to know more about Elon's plans before extending himself too far—had led to the group scheduling a dinner between Parag, Bret, and Elon just days before this revelation about Elon's stake in Twitter, on March 31.

The occasion had been one of the oddest meetings, and venues for a meeting, that Parag had ever attended. Elon would later describe the private residence outside of San Jose, close enough to all of them to be considered neutral ground—which Bret had found via Airbnb—as "post-apocalyptic." The residence had been surrounded by abandoned trucks and farm equipment, and there had been actual donkeys wandering about, braying when anyone got too close. At random intervals, helicopters could be heard flying overhead, circling the valley around them.

But the meeting had been more promising than the setting. Elon had been charming and interesting. The man's patterns of speech could be unnerving—often he took incredibly long pauses, and it was hard to tell if he was engaged in deep thought, or just annoyed. He spoke deliberately, mostly about his two main concerns with Twitter's current state: the proliferation of bots and trolls, which was something Parag and his team had been working very hard to curtail, and the idea of Twitter as a free and unfettered global town hall, a place for conversation with very limited moderation.

It had been instantly clear that Elon took these two subjects extremely seriously. He was passionate about the platform, and he believed strongly that Twitter was failing—especially in regard to free speech. But Parag had left the dinner in good spirits, taking Elon's criticisms and suggestions in good faith.

Now—not even a week later—Parag realized he had misconstrued the entire meeting. The dinner hadn't simply been informational, or a meeting of minds. It had been a shot across Twitter's bow.

Parag took a deep breath, then dialed his chairman's number. Putting the phone to his ear, he didn't need to say anything at first because Bret had already picked up halfway through the first ring, and was speaking fast, and direct.

"Christ. I'm not entirely sure why this is happening—but it damn well seems to be happening. Which means we need to respond—*fast*."

Neither of them knew for sure what Elon's move meant for the future of Twitter, but they had to act quickly.

The conversation was short because the path forward was clear.

Whether because of Jack's prodding, or driven by his own internal reasons, Elon had signaled his intention to play a bigger role in the way Twitter was being run. Clearly, he wanted to go after the bots and trolls in a more effective, precise manner—Parag immediately saw that as more of an engineering problem than anything else, and hardly controversial. Nobody liked bots, and though trolls were a bit more complicated, since they were by definition real people, there was a lot of territory for improvement.

But Elon's more primary interest: freedom of speech, keeping Twitter an unfettered global town hall—that's where things became exceedingly more complicated.

In the past, Parag had stated publicly that he did not believe Twitter's role was to be "bound by the First Amendment." Rather, Twitter's responsibility was to "serve the public conversation." Healthy conversation, in his opinion, had to have boundaries. That didn't necessarily mean bans, or restrictions to speech; speech, as

Parag had also said before, was easy on the internet. Most people could speak. But that didn't mean everyone could be *heard*.

Twitter's real power wasn't in banning speech, but in creating systems to recommend certain speech over others. The goal, in Parag's view, was always to push speech in a healthy, participatory direction.

In Parag's opinion—and, it appeared, in stark contrast to both Jack's and Elon's—Twitter wasn't meant to be a neutral platform. As he'd stated in a podcast while he was still CTO, "We don't adjudicate what's true and false. [W]e do, however, have the privilege of being able to steer the conversation so that more voices can be heard."

Parag would have been the first to admit, he wasn't a philosopher. He was an engineer. And when he looked at Twitter, he saw the platform through the eyes of an engineer. Twitter was a machine, with levers and dials and gaskets that could be twisted and turned: pushing comments and conversations upward, toward higher engagement, or downward, toward obscurity. But the overarching goal of the levers and gaskets—the algorithms behind what you saw on Twitter, and more important, what you *didn't*—wasn't speech that was free, but speech that was *healthy*—meaning, at its most basic, speech that didn't alienate users or advertisers.

Parag began typing into his phone, constructing the text he would soon be sending to Elon—aiming for just the right amount of eagerness and excitement, inviting the celebrity billionaire to officially join the Twitter board.

Beneath the trappings, the billions, the tabloid headlines, Elon was an engineer, like him. He believed they'd get along, or at least find a way to work together. If they didn't, well, perhaps Parag could just wait it out. Billionaires were notoriously fickle; the wind would blow and suddenly, Elon's attention would be elsewhere. Maybe he would go to a particularly exciting basketball game, and then decide to buy the team. Or read some headline that made him angry, and decide to buy the newspaper.

Or perhaps, once Elon saw how Twitter actually worked—saw the levers and dials and gaskets for himself—he'd quickly change his mind.

As the saying went, the sight and smell of sausage might make you hungry; but sometimes, when you saw how sausage was made— you never wanted to eat sausage again.

## CHAPTER FOUR

**Twenty-five hundred miles** and two time zones away, Jessica Kittery, thirty-four, breezed through the glass doors of 245 West Seventeenth Street, Twitter's New York headquarters: a pair of red-brick former warehouses perched on a busy corner in Chelsea, one of Manhattan's chicest neighborhoods. As usual, she was moving fast, her fashionable flats gliding over hardwood floors as she piloted through the lobby. She made her way through a maze of modern furniture and glowing touchscreens, past the lobby coffee bar and the stairs leading down to the speakeasy café (*Beer and rosé on tap! A Ripple Maker that drew pictures of Jack Dorsey's face in the foam of your latte!*), then hopped into an elevator, riding up to the tune of Japanese pop, upbeat and electric enough to match the caffeine coursing through her veins, the result of the oversized Starbucks she'd downed on the train in from Brooklyn.

It was already past ten a.m. when the elevator doors opened, depositing her on the third floor: a massive, open workspace with row upon row of long desks cluttered with computers, and more touchscreens. There were enough workspaces for a few hundred Tweeps, though Jessica counted barely a dozen scattered around the circumference of the room. To be fair, more would trickle into the building by noon, when the cafeteria upstairs kicked into full gear, its pizza station churning out restaurant-grade creations, its Olympic-length salad bar brimming with options.

Out the elevator and into a short hallway leading to the handful of interior conference rooms that actually had doors (though hardly anyone ever closed them), Jessica rushed past a familiar neon sign, a glowing rendition of the company's unofficial hashtag/motto: #lovewhereyouwork. The provenance of the quote was actually quite sad—a tweet from an employee in the London office who had unsuccessfully battled cancer. She had posted it after her team had gifted her a knit blanket—and seeing it always made Jessica smile, because for her it was endurably true. She loved where she worked. Who wouldn't?

She turned another corner, and nearly collided with a disembodied, smiling face, hovering shoulder-high in the middle of the hallway. The face was on a screen, perched atop a long metal stalk and wheels, and lurched backward to avoid Jessica—and then both she, and the face, were laughing. She still hadn't gotten used to the damn things: virtual teleconferencing units, which allowed people who wanted to be in the building without actually *being* in the building to wander the halls, take meetings, and even hang out in the various in-house cafés. *There was no reason work from home had to mean antisocial, did it?* You could always zap your face onto an electric pogo stick and then hit the salad bar, because nobody really liked lettuce, anyway (no matter which organic farm it had just been flown in from).

Jessica laughed again as she sidestepped the teleconferencing robot and continued toward an open glass door near the end of the hall. Although she had nothing against work from home, she had made an effort to make it to the office at least three times a week, ever since New York had reopened after the worst months of the pandemic. Partially because her apartment in Brooklyn wasn't huge, and she shared the three-bedroom walk-up with her husband and daughters. Her husband was mostly back at work as well. He was a financial analyst for one of the big Manhattan banks, which had been the first genre of business to return to the steel skyscrapers of lower Manhattan, though not the bosses. The bosses were still in Palm Beach and Montauk. Yet even with her husband back at work, she found their apartment confining. Before the pandemic they'd considered moving farther out of the city, to something more suited to a family of four—but Jessica hadn't liked the idea of anything longer than the forty-minute commute she already endured.

In the end, they'd stayed put, and to be honest, she had nothing to complain about. She was used to cramped living conditions. She'd been raised in upstate New Jersey; not the New Jersey of Princeton, or the beach, or the dairy farms you drove by on your way toward Pennsylvania. Upstate upstate, around towns like Newark and Jersey City. Her childhood home could have technically been labeled suburban, but the aging, brick townhouses were so jammed together that you basically shared walls with your neighbors.

Her father worked at Rutgers, but he didn't wear the tweed of a professor; he wore a uniform and managed a team of maintenance workers who took care of the university's utility system. Her mom was stay-at-home, although between Jessica and her two sisters, they had spent more time crammed into the family hatchback going to piano recitals, field hockey games, and sleepovers than they had in their warm, if cramped, living room.

She hadn't gone far, physically, matriculating to NYU and then receiving her master's at Columbia, both on scholarship and loans that she was still paying back, but it felt like worlds apart. She'd always known she was going to end up in marketing or advertising, because she genuinely *liked* people, liked talking to people—as her husband often described it, she had the energy of a Christmas tree.

And she'd been a perfect fit for Twitter. Twitter's offices were sparkly and *felt* like Christmas, a place filled with secret perks and hidden gems that spun and sparkled like ornaments. Although she mainly worked out of the New York offices, she was a frequent visitor to the mother ship in San Francisco, the cavernous main headquarters that towered over the edge of the Tenderloin district—a workspace that made even Twitter's wondrous New York offices seem almost banal. She knew that the speakeasies, coffee shops, and pizza stations weren't unusual for tech companies, a holdover from the go-go years before the 2018 crash had brought everyone back to Earth. Pre-2018, Microsoft and Google and Facebook and yes, Twitter, had been locked in mortal combat for the choice employees; when packages and bonuses weren't enough, you added rosé on tap and foosball machines on the roof. In the greater scheme of things, perks didn't cost the company much, and they made people happy. When things got rough, as they were now, at the (supposed) tail end of the pandemic, it was much easier, and more humane, to get rid of a foosball table than it was to fire a dozen marketing representatives.

Jessica's job was to keep enough money flowing into the company to protect both the foosball tables and the marketing reps. As a manager of global sales—a catch-all title that meant she ran a team tasked with coddling major advertising clients who chose to work with the platform—she was responsible for safeguarding ad money coming into Twitter. Titles, on their own, didn't mean much at Twitter; lines of authority could be confusing, and often Tweeps chose to take on various responsibilities without much oversight at all. No doubt, the often messy corporate structure of the company was the result of Jack's relaxed management style, which had trickled down to every level since he'd returned to the helm in 2015; Parag was certainly more by the book, but he was also an engineer, with limited experience running people. Twitter's hierarchy had remained, in a word, amorphous.

But Jessica's job was one of the more essential, her responsibilities more defined, because what she did had to do with the company's economic bottom line. When fires broke out—and at Twitter, this seemed constant—it was her job to try to put them out, or when that was impossible, to find a way to contain the flames in a way that didn't send advertisers running.

Thankfully, this morning's bit of news caused more smoke than actual fire; the sort of thing that would inspire a lot of chatter on the company's internal Slack channels and a bunch of Zoom calls—but hardly require a face-to-face. Only a lucky coincidence of geography and timing had made this upcoming face-to-face meeting possible, bringing her to one of the private conference rooms on the third floor, saving her an hour of squinting into the floating Zoom box on her laptop.

As she stepped through the open doorway and into the small, brightly lit conference room, sporting a circular table and a kitchenette along one wall, she saw that her colleague from the San Francisco office had already arrived. Thin, slight, with cropped hair bordering on a fade and chiseled cheekbones, he was dressed fashionably, as usual. Dark skinny jeans and a dark zippered jacket that looked tailored to his narrow frame. He was on the phone, of course, because he was almost always on the phone; the device was propped between his ear and shoulder as he leaned against the kitchenette's counter, making himself a cup of tea. He smiled at her as she came into the room, then rolled his eyes at whoever was on the other end of the line. Truth was, it could have been anyone. The CEO of one of their biggest advertisers, Parag or Bret, Jack himself, even though he was no longer officially with the company, a congressman or senator, heck, the head of some task force with the FBI. If Jessica's job was putting out fires and trying to keep the money flowing, the young man making himself tea ran the entire fire department.

Yoel Roth wasn't officially what Jessica would consider upper management; he wasn't responsible for the day-to-day operation of the company, didn't sell or manage advertising, wasn't an engineer, and didn't hire or fire people. But Yoel was one of the most powerful people at Twitter, because in essence, he led the team that decided what was allowed on the site, and what wasn't.

Yoel's title—as all Twitter titles seemed to be—was somewhat slippery. Head of Site Integrity, which would soon morph into Head of Trust and Safety. Basically, his team was responsible for monitoring and safeguarding "Twitter": the conversations, comments, trends, and accounts, and in real time. That meant he didn't just run the platform's fire department; he was a fireman, a sanitation officer, and the chief of police. It was his team's job to identify and squelch hate speech, threats of violence, and more and more, "misinformation," a nebulous term with as many interpretations as there were political, scientific, and religious points of view. Yoel's purview wasn't simply to react to issues as they cropped up; his team's job was also to *proactively* try to keep the platform free from harmful tweets and accounts, by making rules and designing algorithms—with the help of computer engineers—that acted as guardrails against actors both malignant and inadvertently dangerous.

It was an impossible job, the sort of behind-the-scenes role that only garnered attention when something went wrong. But Yoel seemed perfectly suited to the work; he was a private person who didn't need accolades, took his responsibilities seriously because he loved the platform, and philosophically believed in what he was doing. He'd gone to Swarthmore and the University of Pennsylvania, where he'd received a PhD in communication, studying how governance and policy could make online communities safer.

Jessica had worked closely with Yoel on numerous occasions since he'd joined the company in 2015. Without the work that Trust and Safety did, you couldn't sell advertising, at least not to the sort of big-brand clients that she was responsible for; brands like Coca-Cola, Microsoft, Apple, and GE. Reputable brands didn't want their ads running next to hate speech, and time and again, social media had proven that without constant moderation, online conversation was always infiltrated, and eventually overrun, by bad actors. The dark corners of the internet were real and many, and more often than not, inhabited by teenagers.

In his work, Yoel had always been careful to emphasize that content moderation shouldn't be governed by "dictatorial edict." As he would later explain, in an interview with tech journalist Kara Swisher, what was important wasn't "the decisions you make, but how you make those decisions." The rules couldn't be arbitrary; they needed to be well communicated and transparent. Even so, as he'd told Swisher, "the work of online sanitation is unrelenting and contentious."

Unfortunately, even when you did your best to make rules of content and stick by them, you couldn't avoid controversy. One of the more public debates that Yoel had found himself caught in the middle of had revolved around the temporary banning of the *New York Post*'s Twitter account. This decision had been made after the *Post* had published an article exposing the contents of a laptop owned by Hunter Biden, the troubled, drug-addicted son of the former vice president, Joe Biden, who was, at the time, running for president against Donald Trump in arguably the most heated election in American history.

Interestingly enough, Yoel had actually been *against* the harsh moderation of the *Post*'s account and article, although the circumstances around the *Post*'s exposé had been confusing and more than a little absurd. According to the story, in April 2019, Hunter Biden had dropped off a water-damaged MacBook Pro at a Delaware repair shop run by a legally blind, albino Trump supporter named John Paul Mac Isaac, who had noticed what he determined to be potentially illegal material on the MacBook's hard drive. Isaac had contacted the FBI, and then, when the FBI hadn't reacted as quickly or thoroughly as Isaac might have preferred, he delivered the laptop to Trump lawyer and associate Rudy Giuliani. Giuliani, in turn, handed the materials over to the *Post,* three weeks before the presidential election. But there was no question that the contents of the hard drive at the center of the exposé were salacious—including sexually explicit conversations and pictures of the vice president's son.

More pressing, to Yoel's thinking, than the contents of the computer had been questions of veracity, chain of custody, and if, indeed, any of it was actually *real.* It was easy, in retrospect, after many aspects of the *Post*'s reportage were eventually corroborated by more news agencies, to judge Twitter's actions in subduing the story—but it was also easy to forget how chaotic that moment in time was. Or how heated the social media environment had become after the events of the previous presidential election of 2016.

During that election, America's security organizations—the FBI, the CIA, and the Department of Homeland Security—had determined that foreign interests had worked to manipulate voters using platforms like Twitter and Facebook. In light of this, as would later be revealed by journalist Matt Taibbi in one of a series of drops of internal reports from Twitter's servers that would be known as the "Twitter Files"—beginning in 2018, over a hundred and fifty emails had been sent between the FBI and Yoel. As Yoel later told Swisher, the FBI had told him at the time to expect "hack and leak operations by state actors . . . before the 2020 election. Likely in October. The material obtained in hacking would be thrown onto the site . . . and would involve Hunter Biden."

When the *Post* exposé hit Twitter, Yoel and his team had been primed to expect exactly what they were seeing: a story with confusing provenance that would impact the upcoming election.

It would have been easy to do nothing, to let the story proliferate unheeded—freedom of speech, after all. But not responding, not moderating the story in any way, was itself an action that could have potentially immense repercussions. If it were to be shown, after the fact, that the story was the result of hacked materials and a foreign agent, Twitter's inaction could be responsible for allowing misinformation to sway a presidential election.

The back-and-forth between Yoel and his team, as revealed in another Twitter files drop by author Michael Shellenberger, included a mix of wanting to cover their own actions—or asses—and coming to what seemed to be the best conclusion at the time.

"I'm struggling to understand the policy basis for marking this as unsafe," one of Yoel's team wrote, "and I think the best explainability argument for this externally would be that we're waiting to understand if this story is the result of hacked materials. We'll face hard questions on this if we don't have some kind of solid reasoning for marking the link unsafe."

Yoel had responded: "The policy basis is hacked materials—though, as discussed, this is an emerging situation where the facts remain unclear. Given the SEVERE risks here and lessons of 2016, we're erring on the side of including a warning and preventing this content from being amplified."

In the end, Twitter's deputy general counsel, Jim Baker, who had also been the leading counsel for the FBI during the investigation into potential Russian manipulation during the election of 2016, had signed off on the decision:

*I support the conclusion that we need more facts to assess whether the materials were hacked. At this stage, however, it is reasonable for us to assume that they may have been and that caution is warranted. There are some facts that indicate that the materials may have been hacked, while there are others indicating that the computer was either abandoned and the owner consented to allow the repair shop to access it for at least some purposes. We simply need more information.*

Yoel, despite his initial misgivings, eventually went all in on the Twitter suppression of the story:

*The key factor informing our approach is consensus from the experts monitoring election security and disinformation that this looks a lot like a hack-and-leak that learned from the 2016 WikiLeaks approach and our policy changes. The suggestion from experts—which rings true—is there was a hack that happened separately, and they loaded the hacked materials on the laptop that magically appeared at a repair shop in Delaware and was coincidentally reviewed in a very invasive way by someone who coincidentally then handed the materials to Rudy Giuliani. Given the severe risks we saw in this space in 2016 we're recommending a warning + deamplification pending further information.*

Although Jack Dorsey would later call the "blocking of URL sharing via tweet or DM with zero context as to why we're blocking unacceptable," Yoel's Trust and Safety team had done what they believed to be their job: protected the platform from what they had determined was potentially dangerous content, at least temporarily, until they could gather more facts.

Jessica knew, because she'd been there, often a fly on the wall witnessing Yoel in action, that the Biden laptop story wasn't the last controversial decision Yoel's team had been forced to make. But it was a precedent; the tools used in the suppression of the *Post* story—banning of accounts, moderating tweets, DMs, and trending topics—went into common rotation, especially as the pandemic moved into high gear and Covid misinformation proliferated on the platform.

The quagmire of policing Covid misinformation paled in comparison to the madness surrounding what brought the most attention to Trust and Safety, and to Yoel personally: the permanent banning of Donald Trump's Twitter account, on January 8, 2021, after the seismic events at the US Capitol building on January 6.

Yoel's personal feeling toward Trump was no secret among people who knew him, or to the numerous internet sleuths who had uncovered some of Yoel's own tweets from his past, most egregious of the bunch, a tweet from 2017: *"Yes, that person in the pink hat is clearly a bigger threat to your brand of feminism than ACTUAL NAZIS IN THE WHITE HOUSE."*

But even so, the removal of Trump hadn't come easy, even though there had been growing calls to ban the president's account since 2016. The public's reaction toward his use of Twitter had grown so furious by 2018 that Twitter's own public policy account had to explain why they hadn't yet removed the president, in a tweet on January 5 of that year:

> Blocking a world leader from Twitter or removing
> their controversial tweets would hide important
> information people should be able to see and
> debate. It would also not silence that leader, but it
> would certainly hamper necessary discussion
> around their words and actions.

But the events of January 6, 2021, and Trump's own tweets during the protest-turned-assault on the Capitol had forced Twitter's hand. The riots had led to more than 840 arrests, multiple deaths and injuries, investigations, and massive ongoing litigation, and had clearly been instigated by the perception that the 2020 election had been fraudulent. Extreme manifestations of that idea were considered worthy of suppression by Trust and Safety, and the idea's greatest proponent had been Trump himself.

The decision to remove Trump from Twitter had been the result of frenzied internal debate between January 6 and January 8. Jack, who had been CEO at the time, had been on vacation in French Polynesia during the discussions, which had left Yoel with an outsized voice in the situation. The direct incentive to ban the president had been two tweets, which Trump had posted on the morning of the 6th:

> The 75,000,000 great American Patriots who voted
> for me, AMERICA FIRST, and MAKE AMERICA
> GREAT AGAIN, will have a GIANT VOICE long into

the future. They will not be disrespected or treated unfairly in any way, shape or form." – at 6:46 a.m.

And then, at 7:44 a.m.:

To all of those who have asked, I will not be going to the Inauguration on January 20th.

These tweets, and the riots that came after had caused a tsunami of action within Twitter. Jessica herself remembered the day vividly, as Slack messages, emails, and tweets flew between the Tweeps, demanding some sort of action. By the end of January 8, it had been clear to Yoel and his team that Twitter had to act, which they publicly explained on the Twitter company blog:

*After close review of recent tweets from the @realDonaldTrump account and the context around them—specifically how they are being received and interpreted on and off Twitter—we have permanently suspended the account due to the risk of further incitement of violence.*

In Jessica's mind, Yoel's team had reacted to the events in a manner that they believed made Twitter a safer environment: identifying what they believed to be a potential conflagration, and reacting swiftly and deliberately.

Compared to the banning of Trump, Covid misinformation, and even Hunter Biden's laptop, the current news that had precipitated Jessica's meeting with Yoel that morning was barely a brushfire. Still, it was just big enough news, at least, that Yoel led with it, even as he hung up his phone and slipped the device back into the pocket of his skinny jeans.

"Elon Musk," he said, shaking his head. "This should be . . . interesting."

The pause told Jessica everything she needed to know. The billionaire—was he still a billionaire? or was it already trillionaire?—now owned 9.5 percent of the company, and word was Parag had already gotten him to agree, at least in principle, to the idea of joining the board. No doubt, Elon was a genius, and powerful, and he sure as hell knew how to tweet. But he was also a notorious Twitter troll: a thrower of memes, who liked to stir things up. Jessica knew that Yoel's Trust and Safety had endured more than a few meetings about things Elon had tweeted, and a few of his tweets had already been flagged for various indiscretions.

Which was why Jessica had arranged the meeting; because right after talking to Yoel and getting the news, she'd be on the phone with her clients, one after another, who all would want to know the same thing. *What does Elon want to change?* And what would it mean for Twitter? More specifically, what would it mean for advertisers, who really only cared about one thing: a safe, stable, healthy environment, the sort of platform that Yoel worked day and night to provide, in which to sell what they wanted to sell?

*Interesting.*

That was one way of putting it. But Jessica was sure Yoel was as curious as she was herself. Most of the Tweeps who had emailed or texted her about Elon's stake had been excited by the prospect of such a brilliant entrepreneur joining the board. But Jessica wasn't as swept up as her colleagues by his aura. In marketing, she worked with a lot of CEOs, many big personalities, who were usually insulated from people with differing points of view. Elon Musk was a legendary businessman, but Twitter wasn't a car company. It was a social media site, providing a platform for hundreds of millions of people from countries all over the world, from every walk of life, to converse.

She reminded herself that it was easy to make things seem more dramatic than they were. Elon hadn't taken over the company, or anything crazy like that—he'd only bought a few billion dollars' worth of shares. But still, it was hard not to wonder:

*What could a man like Elon Musk possibly want with Twitter?*

## CHAPTER FIVE

## Boca Chica, Texas.

It might have looked something like this: a hundred-thousand-acre compound of sand and brush, pockmarked by low-slung buildings; towering, cylindrical chem tanks; and gleaming, futuristic machinery, bordered by a ten-foot-high chain-link fence. A crowd of engineers, some in uniform, some in T-shirts and khaki shorts, stood with their backs to the fence, staring out across a cleared section of brush toward a huge metallic pylon with reticulated arms, braced around something gleaming, suspended twenty feet into the air.

Above the crowd, the air shimmered with heat and a thick, almost visible humidity that had swept in from the Gulf of Mexico, not a hundred yards beyond the highway.

*Command Center to Test Platform.*
*Safety check complete.*
*All systems go.*
*On my mark. Countdown commence.*
*T-minus ten.*
*Nine.*
*Eight . . .*

In the middle of the herd of engineers, Elon might have felt a shiver move through him as the tinny voice echoed through his skull. Not through his ears—but through his *skull*, the fused and interconnected bones themselves. Packets of vibration injected directly into his maxilla at the top of his jawbone, spreading through his viscerocranium, where they were received, digested, and interpreted by the neurons in his brain.

*Seven.*
*Six.*

As space-age as it seemed, the bone-conducting headset, with its vibrating panels resting just above Elon's cheeks, was old tech; the science behind them had been worked out over a century ago, and though they made sense in some instances—like when you were standing in a crowd with a lot of ambient noise, about to experience something that would be immensely, terrifyingly loud—Elon thought of the device as primitive, and extremely inefficient. A simple and quick solution, a stopgap, like giving a blind person a dog or a paralyzed person a chair with wheels, that would one day be replaced by brighter minds with better ideas.

*Five.*
*Four.*

One of his own initiatives, and the end goal of one of his many companies, Neuralink, was an implantable computer-to-brain interface. This would be one such better idea than the bone-conducting headset; the disembodied voice of his Command and Control Team would one day be jacked directly into his brain, skipping bone and cartilage, a seamless marriage of silicon and neuron that was already being beta tested in dozens of monkeys in a laboratory in Fremont, California. Neuralink would be much more than a revolution in the way people would communicate; quite literally, because of Neuralink, the blind would see, the disabled would walk.

But for now, vibrations into bone would have to suffice.

*Three.*
*Two.*

Elon might have blinked, the excitement rising inside him, a feeling he shared with the small crowd gathered around him. He knew there was a much larger crowd behind the fence at his back, across the strip of highway, on the beach. Tourists and journalists and bloggers and YouTubers, aiming cell phones and live-cams from atop the dunes—but he didn't care. It was the sort of moment that deserved to be documented.

He shifted his attention directly forward, past the thirty yards of cleared brush to the test pylon. Beyond the pylon, maybe another fifty yards, he could see the looming structure of the actual launch tower: a latticework of steel and iron rising high above the compound, so high that it appeared to pierce the lowest level of cloud. But today, the launch tower remained dormant, waiting; a backdrop to the much smaller, though equally muscular test pylon, and the precious object it embraced in its tight, mechanical grip.

The thing was shiny and vaguely conical, smooth in places, bristling with knobs and pipes in others. It wasn't particularly large: ten feet in height, four feet in diameter, but it weighed 3,500 pounds. In simple terms, it was one of the most complex feats of engineering in existence, and one of the most powerful objects on planet Earth.

*One.*

Elon might have held his breath, as the crowd around him went suddenly still. There was a frozen moment, as if everything he could see had somehow become pictures splashed across a sheet of glass. And then—

The roar was deafening, a wall of sound and pressure so fierce it actually pushed Elon back on his heels. The conical machine trembled and then burst to life. A massive cylinder of flame erupted downward, colors that were hard to identify: yellow, orange, blue, the very air beneath the cone itself igniting from a heat so intense it could barely be quantified.

A murmur moved through the crowd, as applause burst out from behind the fence. The sound grew louder, the cylinder of flame more powerful, the heat spewing outward across the sand as Elon felt a wild grin spread across his lips. The ground itself seemed to tremble; the flame grew brighter and brighter. He could barely make out the chatter in his headset as Command and Control pushed harder and farther. The cylinder was turning almost pure white, brighter and brighter and brighter—

Until suddenly there was a loud crackle, a sound of metal warping. Fire leapt up the sides of the conical machine and then outward around the arms holding it in place. There was an alarmed gasp from the beach as another crack tore the air—and then the machine went dead, the cylinder of flame extinguished, dark black clouds billowing upward into the sky.

The crowd behind the fence might have assumed that something had gone wrong, but Elon and the engineers surrounding him knew better. The conical device had been pushed to its limit, and then pushed farther, until it had reached its breaking point. Now the engineers would go back, find out what had caused it to explode, fix whatever could be fixed—then try again.

In rocketry, that was often how innovation worked; you blew things up, then figured out how to keep them from blowing up the next time.

Elon might have taken a deep breath, imagining he was inhaling tasteless wisps of superheated methane, then turned and moved away from the crowd of engineers. There were more voices in his headset, but he ignored them, just as he ignored the sirens of the fire trucks moving into place, raising their great hoses filled with flame-deterrent foam, which would flow like living tentacles around the smoldering test platform, dousing the device so the engineers could move in to begin the painstaking task of deconstructing what had happened.

To Elon, the results would have already been clear: his Raptor 2 rocket engine had performed beyond anything of its kind, beyond anything that had ever existed before. A single engine capable of producing 510,000 pounds of thrust, six times more thrust than its predecessor—the Raptor 1—and ten times as much thrust as the engines that carried the Falcon rockets that Elon's private company, SpaceX, had been sending into space for more than a decade. The Raptor 2's internal MCC pressure was far beyond anything that NASA, Russia, or any space agency on Earth had ever achieved, and it was powered by a particularly unique fuel, a mix of cryogenic liquid methane and oxygen. In many ways, the Raptor 2 was the key to everything that SpaceX was working toward, and represented as great a leap forward, perhaps, as Neil Armstrong's famous first steps onto the pockmarked surface of the Moon.

Elon might have shivered, despite the heat, as he started off across the compound, away from the shouts and waves from beyond the chain-link fence. He could feel the cell phones and cameras trained on him; although there were guards at the entrance to Starbase—the kitschy name he'd given SpaceX's main campus when he'd purchased the land back in 2002—and plenty of fences, the work the brilliant men and women of SpaceX were doing was not meant to be secret. Quite the contrary, in fact.

Humanity had evolved, kicking and screaming, on a single, dangerous bit of real estate, upon a fragile, spinning globe, barely surviving and avoiding disaster after disaster, both natural and self-inflicted. Wars, famine, climate change, disease, population decline—human civilization was facing constant, existential threats. In Elon's point of view, because of this, humanity had but one choice to ensure survival: become interplanetary.

SpaceX existed because Elon believed that for the first time in human history, humanity had achieved a level of economic security and technological advancement that made interplanetary life possible. A window was open, but there was no way of knowing how long that window would *remain* open.

Already, what Elon and his engineers at SpaceX had achieved in pushing humankind toward the stars was nothing short of incredible. SpaceX was the first company to privately develop a liquid-propellant rocket that could reach orbit; the first to send a spacecraft to the International Space Station; the first to land a booster vertically, then reuse that booster in a later spaceflight; and SpaceX was the first private company to send astronauts into orbit, then to the ISS. In 2018, SpaceX had debuted the world's first reusable rocket capable of making orbit, the Falcon Heavy, for its maiden voyage. The Falcon Heavy, the fourth largest ever built, had carried along a payload that Elon had called "the silliest thing he could imagine": his personal 2010 Tesla Roadster, a mannequin in a spacesuit behind the steering wheel, and a copy of *The Hitchhiker's Guide to the Galaxy* in the glove compartment (along with a towel, a major prop from the Douglas Adams book). The rocket was adorned with a sign on its exterior imploring: "Don't Panic!"

But the Falcon Heavy had only been an appetizer, the first step toward SpaceX's eventual goal. For humanity to extend beyond Earth's atmosphere, you had to do more than get people to orbit: you needed to cross a vast expanse of space, land them on a suitable planet, and keep them alive long enough to build a self-sustaining colony.

Already, Elon and his engineers at SpaceX had calculated what that would mean. Not one rocket, but a *thousand* rockets, carrying tens of thousands of colonists, machinery, and raw materials. In the end, as with everything, it came down to math and physics. It was math and physics that had convinced Elon that the most likely candidate for humanity's second home was the planet Mars. At 33.9 million miles during its closest orbit, Mars was the most accessible planet to Earth; it had a thin atmosphere that could one day be thickened with the help of technology, and had abundant water in the form of ice. There were also significant deposits of minerals and other resources that could sustain human life, such as iron and nickel.

It was math and physics that had allowed Elon to estimate that it would take at least a million tons of cargo to build a self-sustainable Mars colony. For such an endeavor to be economically possible, let alone practical, SpaceX had needed to solve for the holy grail of rocketry—a rocket that was both powerful enough to reach Mars, and wholly reusable.

Elon's Raptor 2 engine was a key component of that holy grail. Not just because of its power, which was magnitudes higher than the thrust produced by the engines that had put men on the Moon half a century ago, but also because of its unique source of fuel— the frozen methane and oxygen, which would be plentiful under the surface ice of their destination. Enough Raptor 2 engines in parallel could lift a rocket with an immense payload into orbit, hurl it 33.9 million miles across the darkness of space, and then back again, to be reused over and over. That was why SpaceX was already pumping out Raptor 2s at a breakneck pace: one a day, seven days a week.

Elon would have passed through the shadows of a pair of huge satellite dishes. These were components of the Starlink system, an offshoot of SpaceX's mission to colonize the solar system: a network of low-orbit satellites that could provide seamless internet to anyone on Earth. He approached a low-slung building with the word STAR-GATE running up the side in bright red lettering, another kitschy nod toward Hollywood science fiction, but to Elon a fitting label for the central building that housed engineering labs, teaching facilities, and his Command Center's mission control. He paused when he reached the doorway, taking a moment before he stepped inside.

In the distance beyond the Stargate building, he would clearly make out a triumvirate of shiny, cylindrical steel towers, rising hundreds of feet into the air. Just the sight of them made Elon's chest rise. Even one of the glistening behemoths would have put Babel to shame, and yet Elon knew, this was only the beginning. He could close his eyes and imagine the SpaceX compound bristling with the magnificent constructs, row after row after row, like a gleaming field of high-tech terra-cotta soldiers.

To him, these objects, paired with the Raptor 2, smoldering on the test platform behind him, represented hope, and the future, not just of SpaceX—but *humanity's* future. They represented two decades of his life, and much of his mental bandwidth, a dream, coming to fruition right in front of his eyes. The centerpiece of his existential mission, finally real, solid, and, he wanted to believe, inevitable. But he also knew that success was never guaranteed; his experience with Tesla had taught him that threats loomed behind every corner.

Something about the thought might have made him instinctively reach into his pocket and withdraw his phone. As he scrolled back through the past few days of texts, he decided that Stargate and mission control could wait a moment longer.

On the face of it, his newest project, the one that had inspired the barrage of texts that seemed to be palpably weighing down his phone, might have seemed foolish. Indeed, it had begun as something of a whim, but it was fast consuming more and more of his attention. He now firmly believed that in many ways, the attention was warranted.

Twitter, in his mind, was clearly broken. Jack Dorsey's vision of a global town hall, a place where people from all over the world could speak freely, had been overrun by bots and trolls, and constrained, *constricted*, by subjective moderating forces, operating behind a curtain.

Twitter was broken. To Elon, this was more than the tarnishing of a product he enjoyed, more than the deterioration of something that had started with so much promise. It represented a danger to his central mission, to the vision that had led him to Tesla and had powered everything he had built at Starbase.

If human civilization had finally reached that window where becoming interplanetary was possible, to keep that window open as long as was needed, civilization had to continue forward, not fall backward into a dark age. Elon believed that a global town hall, a place for a truly free exchange of ideas, was like a rocket booster, and necessary for that forward motion; conversely, an assault on free speech and the sharing of ideas acted as an air brake, slowing progress, threatening to reverse whatever achievements had brought humanity to the starting gate. To *Stargate*.

Elon was determined to keep that from happening.

His quiet accumulation of shares in Twitter had been a first step in trying to right what had gone wrong with the platform. But his dinner with Twitter's upper management at the donkey-infested Airbnb outside of San Jose had been more of a shuffle backward. He had

nothing yet against Parag and Bret, both of whom had seemed
grounded and smart, yet he'd come out of the session less than confident that talking about Twitter's issues would lead to any real change.
Upper management seemed good at conversation, less so at action.
Elon knew, you didn't make Raptor engines by talking about them.

---

By the afternoon of April 4, after his SEC filing had been made public, he'd decided against joining the Twitter board, and fired off a
text to Parag: "Thank you for considering me for the Twitter board,
but after thinking it over, my current time commitments would pre-
vent me from being an effective board member. This may change in
the future. Elon."

This, no doubt, had led to much consternation and confusion at
the company. Likewise, he knew the revelation of his shares had
caused a ripple of nervous concern within Twitter—while outside, at
least in Elon's circle of friends, it had inspired a more celebratory
form of excitement.

One of the many texts of congratulations he'd received was
from the conservative podcaster and comedian Joe Rogan, with
whom Elon had famously smoked pot on air (earning him a daily
drug test at his publicly traded Tesla), and who had asked: "Are you
going to liberate Twitter from the censorship happy mob?"

Elon had laughed at that. He didn't consider himself right-wing,
nor did he even identify as a Republican. He'd voted for both Obama
and Biden, had gotten vaccinated, though he later seemed to regret
it—how odd that somehow even medical decisions had become signals of partisan tribalism—and would have called himself mostly
centrist. But in recent months, there had been a noticeable shift in
the sort of friends and advisors he'd surrounded himself with, who

now tended toward the righter side of libertarianism, with a few true Trumpers in the mix. Elon might have argued that it was the rest of the world that had shifted left, making him seem more conservative in the process, but his cultural views seemed more and more aligned with the pundits and think tanks of the Republican right.

Still, Rogan's point, though likely inspired by the muffling of conservative voices on the platform, made sense whether Elon looked at it from his past, centrist persona, or his current, right-leaning posture.

"I will provide advice," he'd shot back to Rogan, "which they may or may not choose to follow."

It was an elaboration on that strategy which had pushed him to change his mind; he must find a way to give them advice, whether they wanted it or not. And so on April 5, he'd given Parag the go-ahead to announce to the Twitterati:

*I'm excited to share that we're appointing @elonmusk to our board! Through conversations with Elon in recent weeks, it became clear to me that he would bring great value to our Board. Why? Above all else, he's both a passionate believer and intense critic of the service which is exactly what we need on Twitter, and in the Boardroom, to make us stronger in the long-term! Welcome Elon!*

Elon would almost see the rain of emojis that might have danced among such a forest of exclamation marks, but inside he wondered if a newly appointed CEO like Parag would really want an "intense critic" in Twitter's boardroom.

Perhaps envisioning Elon's concerns, Jack Dorsey had quickly texted Elon to try to set him at ease: "Parag is an incredible engineer. The board is terrible. Always here to talk through anything you want."

That had gotten another grin out of Elon; Jack, after all, had been the impetus for much of what had already happened. And Jack had good reason to hate the board, which had wrestled control of Twitter from him—not once, but twice. Jack probably saw Elon's ascension as a way of fighting back.

"I've wanted it for a long time," Jack had added in his texts, on Elon's joining the board. "Got very emotional when I learned it was finally possible."

Partially for Jack's sake, partially because it was the angle of least resistance to effecting change, from there Elon had engaged in a back-and-forth with Parag, texts so fast and furious they read more like the first hours of a budding romance than the initial conversations of prospective business colleagues.

"I have a ton of ideas," Elon had written in gingerly making the first move, "but LMK if I'm pushing too hard. I just want Twitter to be maximum amazing."

Followed, cautiously, with "I would like to understand the technical details of the Twitter codebase. This will help me calibrate the dumbness of my suggestions."

And, adding a bit of peacock: "I wrote heavy duty software for 20 years."

Parag had responded in kind: "I used to be CTO and have been in our codebase for a long time."

The way Elon perked to this was evident even in the glowing pixels of his text screen: "I interface way better with engineers who are able to do hardcore programming than with program manager/MBA types of people."

Parag, flirting even harder: "In our next convo—treat me like an engineer instead of CEO and let's see where we get to."

"Frankly," Elon had coquettishly acquiesced, "I hate doing mgmt. stuff. I kinda don't think anyone should be the boss of anyone. But I love helping solve technical/product design problems."

But as optimistic as Elon had felt after that first day of texts, now, in the doorway to Stargate, he realized that again, it was nothing more than conversation.

By the next day, the beginning of the weekend, Elon expressed his frustration the way he often had in the past: he'd launched a fiery tweetstorm to his now over eighty million followers.

He'd started by posting a poll, a vote on whether or not Twitter should turn its San Francisco headquarters into a homeless shelter.

He'd followed that tweet with a comment about Twitter Blue, the platform's subscription service, suggesting that users should be allowed to pay for Blue with Dogecoin, and in turn receive one of the precious blue "authentication checkmarks" that were normally reserved for celebrities, journalists, politicians, and other notables.

*"Everyone who signs up for Twitter Blue (pays 3$/month) should get an authentication checkmark, and no ads,"* he'd tweeted. *"The power of corporations to dictate policy is greatly enhanced if Twitter depends on advertising money to survive."*

He wasn't simply trolling with the tweet; he believed that separating Twitter from advertisers was indeed a free speech issue. During the dinner at the Airbnb, Parag had offhandedly explained that Twitter's sometimes heavy-handed moderation was often in support of advertising. Since advertisers didn't want their ads running next to controversial content, the greater the restrictions, the higher the ad revenue. If this was the case, as long as Twitter relied on advertising dollars to survive, how could speech on the platform ever truly be free?

From there, as the weekend had progressed, Elon's inhibitions had begun to recede and a more trollish persona had crept out. He'd begun with a poll asking people to vote on whether Twitter should drop the *w* from its name. But by the morning of April 9, his emotions had turned darker.

At 9:32 a.m., he'd tweeted a pointed question:

> Most of these "top" accounts tweet rarely and post
> very little content. Is Twitter dying?

He'd followed that with a list of the platform's biggest users in terms of followers, accounts including Barack Obama, Justin Bieber, Katy Perry, and Taylor Swift.

It was that tweet in particular that had apparently caught management's attention. Elon had just finished dinner when he'd received Parag's text, which had caught him by surprise, not for its content, but for its vehemence:

> *You are free to tweet "Is Twitter dying?" or anything else about Twitter—but it's my responsibility to tell you that it's not helping me to make Twitter better in the current context. Next time we speak, I'd like to provide you perspective on the level of internal distraction right now and how it's hurting our ability to do work.*

Even now, standing in front of the entrance to Stargate, Elon might have remembered the swell of anger he'd felt as he'd read Parag's text. Admonishing him, like he was some sort of schoolkid—people in Elon's life simply didn't talk to him like that. Perhaps as a result of his lonely childhood, or his inability to properly read social cues, he had never responded well to criticism, something many interpreted to be a sign of thin skin.

"What did you get done this week?" Elon had shot back to Parag.

Followed quickly by "I'm not joining the board. This is a waste of time."

Then, in his fury, he'd launched a text of eight words, eight fateful words, that solidified in his mind almost as he typed them, like methane gas suddenly hit with a cryogenic hose.

*Will make an offer to take Twitter private.*

Elon might have closed his eyes, envisioning the plumes of flame bursting out of the sides of the Raptor 2 engine, as it had been pushed past its limit.

"Can we talk?" Parag had immediately responded, realizing what had just happened—what he'd just done.

Bret Taylor, the company's chairman, had also suddenly chimed in: "Parag just called me and mentioned your text conversations. Can you talk?"

But Elon had made up his mind.

"Please expect a take private offer," he'd texted Bret.

"I saw the text thread," Bret had tried again. "Do you have five minutes so I can understand the context?"

*Backpedaling. Whining. Weakness.*

"Fixing Twitter by chatting with Parag won't work," Elon had succinctly responded.

You didn't make a better Raptor engine by talking about it. You made a better one by, well, *blowing the fucker up.*

Once again, he was firing off text after text, but this was no longer the dance of two potential romantic partners. This was the sharpened rapier thrusts of an impending and violent divorce.

"Drastic action is needed."

"This is hard to do as a public company, as purging fake users will make the numbers look terrible, so restructuring should be done as a private company."

"This is Jack's opinion too."

*A twist of the knife.* Parag and Bret and the board had thought they'd excised Jack, but Jack was back, in a much more potent form.

Bret, panicked, had tried once more: "Can you take 10 minutes to talk this through with me? It has been about 24 hours since you joined the board. I get your point, but just want to understand about the sudden pivot and make sure I deeply understand your point of view and the path forward."

But Elon was finished playing games. He'd proceeded to ghost both Bret and Parag for the next ten hours. In the meantime, he did delete many of the tweets from the weekend, but he'd left the most vicious one, which had asked if Twitter was dying. On top of that, he'd taken the time to like a tweet from a user calling himself "Tank" that explained the now-missing tweets, which everyone had already seen:

> Let me break this down for you: Elon became the largest shareholder for Free Speech. Elon was told to play nice and not speak freely.

But Elon had never been great at playing nice.

Then, two days after his weekend tweetstorm, three days after joining the company's board, Elon had fired off an official letter to Bret, which he'd then added to the required filing he would simultaneously submit to his favorite government organization, the SEC:

> *I invested in Twitter as I believe in its potential to be the platform for free speech around the globe, and I believe free speech is a societal imperative for a functioning democracy.*

*However, since making my investment I now realize the company will neither thrive nor serve this societal imperative in its current form. Twitter needs to be transformed as a private company.*

*As a result, I am offering to buy 100% of Twitter for $54.20 per share in cash, a 54% premium over the day before I began investing in Twitter and a 38% premium over the day before my investment was publicly announced. My offer is my best and final offer and if it is not accepted, I would need to reconsider my position as a shareholder.*

*Twitter has extraordinary potential. I will unlock it.*

Elon's offer represented a more than forty-three-*billion*-dollar investment.

Elon took a deep breath and stopped scrolling through his texts. It was ancient history, because whatever had led him to this point—and the offer to take Twitter private—he now strongly believed it was the correct, and only, course of action. He also had no doubt that Twitter would eventually have no choice but to accept. He'd even added, to his filing, a series of lettered postscripts:

a. I am not playing the back-and-forth game.

b. I have moved straight to the end.

c. It's a high price and your shareholders will love it.

d. If the deal doesn't work, given that I don't have confidence in management nor do I believe I can drive the necessary change in the public market, I would need to reconsider my position as a shareholder.

    i. This is not a threat, it's simply not a good investment without the changes that need to be made.

ii. And those changes won't happen without taking the
company private.

Twitter was broken.

And Elon was determined to fix it. By taking it over.

In a TED interview on April 14, he had put it succinctly: "My strong, intuitive sense is that having a public platform that is maximally trusted and broadly inclusive is extremely important to the future of civilization."

This subtly referenced what he'd come to believe: that taking Twitter private was now an integral part of his existential mission. It would become part of what he was building, here at Starbase and to a lesser extent at Tesla—to save humanity by making it interplanetary. Tesla and Twitter were two sides to a coin; both were necessary to extend the time that civilization's window of opportunity remained open. Tesla, by weaning the world from fossil fuels, and offering sustainable energy. Twitter, by enabling the free and unfettered exchange of ideas.

That morning, at 7:23 a.m., he'd told his eighty million followers, even more succinctly, *"I made an offer."*

Looking past Stargate, out across the compound toward the trio of silvery, towerlike structures, his own personal, triune Babel, he might have almost heard the countdown, deep beneath the bone.

*Three.*
*Two.*
*One.*
*Liftoff.*

## CHAPTER SIX

# June 16, 2022

**Squares, all the way down.**

Mark Ramsey perched on the edge of his chair, staring at the floating window in the center of his laptop computer screen. Still dark and pensive, a square within the square of the virtual conferencing app, within the square that was the laptop itself, resting on the square surface of his desk, in the back corner of his square office, bathed in the light flowing through the square windowpane behind him. The view, if he'd turned to see it: a parking lot baking in the morning heat, more squares of blacktop, almost all of them empty. Mark could have chosen an office on the other side of the seven-story building, something with a view of the financial district, and nobody would have cared. Hell, nobody would have noticed, because he was mostly alone at the Charlotte headquarters. More than 80 percent of the Tweeps who would be watching the videoconference along with him were in their homes, or in their cars, or maybe even at the beach.

His reflection bounced in the screen as he shifted in his chair; even his reflection seemed vaguely square to him. When he was ten years younger, back in his army days, he could have been described as chiseled. Now, in his thirties, he'd gone a little soft, less carved of stone and more blown of glass. But still primarily square, from his closely shorn hair to the boxiness of his shoulders.

Squares, all the way down.

He drummed his fingers against the desk, still waiting. The skin of his fingers looked strangely dark to him, which made him smile, reminding him that two days ago, he too was on a beach, with Gina, his wife. *Wife*—the word seemed so strange to him. Being from the South, waiting to get married until his early thirties was almost scandalous, but four years in camouflage between college and business school had delayed what had been inevitable since he'd met Gina in his freshman year of high school. Both had been new kids at a new school, and had gravitated to each other mostly because of proximity—same bus stop, same homeroom—but they'd soon found they had a lot more in common than a lack of driver's licenses. They'd both grown up in small towns, both loved classic rock, and both wanted to travel the world. On top of paying for college and business school, the army had given Mark enough of a cushion to take her across Europe; he'd smuggled an engagement ring from London to Paris to Berlin before finally getting up the nerve to propose in Copenhagen, while wandering the Rosenborg Castle Gardens, after which they'd traded their brief but romantic vagabond lifestyle for the practical life back in Charlotte.

Even the two-week honeymoon they'd just spent in Hawaii had been carefully planned and budgeted; Mark had never been the sort of person who could just relax, so they'd spent much of the first week hiking through lush rain forests, snorkeling in crystal-clear waters, and diving off perfectly good cliffs—before Gina had finally put her foot down, negotiating for a half dozen days of lying on the beach until sunset, by the end of which Mark had been jumping out of his skin to get back to Charlotte and his empty office building.

Part of the reason he'd been unable to simply shut down and enjoy his first two weeks as a newlywed had to do with the moment, now almost two months before, when that lightning strike of news had first hit Twitter, almost simultaneously as it had hit most of the major media outlets.

Mark had been sitting in this exact spot when his office had erupted in a cacophony of sound: his cell phone chirping as its vibrations threatened to send it clattering to the floor, his desk phone clanging, which had surprised him the most because who the hell still called him on his desk phone, and his computer signaling a flood of incoming messages, on the multiple email servers he used inside and outside of work. It had seemed like everyone had seen the news before he had; after opening Twitter, Slack, and his text app, he'd immediately understood the commotion.

Elon Musk's offer to take Twitter private had hit everyone by surprise. To Mark, the numbers had seemed insane—a 40 percent bump over the stock's price, almost $44 billion—but he'd also realized it was a number that would be almost impossible for the Twitter board to turn down. Though they'd initially adopted a "poison pill" strategy—announcing that they would offer shares at a discount to other shareholders to try to dissuade Elon's private offer—they'd very quickly flipped in the opposite direction, understanding that they served at the pleasure of the shareholders. It would be a dereliction of their duty to turn down such a premium, no matter how much they might have wanted to. In short order, Parag had informed the Tweeps that the board had voted to accept Elon's offer.

Mark's colleagues inside Twitter had responded with a mix of fear and dismay; the riotous applause Elon had garnered as a virtual guest—and cheerleader—at the Houston conference almost three years earlier had morphed into a terrified circling of the wagons at the thought of the unpredictable billionaire taking the reins of the company. There was also an undercurrent of disbelief. Didn't Elon have enough on his plate with Tesla and SpaceX? Did he really want to step into Twitter, a social media company that seemed to lurch from one controversy to the next?

Meanwhile, Mark's colleagues outside Twitter had barraged him with texts and emails of congratulations; for some reason, most of them had assumed that the richest man in the world taking over Twitter meant that Mark himself had somehow just hit the jackpot, and would soon be retiring to the sort of beach he'd just spent a month's salary to visit on his honeymoon. Mark's own mother had left two messages pointing him toward real estate listings in the greater Charlotte area, houses that would have been oversized for a family of five, let alone a newly married couple. He assumed that his mom pictured herself occupying one of the many bedrooms; Mark's father had passed away when Mark was in his twenties, and since he was an only child, his mother had leaned on him pretty heavily for support during the traumatic decade that followed. But Mark knew that, in her own way, she only wanted the best for him—and she'd obviously assumed that Elon taking over Twitter would translate into a six-bedroom estate in Myers Park.

The general public seemed to share Mark's mother's enthusiasm, as evidenced by Twitter's stock price jumping as much as 28 percent in the day after Elon had announced the offer. But weeks later, by the time Mark had been trading vows with Gina at a church two blocks from the house where he'd grown up (his mother and two cousins he hadn't seen since elementary school representing his family in a sea of Gina's relatives), there had been signs that the road forward wasn't going to be anywhere near as smooth as the optimistic public might have hoped.

Within a day of Twitter officially accepting Elon's offer for the company, Tesla's stock had cratered 12 percent—losing more than

$100 billion in value in a single market day. That meant Elon's car company had lost more than twice what Elon was going to pay for Twitter: a pretty unavoidable signal that Tesla shareholders had a very different view of Elon's takeover of Twitter than Twitter's own investors did. Three days later, when it became public that Elon had sold $8.5 billion worth of Tesla stock to boost his own cash position ahead of the deal, Tesla stock descended further, beginning a spiral that seemed to have no end in sight.

Though Tesla's plummeting stock price could also be blamed on the wider market pullback, it seemed obvious that Tesla investors feared Elon's divided focus, and perhaps the sort of public attention that running Twitter would surely bring Elon's way. Elon had caused enough problems with his tweets when he was just another registered user; what was it going to be like when he was tweeting as the platform's CEO?

Elon himself seemed to be taken aback by the sudden negative sentiment from the Tesla community; likely he was not accustomed to the Tesla faithful treating him as anything but a savior, considering that he'd carried the company on his shoulders through multiple potential disasters. Quite frankly, in anything Tesla related, there had been very few times Elon's name had been mentioned in a paragraph that didn't also include the word *genius*.

Then Elon's sudden announcement—two weeks later, on May 13—that he was putting his Twitter deal "on hold" seemed too much a coincidence with the plummeting of Tesla's value (slicing away at Elon's net worth along with it) to be anything but a reaction. Elon's own explanation of the pause on his purchase had nothing to do with Tesla stock, of course: he had put the deal on hold, he'd announced, because he had reason to believe that Twitter had inflated its calculation of its user base by claiming that less than 5 percent of its users were fake or spam accounts. Elon believed that number was wildly underestimated, suggesting in a tweet on May 17 that even 20 percent of Twitter's users being fake might have been an underestimate.

Although in public, both Elon's and Twitter management's rhetoric had begun escalating toward outward animosity, within Twitter, Parag and his team were proceeding as if Elon's purchase would be going forward, no matter what the billionaire was tweeting. Through internal channels, Mark had heard that a legal team was already being assembled on the chance that Elon's "hold" on the deal turned into a true retreat.

A month later, newly tanned and back at his desk, Mark had no reason to suspect it would ever come to a lawsuit; quite the opposite, as the floating square in the center of his laptop's screen suddenly flickered to life, revealing a live image of Parag in a cramped office with walls that seemed to have been papered in fifteen different shades of beige. Mark felt like he had a front-row seat—alongside the nearly seventy-five hundred other Tweeps who were attending the all-hands call along with him—of what Twitter would soon look like.

After a brief and overly obsequious introduction, Parag's visage was replaced by Elon's; the contrast between the two engineers, and the backgrounds they'd chosen to beam into the gathering, could not have been more stark. Parag's black shirt, collarless and clingy, morphed into Elon's crisp white dress shirt, open at the neck in a style that seemed both effortless and debonair. Parag's tiny, cramped beige office was offset by the vast and airy setting Elon had chosen for the call: some sort of conference room or business cafeteria with ridiculously high ceilings, decorated in tones of gold and softly lit wood, with what appeared to be a galley kitchen behind him, complete with the shiny chrome of a large refrigerator.

Parag couldn't have slunk off the screen any faster, quickly pass-ing the baton to Leslie Berland, Twitter's chief marketing officer. Mark was pleased to see Leslie conducting the conversation; Mark had worked with her directly on numerous campaigns, and knew her to be extremely competent. He also felt it was telling that Parag had tapped his CMO to run the call, perhaps a sign that he under-stood that his background as an engineer, and his lack of experience in management, hadn't prepared him for handling someone like Elon Musk. The way Mark saw it, Parag had already "managed" Elon into quitting the Twitter board, making an offer to take the company private, and then putting that offer on hold.

Leslie started off the call with a softball, giving Elon a moment to tell the camera how much he loved Twitter: "I've literally tweeted—I love Twitter," he answered. She followed up by asking why. Because, he explained, it allowed people to communicate with large numbers of other people without being filtered by the negative lens of mass media. He continued by clarifying comments he'd made about the importance of Twitter being "a digital town square."

"You can't have millions of people in a town square," Elon told Leslie. "You have millions of people on Twitter, which is incredibly important and essential for a functioning democracy. To function well, I think it's essential to have free speech and communicate freely."

Then Elon dug deeper:

*I think there's also freedom of speech and freedom of reach. Freedom of speech is one thing. Anyone can go to Times Square right now and say anything they want. They can deny the Holocaust, okay? That doesn't mean that it needs to be promoted to millions of people. So I think people can say out-rageous things within the bounds of the law, but it doesn't*

*have to get amplified. And I think an important goal for Twit-*
*ter is to try and include as much of the country, as much of*
*the world as possible.*

On the one hand, Elon seemed to be saying that he did agree
that the sort of moderation that Twitter had been performing, often
led by Yoel Roth's team, was sometimes necessary, but that it could
be applied without truly limiting "legal" free speech. But it was also
clear that Elon wanted to expand Twitter's user base—giving more
people the opportunity to join in on the conversation.

"You want as much of the world on Twitter, you want to be
inclusive as possible for the broadest demographic," the billionaire
continued. "In order for that to happen, people must like being on
Twitter. If people are, like, being harassed or they're uncomfortable,
they're just not going to use Twitter."

Elon was saying all the right things, at least this far into the all-
hands, and off to the side of Mark's conferencing window he could
see optimistic Slack channels sprouting up.

"So we have to strike this balance of letting people say what they
want to say, but also make them comfortable on Twitter, or they
simply won't use it."

Mark didn't think anyone in the company would have a problem with that line of thinking; Christ, Yoel could have stated that
himself, and nobody would have blinked an eye. Rather than push
deeper on the concept of moderation, Leslie changed direction,
giving Elon a chance to touch on the bot issue, leaving out the fact
that it was the central point of dispute that had led him to pause his
takeover.

"There's definitely an ongoing challenge with bot accounts and
spam accounts," Elon said, nearly bouncing in his seat, the camera
fighting to keep him in the center of the chat square. "There are quite

a bit of scams on Twitter. . . . There are also people, it may not be bots, but one person operating hundreds of accounts and trying to make them look like individuals but they're not. In order for people to have trust in Twitter, it's extremely important there's transparency."

Again, nobody at Twitter would have argued with Elon's point— that bots and trolls were an issue—but then he advanced one possible solution that set the Slack channel on edge.

"I have a thought in this regard," he began. "If there was a little Twitter Blue authenticated, not like a celebrity, but authenticated by Twitter Blue payments. Piggybacking on the payments system to do authentication . . . Some authentication to my name, that means I'm probably not a bot or spam or someone operating hundreds of accounts. That's like three dollars a month. I believe that would be helpful. . . ."

Mark leaned back in his chair. If he had heard Elon correctly, Elon was talking about people *paying* for the Blue Checks that Twitter currently gave out to celebrities, journalists, politicians, and the like. Would anyone be willing to pay for "authentication" when that authentication would no longer mean anything other than the fact that you could afford three dollars a month? Even putting that aside, Mark wondered how that would impact the level of dialogue on the site. Though the Blue Check system had its flaws, particularly in the murky way the checks had been historically distributed, it had at least offered some way of vetting accounts based on the quality of information they might be able to bring into the conversation. All tweets were equal, but there had always been a sliding scale of tweeters.

From the point of view of someone who worked closely with advertisers, this made sense; if a celebrity, journalist, politician, or company representative tweeted something controversial, you at least knew who it was coming from, which meant there was some level of responsibility, authority, and the potential for consequence behind the tweet. You could disagree with it, you could complain about it, you could ignore it, you could embrace it, but at least theoretically, you understood its source. But if anyone could have a Blue Check, you would have no way of judging the provenance of a tweet; you could no longer assume Twitter had verified anything about a tweeter beyond his ability to own a credit card.

Maybe this would be a fairer platform, but Mark couldn't see how, in practice, it would lead to a safer, more elevated platform. Mark wondered if it was something Elon had actually thought through, or if it was something he'd just thrown out, on the spur of the moment. The way he spoke made it seem like everything he said was deliberate, but then again Mark didn't know the man at all; perhaps it was simply his style.

If Leslie had concerns about Elon's Twitter Blue suggestion, she didn't show them; instead, she shifted the conversation to a topic with a more direct impact on her audience.

"Distributed work has been core to our strategy," she said in the beginning of this new line of questions, leaning heavily into some corporate euphemisms. "Most of our people work in a hybrid model. About 1,500 people work remotely full-time. You've sent communications to Tesla executives on remote work. Can you share what your point of view is on remote work and specifically for Twitter?"

Elon shifted perceptibly in his seat, but then offered a little wisp of a smile.

*Yeah, so Tesla makes cars and obviously you cannot make cars remotely . . . the bias needs to be strongly towards working in person, but if someone is exceptional, then remote work can be okay. . . . The bias is very much toward in-person work. It would obviously be insane if someone is excellent at what they do but can only work remotely to then fire them. That would be insane. I'm not in favor of things that are, like, mad. I'm in favor of things that build the business and make it better.*

Sitting in his office in an empty building, Mark had to grin at that; certainly, he understood why most people preferred to work from home. Some people were even more productive in the comfort of their home offices, not having to deal with commutes, unnecessary face-to-face meetings, wasted time in elevators, cafeterias, smoothie bars. But on the whole, Mark had found the shift to "distributed work" a gateway drug toward the weakened work culture at Twitter, which had made it harder and harder to get things done.

From remote work, Leslie moved right into a question that was central to her audience's concerns: "Can you speak to how you're thinking about layoffs at Twitter?"

Mark doubted Elon's response put anyone listening at ease: "Well, I think it depends, the company does need to get healthy. So right now the costs exceed the revenue so that's not a great situation to be in . . ."

But in a roundabout way, he at least tried to be optimistic: "Anyone who is a significant contributor should have nothing to worry about. I do not take actions which are disruptive to the health of the company, so, you know, yeah."

Not exactly comforting words, but Mark didn't disagree with the sentiment; the company had surely become bloated, although with so many employees "distributed" it was hard to know, day to day, who was necessary and who was simply out there living their best Silicon Valley life.

From there, Leslie gently prodded Elon through a variety of topics—from his views on diversity: "we want at least a billion people on Twitter, maybe more . . . so that's the most inclusive definition of inclusiveness. That's all humans. That's important"—to his own political beliefs: "I think I'd be pretty close to the center. I voted Democrat in every election until a recent one this week. . . . I'm in favor of moderate politics, but allowing people to have relatively extreme views, to express those views within the bounds of the law . . . let's say the far left ten percent and far right ten percent were equally upset on Twitter, then that would probably be a good outcome"—then back, briefly, to authentication: "Essentially it needs to be much more expensive to have a troll army"—to his own tweets: "I'm not an angry person. I almost never raise my voice. Like, in a year I might not have raised my voice, literally."

It was clear to Mark that the longer the all-hands went, the more Elon's attention seemed to be drifting: his eyes shifting upward more and more often, his head tilting away from the camera. But as Leslie tried to steer the conversation toward whether Elon himself would step into the role of CEO at Twitter, as he had with Tesla and SpaceX, the billionaire launched into what could almost be described as a monologue, and as he spoke, Mark realized that what he'd first interpreted as a lack of focus was actually something else: an almost dreamlike intention, passion, even, as if Elon was suddenly trying to break away from the mundane chatter about layoffs, advertising, politics, moderation.

"What is the unifying philosophy, for me," he was suddenly revealing, in words veering almost to poetry. "We should take the set of actions most likely to extend the scope, scale, and life span of consciousness as we know it. And so that's like what set of actions improve things at a civilizational level and improve the probable life span of civilization."

It was the strangest thing Mark had ever heard on a business call, and it literally made him sit up straight in his seat. Parag, certainly, had never spoken like this; Jack might have had these sorts of thoughts, but he would never have expounded on them during an all-hands conference call, right after implying that he might fire a lot of people.

"Our civilization," Elon continued, "will come to an end at some point, but let's try to make it last as long as possible. It would be great to understand more about the nature of the universe. Why we're here, the meaning of life, where are things going, where do we come from, can we travel to other star systems and see if there are alien civilizations? There might be a whole bunch of long-dead one-planet civilizations out there that existed, you know, five hundred million years ago. If you think about the span of human civilization from the advent of the first writing, it's only been about five thousand years, which is nothing. Earth is roughly four and a half billion years old. So all of civilization as measured from the advent of writing is a flash in the pan. And we want to take whatever actions we can to extend that flash in the pan to hopefully be a flame that lasts a long time."

Mark stared at the man. For a brief moment, it seemed like Elon had somehow *transcended* the video chat; for a brief moment the square borders containing the billionaire, in his billowing, ivory white shirt, in his gold-hued conference room, or cafeteria, or hell, cockpit of some intergalactic spaceship—the square borders seemed inconsequential, faded, irrelevant.

*What the hell?* Mark wanted desperately to toggle to the Slack convos, to see if the rest of the Tweeps were as blown away by the sudden shift in the conversation as he was, but he also didn't want to look away.

Leslie's eyes looked as wide as Mark's felt, as she stumbled to bring Elon back to Twitter. "I can't believe I have to transition this from aliens—this conversation—to Twitter—"

"I'm not saying it's aliens, but it's aliens," Elon joked, and as Leslie tried to get her question out, Elon was clearly in his own world now.

"I've got to stop trolling people about aliens. To be clear I have seen no evidence of aliens—I get asked that a lot, and I think I'd know . . ."

Finally, Leslie got her question out.

"About Twitter, when you look five to ten years from now, what do you consider successful for yourself . . . and for all of us?"

Back to the mundane:

"I think success would be a substantial increase in daily active users. . . . Can we get daily active users over a billion?"

But clearly, the mundane couldn't hold Elon's attention.

"I guess broadly speaking, is Twitter helping further civilization and consciousness? You know are we—is Twitter—contributing to a stronger, longer-lasting civilization where we are better able to understand the nature of reality?"

Mark leaned back in his chair. If he'd read the words in some magazine, he might have thought that Elon was putting on a show, but seeing the man speaking, seeing the intensity behind his words and the thoughtful way he presented them, he clearly meant every syllable. He was charismatic, esoteric yet somehow relatable. Yet it all seemed a little *unhinged*. Twitter was a social media company. A place where people posted random thoughts, moments from their daily lives, political philosophies, jokes, memes, news stories, whatever the hell they wanted, whenever they wanted. Twitter, the company, sold advertising to intersperse between the tweets, and did its best to keep the platform free of violence, hate, and misinformation.

*What company did Elon think he was buying?*

"I would say," Elon continued, looking more and more swept up in his own thoughts, "my philosophy is one of curiosity, of trying to understand the nature of the universe as much as it is possible to understand. In order to understand the nature of the universe, we must expand the scope and scale of consciousness to expand the life of consciousness."

Then he seemed almost to shrug, as he went on to finally answer Leslie's question—what Elon would consider the successful result of his acquisition of Twitter.

"I guess, broadly speaking, has Twitter meaningfully improved the strength and longevity of civilization?"

Moments later, Leslie thanked the billionaire, and the video-conference window went black.

Mark sat at his desk, still staring at the screen. His cell phone was chirping in his pocket, and Slack was boiling over, but he remained focused on what was now, once again,

just a square,

within a square,

within so many other squares.

## CHAPTER SEVEN

# October 4, 2022

**Paradise in a tin can.**

Elon stared at the image that had suddenly appeared on his laptop's screen. Not a desk in a stark office, or a view of a glass-walled conference room; no whiteboards or steel-framed table or videoconferencing machinery. Not even a chair—but a *lounger*, something white and glimmering and reclined, maybe made of lacquered wood, or even *wicker*, could it actually be wicker? And behind the chair, a balcony that stretched a dozen yards to a low railing and beyond that, sand and water and goddamn palm trees, swaying in what could only be a tropical breeze.

Elon could almost smell the coconuts, cracked by machetes or blended into sunscreen or milked into frilly drinks.

*Paradise in a tin fucking can.*

Elon almost closed his laptop right then and there. In contrast, his own accommodations were zero paradise and all tin can: a twenty-by-twenty prefab one-bedroom, portable home that had been towed into place, parked in a quiet corner of the SpaceX compound, erected in under six hours. Basically, a studio apartment that could be dropped anywhere and divided into four equal spaces: a bedroom, a kitchen, a bathroom, and a living room. A living room where he now sat on a low-slung couch of vinyl, surrounded by laminated walls of steel, concrete, and foam. Hurricane-, fire-, and flood-resistant, powered by solar panels and batteries not unlike the cells that ran his Tesla fleet. The future of portable, sustainable living, made by a company called Boxabl—fifty thousand dollars all in if you could get off the wait list, or happened to be Elon Musk, for whom there was no such thing as a wait list.

Despite Elon's initial impulse, he left the laptop open. It wasn't long before a shape moved into view from somewhere off to the left of the balcony and the palm trees. The camera fought against the sudden movement to translate the reflected light from the shape into pixels, tracking and stabilizing and transmitting. In his better moments, it was as if Elon could close his eyes and actually see the lines of computer code that enabled things like laptop cameras to work, bits and bytes running down in front of his eyes like some scene from *The Matrix*. But right now he was too fixated on the shape on the screen, the form that was now a person, settling awkwardly down onto the lounger. Not reclining, not sitting, somewhere in between; an artful lean against the edge of the wicker, meaty limbs akimbo.

A chubby young man, with a shock of curly hair, sloping shoulders, and a panda's physique, head lowered so Elon could barely make out his inset, pincushion eyes.

Even without the lines of code running down in front of Elon's eyes, there was something unreal about the young man on the screen. The palm trees and the beach, the kid's plump features that made him seem almost more cartoon than human—the moment had a sudden, dreamlike quality to it, which Elon found oddly comforting.

For a long time, Elon had flirted with the concept—worldview, really—known as simulation theory; the idea that reality was a simulated construct, perhaps created by an advanced civilization. What we perceived as the "real world" might actually be a computer-generated sim, built on a framework of insanely complex computer code, designed to mimic reality.

Consciousness, experiences, moments such as the video call Elon was about to have: they might simply be by-products of this simulated reality, while the rules and laws of physics that we believe to be fundamental to our existence could be mere programming.

Although simulation theory sounded like science fiction, it was actually grounded in simple math. As the idea went—expounded by the scientist and philosopher Nick Bostrom in a paper and subsequent book in 2003—advanced civilizations would eventually develop the technology to create computer simulations that were indistinguishable from real life. Such societies wouldn't simply create one simulation, but would create many. The civilizations within the simulations would eventually likewise create simulations, also indistinguishable from real life. Eventually there would be trillions upon trillions of simulations, and still only one base reality.

Which meant, mathematically, that the odds that you were living in the one base reality, and not one of the near-infinite, indistinguishable simulations, tended toward zero.

Further, even if a simulation were built around a specific base character, each simulation contained a near-infinite number of "non-player characters" (NPC). So not only were the odds that you were, at this very moment, living in a simulation; the odds were also that you weren't even a self-functioning character. You were, in all mathematical likelihood, an NPC.

Elon did not believe that he himself was an NPC, but in numerous interviews, tweets, and comments, he had made it clear that he was captivated by the beauty and logic of the simulation worldview. No doubt, the arbitrary and absurd twists and turns of his life gave off an aura of unreality that was sometimes hard to ignore.

He could certainly imagine and admire the sort of creative computer code that might have gone into designing his current timeline, the "if-then" algorithms that had led him to this Twitter video call, which capped off a week of similarly absurd diversions.

He'd already spent an entire summer learning that the only thing more complicated than embarking on the hostile takeover of a multibillion-dollar social media company, in public and in broad daylight, was trying *not* to take over that same social media company.

The decision to try to step back from the takeover hadn't come easy to Elon, even though he'd paused his plans to take Twitter private earlier in the summer. While he'd cited the much larger number of bot and fake accounts than had previously been made clear, it hadn't been until he'd gotten a deeper look into Twitter's abysmal financial situation that he'd realized how costly it was going to be to try to fix the global town hall. Not only did Elon believe that Twitter had misrepresented how many of its users were actually real people, but he was beginning to suspect that their balance sheet was likewise more smoke than solid. "If I understood them correctly," he'd texted on June 16, "Ned and Parag said that cash expenditures over the next 12 months will be $7B and that cash receipts will also be $7B. However, the cash receipts number doesn't seem realistic, given that they expect only $1.2B in Q2, which is just $4.8B annualized."

He'd followed up that text with another a day later, summing it up more succinctly: "Their revenue projections seem disconnected from reality."

It wasn't simply the financial swamp he'd be stepping into that had given him extreme vertigo at the thought of consummating the deal. The downward spiral in Tesla's stock price—and Elon's net worth along with it—had likewise taken him by surprise. Besides the sheer economic consequences of the dive in value that would eventually knock *$200 billion* off his personal net worth (breaking the record for the biggest loss of wealth in history), even more immediately there was the vehemence suddenly directed toward him by fans and foes alike.

He'd expected a level of pushback from the predominantly liberal media. They had interpreted many of his tweets leading up to the takeover offer as signals that Twitter's moderation policies had unfairly targeted the right. He knew that in general, billionaires were an easy target to rile up public opinion against.

But he hadn't expected the wave of backlash aimed at him from what he'd always considered his own base: the legions of Tesla fans and investors, who were concerned that he was sacrificing Tesla in his bid to go after Twitter. Not only was he diverting his attention from his core companies—Tesla and SpaceX—but many of his investors believed, correctly, that he'd soon need to sell more Tesla shares if his $44 billion purchase were to go through.

Elon was not immune to the sudden outcry from his base; over the past decade he'd developed an almost untouchable reputation— the genius who had lifted Tesla out of near bankruptcy more than once, who had built SpaceX with his bare hands, who had dedicated his life to saving humanity—and for the first time, he was facing intense criticism from those who were normally his biggest fans. Eventually the outcry would get so bad that a group of prominent investors would even petition Tesla's board to have Elon replaced as CEO.

Elon had the sort of relationship to outside attention that one might expect from a person who saw the world the way a computer, or an avatar in a simulation, might. Outside attention and emotion had to be analyzed and digested, with a certain amount of turning gears.

The angry backlash from his Tesla following, combined with what he was seeing the deeper he looked into Twitter's financials, had set those gears spinning, and Elon had responded in the only way that had seemed rational at the time. He'd officially rescinded his offer to take over Twitter.

The barbarian had backed away from the gate, and Twitter had responded by promptly suing him.

The same board that had enacted a poison pill to battle his initial entreaties, that had instigated numerous op-eds and articles about the dangers of such an unpredictable billionaire taking the helm of the social media company at the heart of the global conversation, now demanded that the barbarian return to the damn gate, bash right through, and take them over, hostile and without mercy, just as he'd promised.

Elon knew why the board was suddenly begging him to finish what he'd started. Since he'd officially withdrawn his offer, Twitter's stock had tanked; the shareholders were losing their shirts, and Elon's offer of $54.20 was now nearly double the value of the company's shares. If the board had let him walk away, the shareholders would have started sharpening their pitchforks.

Instead, the board had hired the same law firm they'd used to enact their "poison pill" share maneuver to keep Elon from taking over Twitter, now to fire off a lawsuit demanding he finish the job.

*In April 2022, Elon Musk entered into a binding merger agreement with Twitter, promising to use his best efforts to*

*get the deal done. Now, less than three months later, Musk*
*refuses to honor his obligations to Twitter and its sharehold-*
*ers because the deal he signed no longer serves his personal*
*interests. Having mounted a public spectacle to put Twitter in*
*play, and having proposed and then signed a seller friendly*
*merger agreement, Musk apparently believes that he—unlike*
*every other party subject to Delaware contract law—is free to*
*change his mind, trash the company, disrupt its operations,*
*destroy stockholder value, and walk away.*

*Apparently, hell hath no fury like a social media company*
*scorned.* Although Elon fired back with his own legal arguments,
elaborating on what he believed were misrepresentations made by
the board, by the end of the summer it had become clear that getting
out of the deal was going to be almost as costly as seeing it through.
The only people benefiting from the protracted legal battle were the
lawyers.

From hostile to reluctant, almost overnight. Though there was
no way Elon was going to avoid bearing the brunt of the expense of
buying Twitter, from the moment he'd hinted at his plans to take the
platform private, his wealthy friends and associates had been lining
up to help out. In many cases, raising billions from the sorts of people Elon had in his contacts seemed no more difficult than borrow-
ing change to top off a parking meter.

As far back as April, he'd reached out to billionaire Larry Ellison, asking how much Ellison might be able to chip in:

"A billion . . . or whatever you recommend," Ellison had texted
back.

"Whatever works for you," Musk had nonchalantly responded.
"I'd recommend maybe 2B or more. This has very high potential
and I'd rather have you than anyone else."

To which Ellison had happily agreed: "Since you think I should come in for at least 2B . . . I'm in for 2B."

Musk had also secured financing from banks such as Morgan Stanley and Bank of America, who together committed $13 billion to the purchase in-debt financing. Saudi prince Alwaleed bin Talal had joined in as well, rolling over his $1.9 billion worth of Twitter shares to Musk's effort, making the prince the second-largest shareholder. On top of the investment by the Saudi prince, Qatar Holding, the country of Qatar's sovereign fund, had added an undisclosed amount.

Although initially, Elon had hoped to keep his personal commitment below $15 billion, he'd ended up coughing up closer to $27 billion in cash, in part funded by the $15 billion worth of Tesla shares he'd sold, to the chagrin of his Tesla faithful.

Depending on the day of the week, and the price of Tesla shares, $27 billion represented anywhere between 7 and 15 percent of Elon's total personal wealth. If anyone had believed Elon's move on Twitter was little more than a vanity project, this alone might have given them pause.

On top of Ellison and the Saudi prince, there had been plenty of opportunities to lower his own exposure even further, but Elon's motivation had never been about money. In this instance, money was truly a means to an end; a philosophy, which, ironically, had led to this morning's video chat.

The initial entreaty that had led to this call had come via Scottish philosopher and social entrepreneur Will MacAskill. MacAskill was one of the originators of the "effective altruism" movement, and a guru to many a billionaire looking for ways to make the world better by giving away wealth. Effective altruism encouraged its proponents to be strategic in using wealth to make the world better, by focusing resources on interventions with proven positive results.

Although Elon had never specifically identified with the theory, he'd also never been a fan of traditional philanthropy, which he believed was often ineffective and wasteful. The idea of using data and research to identify ways to make an impact on the future spoke to him. So initially he was receptive to MacAskill, when the philosopher reached out via text, explaining that he had a "collaborator" who had been considering buying Twitter for quite some time, with the purpose of "making it better for the world."

At the time, Musk had cagily responded: "Does he have huge amounts of money?"

"Depends on how you define 'huge,'" MacAskill had come back. "He's worth 24B, and his early employees with shared values bump that to 30B. I asked how much he could in principle contribute and he said "1-3B would be easy 3-5B I could do 8-15B is maybe possible but would require financing."

Elon was cautiously intrigued—MacAskill's theories had merit, but Elon wasn't a disciple—and these were not the sort of numbers even a man as wealthy as Elon could ignore.

Looking at the awkward panda of a kid on the other end of the video chat, his untucked, oversized T-shirt billowing in the tropical breeze, it was hard to believe that mop of curly hair was sitting on a $24 billion fortune. Even for Silicon Valley, the vision on the screen seemed unkempt; as the panda started talking, his words coming so fast they were nearly slamming into each other, the alarm bells began to ring.

Elon was no stranger to the mythology that had grown up around the kid: Sam Bankman-Fried, or SBF as he was generally known in the tech press, was considered one of the most brilliant young entrepreneurs of the past decade. After first making a name for himself at Jane Street Capital, then starting his own quantitative trading firm, called Alameda Research, at thirty, SBF had founded FTX, one of the fastest-growing crypto exchanges in the world. The stories about SBF were legendary, and unavoidable. How he'd first pitched FTX to a room full of Sequoia Capital VCs, waxing poetic about making his exchange "a place where you can do anything you want with your next dollar," from buying crypto to art to goddamn produce, all the while his head hovered inches above his laptop, never once breaking from the screen to make eye contact. It was only after most of the room had committed to funding the idea that someone had walked close enough to see SBF's computer screen. Apparently the kid had been playing the video game *League of Legends* through the entire meeting, securing $150 million from Sequoia without ever breaking game play.

Elon could respect a little Zuckerbergian disassociation when it came to dealing with VCs, but other stories he'd heard about SBF and the work culture at FTC and Alameda had a darker tinge. Crypto exchanges, especially those with headquarters overseas, were notoriously sketchy. Though FTX had a US component and engaged in massive mainstream marketing—Super Bowl ads! Stadium naming rights! Celebrity endorsements as varied as Tom Brady and Larry David!—SBF had moved all of his upper management to the Bahamas, installing his coterie of crypto whiz kids in a lavish, $60 million campus. In all, SBF and his team had spent nearly *three hundred million dollars* in real estate on the island. SBF himself shared a $40 million penthouse with nine roommates, including the titular heads of Alameda and FTX—and according to the rumors, there was a lot more going on in that tropical, crypto Valhalla than the late-night tweaking of trading algorithms. Stories of massive amounts of drug use and rampant polyamorous relations abounded; at one point or another, all ten roommates had paired or tripled up. Like Elon, SBF was a prominent believer in simulation theory, but it appeared the quest he was playing in the video game of life had veered NC-17.

*Simulation theory, meet stimulation theory.*

Watching SBF, as the kid rocked back and forth on the edge of the wicker, spouting phrases like "vision lock" and "social block-chain integration," pinpoint eyes darting every direction but the camera, it was clear he was smart; likewise, considering the setting, and the stories surrounding him, his embrace of effective altruism made perfect sense. The idea that you could fix the world by making as much money as you could—in other words, get stinking rich to make the world better—meant not only did you get to solve world hunger or cure malaria, but you were able to do it from a wicker lounge chair on the balcony of a $40 million penthouse, overlooking a tropical beach.

Despite what SBF appeared to be offering, though, Elon was far from sold. The doughy kid might have been a genius, and he might not have been an NPC—but he was clearly playing a very different game.

Elon had nothing, personally, against hedonism, when properly applied. He'd dated numerous celebrities and pop stars, been divorced three times, and had ten children. And he understood the logic of effective altruism, the primacy of Ends over Means.

But in Elon's simulation, the End he was striving toward was bigger than curing malaria or defeating world hunger. He was trying to save human civilization, and it would take more than carefully applied wealth to reach that goal. Twitter was a Means, not an End, and now that Elon had been dragged back into the deal to take it private—brought right back to the gate, which was primed and ready for him to bash through—there was no room for a partner who had calculated his way to paradise, no matter how many zeros he could draw on a check.

Quite frankly, Elon didn't trust the doughy genius. They might have been on two ends of the same spectrum, watching the same computer code float down in front of their eyes, but SBF was clearly still playing a multiplayer online battle arena game as he had been in the offices of Sequoia. When MacAskill had first reached out, Elon had shown skepticism that SBF had the sort of wealth that MacAskill had claimed—"Does Sam actually have 3B liquid?" he'd texted back. After listening to SBF's pitch, he was even less confident that there was anything solid behind the layers of PR, philosophy, and myth.

Elon's decision was made; he wouldn't be accepting any money from SBF, even if the Twitter deal was going to cost him a significant portion of his personal wealth.

There was no more time for backpedaling, concerns about funding, or absurd diversions.

It was time for Elon to take Twitter, fix Twitter, and if he needed to, along the way—break Twitter even further than it was already broken.

A Means, to the only End that really mattered.

## CHAPTER EIGHT

**Fyodr Drovosky** was already counting rubles as the voice on the other end of his cell phone was abruptly replaced by a crackle of feedback. With a grin, he tossed the device toward the hard surface of his steel-framed desk, where it landed with a clatter, an instant spiderweb of cracks exploding across its still glowing screen. He didn't give a damn about the phone. It was a burner, like the hundreds of others wrapped in Styrofoam and stacked up in cardboard boxes along the far wall of his stark office. Cheap, disposable, untraceable, and infinitely useful; Chinese tech by way of an Albanian middleman with an elaborate mustache and no last name, who worked out of the back room of a pharmacy in the center of town.

Of course, the Albanian probably did have a last name, but Fyodr had never asked and the mustache had never volunteered. After all, the man's last name wasn't going to appear on any purchase form or accounting ledger, and Fyodr didn't have any interest in developing anything resembling a social relationship with the Albanian, who wasn't the sort of man you brought home to meet the wife and kids. Fyodr was certain the feeling was mutual. Fyodr was not the sort of man you brought home to meet the wife and kids, either.

It hadn't always been that way; there was a time in Fyodr's life when he might have even been considered respectable. He'd grown up in an elegant suburb north of Moscow to parents who had been active in party politics; he had attended the best elementary and finishing schools, where he'd developed an affinity for numbers and calculation, along with a waning sense of respect for the rules and regulations that had weighed down his parents' generation. He'd even matriculated to the prestigious Moscow Institute of Physics and Technology, Russia's version of MIT, to study mathematics, and had been on his way to a distinguished academic career when the 1990s hit, the Soviet experiment collapsed, Russia's economy went into a tailspin, and his entire universe had exploded.

He'd been barely twenty-two years old when the economic rug had been pulled out from under him, but he'd been agile enough to stay on his feet—choosing, like many of his classmates who shared his abilities and general lack of conscience, to pivot rather than to plunge. Through his twenties he'd dabbled in unconventional ventures, from concocting cost-saving algorithms for an oligarch murdering his way up the ranks of the newly privatized energy industry, to writing software for a group of black market car dealers, who were importing Mercedes and VW Bugs, replacing their engines with much cheaper and decisively less effective parts. By his thirties, he had begun to dip his toes into the more sophisticated world of computer "arbitrage," providing a service to members of the banking industry who wanted to skim from their customers' accounts. It was this last scheme that had landed him in Straflager detention center, two hundred and fifty miles outside of Moscow in the snowy swamps of Mordovia, known charmingly as the "land of prisons," for a two-year forced vacation.

Straflager had turned out to be a crash course in the burgeoning industry of online crime; by the end of the first decade of the new millennium, Fyodr had gained enough knowledge and connections to strike out on his own, using the bit of cash he'd saved up from previous adventures to turn himself into one of the pioneers of a brand-new way to effectively pull rubles out of the digitized, worldwide ether.

He grinned as he pushed his chair back from his desk, the tired iron wheels groaning beneath his excessive girth. Business had never been better—though one might not have guessed how far Fyodr had come in the two decades since Straflager by a simple glance at his current surroundings.

Fyodr's office was a cold and utilitarian space, with walls of bare concrete and a ceiling lit by fluorescent strips that hissed as if they were alive, or maybe just overheating. The room was sparsely furnished: the steel desk and chair and a tattered-looking couch in the far corner. The desk was empty, save for an open laptop and his now-shattered burner. The laptop's screen flickered with activity, and if one looked closely, one might have noticed a cascade of open windows, each blinking out a signature page of a different social media platform. From a royal flush of more well-known, international behemoths like Facebook, YouTube, TikTok, Reddit, and Twitter, to a rainbow of less heralded, less international companies, like Taringa, Xing, VKontakte, and Douban.

Rising up from his chair, Fyodr turned away from his desk and started toward the pair of double doors beyond the couch. As he went, he passed the only window: a pair of winterized panes, so thick they were nearly opaque. Still, through the milky glass, he could see the outskirts of the town, a collection of low-slung buildings huddled together for warmth. Smoke rose from the chimneys, and the faint sound of car engines could be heard in the distance.

Moving away from the cosmopolitan hustle of Moscow had not been as difficult as Fyodr might have imagined; although he might have chosen to stay within Russia, a contact from prison had advised him to look farther, for opportunities in the less policed regions where his native tongue was still dominant enough to give him the edge he would need as a struggling entrepreneur. In truth, he could think of no place better than where he had ultimately settled—the small, semi-urban enclave of Aktobe in the former Soviet republic of Kazakhstan.

Despite the more popular conceptions of Kazakhstan as eternally backward, it was one of the richest former republics, with incredible reserves of oil and uranium, and was modernizing at a breakneck pace. Aktobe, though still village-like in some areas, had supermarkets, internet cafés, even a McDonald's with delivery service. Sure, there were people who pulled carts to work and had chickens in their yards, but there were plenty of internet entrepreneurs like Fyodr as well, men and women who might have made their names in Silicon Valley—if they'd chosen a straighter, narrower path.

Fyodr had grown to love the view from his window, despite the ever-present snow that covered the ground around the former industrial complex where his office sat. There was a sense of resilience and determination in that view; this was a place where people had learned to adapt and thrive, despite the harshness of their environment.

Reaching the double doors to the room he paused, his mind already whirling forward as he contemplated the call he had just received. There was another window set halfway up the doors, its single pane of grimy glass offering a distorted view of the rows of young people sitting at their desks.

It wasn't really *rubles* on his mind. Nobody in his business worked in fiat currency anymore. The job he'd just agreed to would involve a deposit of bitcoin into a numbered crypto account, which would eventually be transferred to a cold storage device he kept in his apartment in the nicer section of Aktobe, right in the center of the McDonald's delivery zone. A much more sophisticated process than the old days back in Moscow, when it was suitcases of cash dropped off in the coatroom of a fancy hotel, or duffel bags left in the trunk of a Lada.

The world had gone digital, Fyodr along with it—a greater revolution than anything his Russian forefathers could have concocted.

He pushed open the doors to the warehouse, his footsteps echoing in the vast space beyond. Rows upon rows of young people spread out ahead of him, each sitting at a long table with ten of the burner phones arranged neatly in front of them. The atmosphere was frenetic, with the sound of tapping against screens and a faint electric glow filling the air.

Fyodr beamed, watching his employees work, engaging in that digital revolution. It was still amazing to him to see how big his endeavor had grown; in the beginning, it had just been him and a handful of savvy kids he'd hired from the local university. Now there were more than a hundred young men and women checking into the warehouse every morning for their six-hour shifts, many of them computer programming students themselves—not that coding was a prerequisite for the work they were doing. All Fyodr asked of his charges were quick fingers and the ability to follow a script.

Compared to writing algorithms that could scrape kopecks off the daily outputs of Siberian oil refineries, Fyodr's current venture was actually quite simple. In fact, there was very little technical chicanery involved.

It was during his tenure in Straflager that he'd first been introduced to the world of social media, witnessing the explosion of websites like Myspace and Friendster, then Facebook and Twitter on the shared computer terminal in the prison rec area. Inmates had been restricted to tight fifteen-minute windows of daily computer time, so Fyodr had bartered cigarettes, toilet paper, and anything else he could get his hands on from the prison commissary to spend as much time as he could surfing this burgeoning new landscape. Eventually the prison's warden had gotten wise to the dangers of allowing people like Fyodr to have unfettered access to networks that connected billions of people to each other, but not before Fyodr had realized that there was an infinite web of fiber-optic cables acting like open veins not only to unsuspecting strangers' personal information and wallets—but even more significant, to their opinions, emotions, and ideas.

Social media wasn't just a place for people to be social. Billions upon billions now used the various social media sites as their primary sources for news, both local and international. They developed their opinions—often their wants, even their needs—from information provided both by people they knew and by total strangers.

That is where Fyodr's entrepreneurial spirit had kicked in. Although he'd never personally used the term *troll farm* to describe the digital "influence for hire" business he had built on the outskirts of Aktobe, he had to admit there was a certain literary charm to the label. Compared to the much larger *Agentstvo internet-issledovaniy* stationed in St. Petersburg, owned by the Russian oligarch Yevgeny Prigozhin, which employed over a thousand "influencers"–who had arguably, successfully influenced the American election of 2016—Fyodr's own "*фабрика мнений*"—roughly translated, "Opinion Factory," was a tiny concern. But his team had boasted growing revenues every year since he'd opened its doors, and was now generating close to seven figures a quarter.

As Fyodr strolled through the warehouse, heading toward the raised platform at the far end of the room, which contained a stool and a microphone stand, connected to the building's PA system, he thought back to the various campaigns his team had completed over just the past two years. His clients came from all over the world, and from arenas as varied as politics, media, commercial product marketing, and even health care. Although a handful of lucrative gigs had funneled in from places with high social media presences like Brazil and Korea, the majority of his big-money business flowed in from the United States.

He had worked for clients from both political parties in America, flooding the internet with propaganda and targeted misinformation in an effort to sway public opinion. He had promoted products for companies in nearly every industry, using social media to create a buzz and drive sales. And he had pushed various points of view for pundits, using his army of internet warriors to drown out opposing voices. Fyodr didn't care who he targeted; he was an equal opportunity troll. One day, his team might be barraging a Democratic senator with false accusations of corruption, and the next day, going after a Republican candidate for president with disinformation about their policies. The more chaos they could sow, the more bitcoin ended up in cold storage.

It was not a business without risks. Creating fake social media accounts to spread comments-for-hire, targeted opinions, and misinformation skated close to crossing any number of laws affecting commerce, advertising, and personal libel; certainly, some of his more controversial campaigns fell into the category of outright fraud. But being a Russian national, operating out of a place like Kazakhstan, had its advantages. It was unlikely his company would ever face any real legal ramifications, especially considering the amount of bitcoin he'd spread to the right people in the judicial and enforcement spheres.

On a personal basis, Fyodr was proud of what his team had accomplished. Although it would be hard to quantify exact results, there was a chance his campaigns had swayed close elections, tipped the balance for companies on the edge of rising or failing, and pushed any number of public debates toward consensus. Troll farms such as his had proved that a correctly placed storm of social media posts, memes, and comments could move economies, at least temporarily, and effect real political outcomes.

Many might see his work as unethical, but he had grown up in a world where ethics was the sort of thing privileged people debated while the less fortunate hoed their wealthy neighbor's gardens, cleaned up their trash, and died fighting their wars. Besides, Fyodr hadn't invented social media, and its system of profiting off emotion, controversy, and debate. Was it really any different, what he did, than what millions of legitimate "influencers" got away with every day? B-list celebrities and pundits hawking products and ideas for pay—was it any different than what digital advertising agencies did? What was advertising, if not an attempt to convince people to buy things they didn't really need, often for more than they could afford? Capitalism was powered by the engine of influence peddling. It didn't matter if you were selling flavored water, electric cars, or a political candidate; push the right buttons, and in an instant you could sway millions to your cause.

Fyodr reached the raised stage at the center of the warehouse and took the microphone off its stand, listening as the PA system coughed to life. A hundred young men and women looked up from their long tables, their expectant and eager faces reflecting the glow from a sea of cell phones.

The job Fyodr had just accepted via the call in his office didn't have anything to do with flavored water, electric cars, or politics. In fact, in this instance, his team wouldn't be selling anything at all; not a product, or a political stance, or even an opinion or ideology. As far as he could tell, it would be trolling at its most pure. An organized campaign of chaos, for a purpose that was well above his pay grade to understand.

He wasn't even sure who had funded the campaign; it had come to him through a middleman, who had been unwilling to give many details other than the target platform and the briefest of scripts for him to circulate to his waiting charges.

But Fyodr didn't really care who was behind the job, or what their intentions might be. In a matter of minutes, his team would begin concocting fake accounts—and soon after, over a period of less than three hours, barrage the target platform with a storm of comments fifty thousand deep.

In this case, for whatever reason, the client wanted chaos. And as long as the client had bitcoin to spend—

Fyodr and his team would happily give them chaos.

# PART TWO

---

"To anyone who I've offended [with my Twitter posts], I just want to say I reinvented electric cars, and I'm sending people to Mars in a rocket ship. Did you think I was also going to be a chill, normal dude?"                    —ELON MUSK

"The problem is that at a lot of big companies, process becomes a substitute for thinking. You're encouraged to behave like a little gear in a complex machine. Frankly, it allows you to keep people who aren't that smart, who aren't that creative."                    —ELON MUSK

"Any product that needs a manual to work is broken."

—ELON MUSK

## CHAPTER NINE

# October 26, 2022

**Ten minutes past noon** on a Wednesday, and Esther Crawford was in the back corner of the Perch, the lively and industrial in-house coffee shop hanging above the ninth floor of Twitter's vast and yawning San Francisco global headquarters, itself an art deco behemoth rising high over the edge of the Tenderloin district. Esther was deep into her second cappuccino as she pretended to focus on whatever Rami Answar—a scruffy moppet of an engineer sitting across from her—was spouting. Rami was one of the top members of her team and as close a friend as she'd made in the year and a half since she'd joined the company.

She'd caught only a handful of words since he'd launched into what she guessed was some sort of arcane product description, something involving way too much code and a lot of fluffy keywords like *sentiment* and *nostalgia* and *engagement*; her mind was far too preoccupied with scanning their bustling surroundings, every nerve in her body tingling with anticipation. The sleek, modern, and industrial-looking interior of the Perch, with its exposed pipes and constant aroma of freshly ground coffee beans, vibrated with an energy that mirrored her own internal sense of excitement.

She could tell that Rami, too, despite his attempt to fill the silence, was similarly preoccupied; even as he spoke, his dark eyes darted around the room, betraying his own anxiety. The cup of black coffee on the low wooden table in front of him sat untouched, the surface of the liquid shimmering with an oily sheen, steam curling into the air.

When he finally reached the end of his pitch, he, too, settled into an uncomfortable quiet, looking at her, while somewhere nearby an espresso machine hissed in the background, a stark contrast to the hushed tones of conversation from the other occupied tables scattered around the coffee shop.

"You haven't really heard a word I've said," Rami finally said, grinning.

His dark wavy hair fell into his eyes as he leaned forward, elbows resting on the table, his voice barely above a whisper.

"It may not be today, you know. It may not happen this week."

He didn't need to elaborate; they both knew what he was talking about. Everyone in the coffee shop was thinking the same thing. The entire company had been on edge for weeks, whispers and speculation spreading like wildfire through the halls, via Zoom chats, over email and Slack and even the Twitter platform itself. They had all endured a roller-coaster ride of false starts.

"Christ," Rami continued, shrugging as he finally reached for his coffee. "It may not happen at all—"

Just then, a buzzing sound erupted from Esther's laptop bag, down by her feet. Her iPhone, she realized—and then a second later, more buzzing, Rami's own phone, going off in his pocket—followed by a frenzy of electronic notices, coming from the surrounding tables.

Esther's fingers froze on her cappuccino mug as she looked at Rami. He was already reaching for his phone, and she realized that across the coffee shop, people were reaching into pockets and hand-bags and backpacks.

It took her a few seconds to find her iPhone in the bottom of her bag. A moment later, she was looking down at the screen as she clicked through to her emails.

The message was from Leslie Berland, Twitter's head of market-ing and a member of the company's top management tier, two or three levels above Esther herself, part of the old guard, directly under Parag, and before that, Jack.

Esther read the email out loud, even as Rami was reading it to himself: "Hey, Elon is in the building. If you happen to see him, say hello!"

The message sounded so bright and cheerful that it may as well have ended in a string of happy-face emojis. Esther had nothing against Leslie, who was sharp and capable, but the email seemed so superficial, considering the gravity of the situation. Elon was in the building? Elon was about to *own* the building.

"Holy shit," Rami muttered.

"Yeah."

Esther tried to steady her nerves. She glanced around the Perch, trying to gauge the reactions of her fellow employees. Some were visibly excited, their faces lighting up with anticipation; others looked a little ill. Although it was impossible to know which of the many rumors concerning Elon's plan for Twitter were based in real-ity, and which were simply the fevered opinions of pundits on CNBC and Bloomberg, there was little doubt that big changes were on the horizon. New management usually meant some level of layoffs; Elon's public displeasure with Twitter's former leadership team, their reported balance sheets, and what he saw as their failings in maintaining an unfettered global town hall hinted at much more than an employee haircut.

Esther wouldn't have been surprised if the rumors she'd heard of a 25 percent culling were in the making; as an entrepreneur and founder, who had joined Twitter by way of the acquisition of her own start-up, she knew that the quickest way to fix a balance sheet usually involved a bit of sudden bloodshed. She was also aware that Twitter had already been contemplating mass layoffs even before Elon had made his offer for the company. She had it on good authority that Parag had lists of names drawn up but had put the firing on hold when Elon had appeared with his deep and initially eager pockets.

Now there was a good chance that Parag himself would be on the chopping block if Elon was "in the building," and beyond Parag, there was no telling how deep the cuts would go. Esther didn't consider anyone safe, including herself, and as frightening as that seemed—for someone in a job she loved, with three kids and a mortgage—it was also strangely exciting. New management could also mean new opportunities. Esther had always been a fighter; she was good at picking her moments, and she knew how to stand up for herself when it mattered. If Elon was going to sweep away the bureaucratic layers that he believed were stifling Twitter's innovative spirit, Esther would simply have to find a way to prove her worth, and pick her moment, as she had so many times before in her life.

She wasn't going to have to wait long to make her first move; barely three minutes after Leslie's email, a hush moved across the Perch, and Esther craned her neck toward the front of the coffee shop just in time to see what had sucked all the attention out of the room.

There he was, Elon Musk, moving quickly through the open space. He looked bigger in person than he seemed on TV, though he'd obviously lost weight. Back in July, shirtless photos of him being sprayed by a hose on a yacht had made the rounds on Twitter, causing no end of online bullying—and reportedly pushing the billionaire into a regimen of diet and exercise that had gotten him back into pretty good shape. He hunched slightly forward as he moved, dressed all in black; black T-shirt, black pants, shiny black shoes. He was trailing an entourage of twenty to thirty Tweeps, all walking behind him at an awkward distance, some actually jogging to keep up with his elongated gait.

As he entered the Perch's main area, heading toward the long counter that bisected the center of the space, people closest seemed to part around him, while others farther back gathered in clusters, forming a sort of ring around the billionaire. The nervous energy in the room was even more tangible than the anticipation of before; yet Esther noticed that nobody was approaching Elon.

She leaned toward Rami, who was also staring at the billionaire— but seemed as frozen in place as the rest of the coffee shop.

"I think we should go say hi," Esther whispered.

Rami glanced at her, then back at Elon.

"You sure? I'm pretty comfortable right here."

She shook her head.

"We've got to shoot our shot."

He raised his thick eyebrows at this, but stayed rooted to his seat. She shrugged, stiffening her jaw.

"I'm gonna do it."

Then she was up and out of her chair and moving across the coffee shop. Elon was now at the counter, his back against the waist-high wood, one of the baristas pouring him something, and Esther quickened her pace. Even so, it was the longest ten yards she'd ever crossed, and it gave her time to add much-needed density to her resolve.

She'd always considered herself an introvert, though she knew that to the outside world—and especially to people who were privy to her background—she might have seemed the opposite. Her route to Twitter hadn't been easy, and the fact that she'd even escaped her childhood, let alone ended up managing multiple teams at one of the most important social media sites on the web, was nothing less than shocking.

She had been born into a household that wasn't so much broken as never whole in the first place, the "secret" child of a man she didn't meet until she was in fourth grade and a disabled mother. From the ages of nine to nineteen, she'd been brought up in a strict religious cult in rural Oklahoma. The cult, a mix of Mennonite and Pentecostal apocalyptic Christianity, engaged in a rigid hierarchy, which meant Esther had to ask permission for even the most basic things; she was homeschooled, forced to dress in conservative clothing, disallowed from watching television or listening to music, taught that the world was six thousand years old and that people had walked with dinosaurs. Her only solace had been the fact that the cult leaders were not technologically savvy, which meant computers—and the internet—had been off their radar. By the time she'd reached high school, she was spending any moment she wasn't under the watching eyes of her fellow cult members online, eventually teaching herself everything she could about web design and the use of social media. At nineteen, she'd become a popular blogger, and after escaping the cult by matriculating to Oregon State University, by her early twenties she had become one of the first people to garner a six-figure sponsorship on YouTube.

Seeing the internet—a place of connectivity and diversity—as an escape from her own past, she'd thrown herself into the world of entrepreneurship, eventually moving to San Francisco to work for various social media–adjacent companies such as Circle and Lyft. Her first attempt at her own company, a short-form video product called Glimpser, had gone under when Vine was acquired by Twitter; her next company, Squad, began as a generative AI endeavor before generative AI was hot. A blowout with her cofounder had led her to pivot the company into a screen-sharing social app, inspired by her seven-year-old daughter's eagerness to find some way to chat with her friends while she played *Roblox*.

Toward the end of 2020, Esther had been contacted out of the blue by Discord with an offer to buy her start-up. Though she'd intended to grow the company on her own, the uncertainties of the pandemic and the competitiveness of the technology sector pushed her toward what she decided was the more responsible decision. She'd grown up on welfare, and she now had kids of her own; turning down an offer that could secure her family's future had felt like a gamble she couldn't afford.

The offer from Discord had led to two weeks of meetings with multiple tech and social media giants; in the end, she'd chosen Twitter—even though Twitter's offer hadn't been the most lucrative of the bunch. Still, she had seen an opportunity to be part of a company with almost unlimited potential. She was a builder and a fighter, and Twitter had seemed the sort of place where someone who knew how to build and to fight could make a real impact.

In the year and a half since she'd been acquired by Twitter, there had been a handful of instances where she'd felt that builder's high; she'd been part of the team that had created Spaces, Twitter's live audio feature, as an answer to the stand-alone app Clubhouse. She'd worked on teams aimed at finding innovative ways to add payment to the platform, which had included an optional subscription service, and had been pitching ideas around crypto and the possibility of monetizing the adult content that was pervasive on the site. But she'd also found herself perpetually bogged down by the bureaucratic hierarchies at the company, a situation that had only gotten worse with Parag's ascension to CEO. Over the summer, Parag had fired her direct superior, head of product Kayvon Beykpour, and her new head of product Jay Sullivan was someone she'd describe as a

nice guy, not a bad human, but uninspiring—a real suit. Since helping create Spaces, she'd struggled to get anything significant off the
ground, and having Jay running defense against any spark of innovation she might try to toss up the command ladder had made it
unlikely that was going to change—

—until Elon and his kitchen sink.

Nervous electricity ricocheted through her limbs as she finally
reached Elon at the counter, and he immediately seemed to notice
her. Luckily, she was wearing her highest heels, softening the
immense height difference between them. She was four eleven on
her best days, though her intensity made her seem taller. Still, Elon
was leaning back against the counter on his elbows, which put them
almost eye to eye.

She held out her hand, introducing herself without pause, and
he smiled back at her.

"And what do you do here?"

She let loose the nervous energy and took her shot, telling him
that she led new products—which included creator monetization
and payments. Elon lit up at that; he suddenly exclaimed that he had
big plans around both of those areas, and that they were both core
parts of his vision.

"We should talk," he continued. "Email me and set up a time
tomorrow."

And just like that, he was giving Esther his email address, which
Esther quickly typed into her phone. Before she could say anything
more, she felt a presence next to her, and saw Leslie Berland sweep
in from somewhere off to the side.

"Of course, Elon," she said over Esther's shoulder, then to Esther,
with a bit of ice, "We can schedule you in."

Esther immediately knew it was the old guard doing the thing
they did, trying to preserve the old hierarchies. Esther smiled back

at Leslie, but inside the thought hit her: *none of you are going to be around much longer.* She could feel it in the air, things were going to change quickly. Elon hadn't officially taken over Twitter yet, no deal had been signed—but it was clear by the jockeying of the nearby employees that they were all angling for their jobs.

As Elon pushed off the counter and started back through the coffee shop, trailing his awkward entourage of Tweeps, Esther hung back, still gripping her phone in her left hand. She was about to glance down to double-check that she'd saved his email address when one of Elon's flock separated and stepped toward her. It took her a moment to recognize Walter Isaacson, the journalist, who she had heard had been tailing Elon for many months now in support of a biography he was writing about the billionaire.

"You do payments at Twitter?" Isaacson asked, quietly.

Esther nodded; no reason to elaborate on the chain of command, or the fact that Twitter was a pretty fluid place: a lot of people did a lot of things at the company, and titles changed so often people googled themselves to find out what management was calling them that particular week.

"I think you're going to be really important going forward," Isaacson said. Then he smiled, and scurried off after Elon.

Esther stared after him, then found that she was smiling herself. She figured that as first impressions went, she could not have done much better. She glanced across the Perch and saw that Rami was just about standing on his chair, peering over the tables between them. He grinned at her and raised both thumbs up in the air. She laughed, then shrugged. It was impossible to know what was going on in Elon Musk's head, but Esther had definitely taken her shot.

---

She waited until nine p.m. to send the email, even though she'd been constructing it since she'd left the office at seven, dictating various versions into her phone on the short, hilly drive to the townhouse she shared with her husband and kids, spitting distance from the affluent neighborhood of Nob Hill. At first she'd done her best to try to get the tone just right, listing her accomplishments without seeming like she was inflating herself or submitting a run-of-the-mill CV, but by the time she'd pulled into her driveway she'd decided that the little she knew of Elon told her he wasn't against a little self-aggrandizement. Still, she'd waited until well after dinner to hit send, not wanting to appear too eager. Then she'd gone to bed—but unable to sleep, she'd happened to check her phone again around one a.m.

To her surprise, Elon had responded at midnight. Not an assistant, not one of his inner circle or even Leslie Berland—Elon himself. *Yeah, let's get connected*, he'd emailed back. *Come see me tomorrow when I get in.* Esther had sat straight up in bed next to her sleeping husband, her head spinning. Sure, Elon wasn't officially CEO of Twitter yet, but even so, that sort of direct communication from someone in his position was not what she had expected at all. Current Twitter leadership would never have responded that quickly, and certainly not in the middle of the night. Parag might never have responded at all, and when he'd eventually checked in, it would have been through a phalanx of assistants, scheduling a meeting a minimum of two weeks out. And Jack Dorsey—well, he had been a different animal altogether.

Esther was reminded of one of her past meetings with the former CEO. She'd spent ten minutes explaining her thoughts on monetizing creator accounts on the platform, after which he'd laced his fingers together and looked her right in the eyes.

"Esther, you are somebody who I hear and see leans toward nobility. What I mean by that is you believe you have good intentions, but the corporation is stronger than any individual."

From there, he'd gone on to tell her that it was a mistake to try to find ways for the company to make more money, because he didn't want to turn Twitter into a casino. She'd come away from the meeting bewildered; the CEO of Twitter had literally just told her he didn't want her working on making Twitter more profitable, because he didn't think Twitter's *purpose* was to *be* profitable.

Obviously, Elon had a different point of view. Esther had a feeling that if she played her cards right, the hierarchies that had held her back at Twitter 1.0 would soon be nothing but a distant memory.

---

The text came in shortly after Esther had arrived back at the headquarters the next morning—Thursday, October 27, the day Elon was supposed to officially take over the company. It caught her by surprise, even though she'd known that it was coming. She was up on the ninth floor, in one of the tiny, glass-walled conference rooms that circled the open workspace. This time the text had come from one of Elon's "inner circle"—a woman named Jehn Balajadia. Jehn was the COO of Elon's underground drilling business, the Boring Company, which had originally been pitched as the future of transportation, promising a network of underground Hyperloop tunnels spiriting electric cars up to a hundred and fifty miles per hour beneath crowded urban hot spots like Los Angeles, Chicago, and Baltimore. So far, the Boring Company's greatest successes were a 1.7-mile long loop connecting the Las Vegas Convention Center with itself, populated by Tesla Model 3s moving at an underwhelming 30 mph; a mail-order personal-use flamethrower; and a fragrance called "Burnt Hair" that provided men and women with an olfactory experience "just like leaning over a candle at the dinner table, but without all the hard work." From what Esther had already heard through the Twitter gossip line, Jehn had temporarily moved over to Twitter with Elon, with undefined responsibilities that appeared to include managing his interactions with the employees of his soon-to-be new company.

Jehn's email was sparse on details, other than that Elon wanted to meet with Esther "in an hour or two." Excited, Esther had been about to head down to the Perch to charge herself up with caffeine when there had been a staccato knocking on the door to the conference cubicle; before she had a chance to respond, the door flung inward. Jay Sullivan was moving so fast it seemed like his shoes were moving an inch above the hardwood floor. His normally pallid face was splotched in red, like a tomato left on the vine.

He didn't say a word until he'd reached the end of the table she was sitting at and placed both fists against the glass. Then he launched right into it.

"Esther, there's a process around here. And I hear you're attempting to circumnavigate the process. Meeting one-on-one with Elon? That's not how it works. You need to get in line."

It only got worse from there. Jay was absolutely seething, as he explained through a comically locked jaw that "we" are "trying to tell Elon a story," that "he's difficult to talk to," that "he doesn't stay focused," that "he doesn't stay on track," that "he doesn't know the business." That Jay and his upper-level colleagues were trying to give Elon everything he needed to run the company effectively, and that this would all work out for everyone if lower level people like Esther stayed out of it.

"You simply can't have one-off conversations with Elon," Jay hissed.

Esther sat in stunned silence as Jay barreled through his lecture. Though she was livid at being dressed down for making a connection with the man who would be taking over the company in the next twenty-four hours, she decided it wasn't worth the effort to respond. Again, she had the premonition that her boss—this suit—was completely irrelevant now. Just from the tiny interaction Esther had already had with Elon, she could guess he wouldn't be "managed" the way Jay was describing. And there was no way Esther was going to let Jay, or Leslie Berland, or anyone be a go-between between her and the new boss.

She waited until Jay was finished speaking, then, without a word, quietly packed up her laptop and headed for the door. She could feel Jay's eyes burning a hole in the back of her neck, but she didn't care, because he didn't matter anymore.

---

It was a short walk over to the nearby building her colleagues called Tenth, on Tenth Street. In the past it had been used as a meeting place for visiting clients; now it was where Elon had apparently set up shop, according to Jehn's follow-up email, which had dropped into Esther's inbox at some point during Jay's tirade. The minute the elevator doors opened on the second floor, she could feel the strangeness in the air. There were people everywhere, which was jarring, since both buildings of the Twitter headquarters had been functioning at less than 10 percent occupancy since the beginning of the pandemic. Though Esther herself tried to hit her office at least a few times a week, she knew plenty of people who had been employed at Twitter for years and had never set foot in either building.

The first people she caught sight of were Tweeps she recognized; the old guard again: Leslie Berland, of course, and a few others from Sales and Marketing moving along with Leslie as she patrolled the lobby area in front of the elevators. There was a head of engineering that Esther also recognized, nervously pawing at a croissant, and at least three heads of product from various divisions, two men and a woman she'd never worked with but had passed a few times in the halls. Then others she didn't know—it was a big company, and she'd only been there a year and a half—but assumed were on Leslie's level, since the CMO hadn't chased them away.

Although Leslie didn't seem to notice Esther as she made quick work of the lobby area, she could feel plenty of gazes moving with her. She didn't know Tenth well, had really only been in the building a handful of times, and never on the second floor. She knew the place had formerly been used to wine and dine well-heeled outsiders—big-money advertising clients, visiting politicos and celebrities—and was stocked with memorabilia from Twitter's past. The far wall ahead of her was covered in a huge, brightly lit projection cycling through various versions of the Twitter logo, and nearby there were dioramas highlighting some of the big moments in Twitter's chronology, from Jack's first tweet—*"just setting up my twttr"* to Barack Obama's victory tweet from 2012, which had been the most retweeted tweet in history. Esther was pleased to see a display heralding the advent of Spaces, her own contribution to the timeline—but then her attention was sidetracked by a group of people she spotted hovering around the entrance to the main conference room that took up the majority of the second floor.

These people were decidedly *not* Tweeps. The first figures she saw were huge and cartoonishly bulky—a pair of enormous men with beards, in tight, light blue suits that barely contained their bulging muscles. No doubt these were bodyguards, at least they damn sure didn't look like *engineers*, and they had taken up posts on either side of the door leading into the conference room.

In front of the bodyguards gathered a smattering of strangers, though Esther did recognize a couple of the faces; specifically, David Sacks, the celebrity VC and official "Friend of Elon" who had gone

from being the COO of PayPal and a member of the so-called "Pay-
Pal Mafia" to becoming one of the most prolific Silicon Valley investors, through his venture firm Craft Ventures. Sacks currently
cohosted a podcast called *All In* and had been publicly egging Elon
on in his takeover bid for Twitter since the spring. Although Esther
didn't see Sacks's *All In* cohost Jason Calacanis, she assumed he
would be somewhere nearby. Calacanis was another well-known
"FOE"; the Silicon Valley investor and tech journalist had also been
tweeting nonstop support for Elon's takeover bid since his offer, and
was reportedly going to be a very hands-on advisor as Elon took
charge of the company.

Next to Sacks she did see Alex Spiro, Elon's lawyer and confi-
dant, who looked almost as terrifying as his reputation; fit, impeccably dressed in a blue suit and power tie, paired with dress sneakers,
a bit of Miami mingling with his Manhattan sheen. Spiro was one of
the top trial lawyers in the country, with a long list of celebrity clients that had included Jay-Z, Mick Jagger, Robert Kraft, and Aaron
Hernandez. A partner at the legal behemoth Quinn Emanuel, Spiro
had the reputation of being a fierce street fighter of a lawyer, and
even his name seemed culled right out of Hollywood casting.

Spiro's imposing presence was mitigated by a cyclone of motion
at his feet; X Æ A-12, Elon's two-year-old son, skirting in and out
between the gaggle of adult legs, a pair of wooden blocks gripped in
his hands. The toddler was grinning and bouncing along as only
toddlers could, oblivious to the important business going on around
him; surely this was just another in a long line of unconventional
moments for X, whose mother, the Canadian pop singer Grimes,
had once explained the toddler's distinctive name in a tweet:

•X, the unknown variable ⚔

•Æ, my elven spelling of Ai (love &/or Artificial intelligence)

•A-12 = precursor to SR-17 (our favorite aircraft). No
weapons, no defenses, just speed. Great in battle,
but non-violent 🩶

\+

(A=Archangel, my favorite song)
( 🕊️ 🐀 metal rat)

Something about seeing X happily playing with his wooden
blocks while, behind Esther, Twitter's C-suite were pacing trenches
into the lobby floor took some of the edge off Esther's nerves as she
continued toward the group in front of the conference room. She'd
almost arrived when she felt her phone buzzing in her pocket, and
she paused long enough to glance down at the screen.

She saw the text immediately—from Rami—and her eyes wid-
ened.

"What are you doing on the second floor?"

Christ. It hit her immediately. She had just stepped out of the
elevator and already the news was making its rounds. She had no
doubt someone had already put together an internal group chat,
monitoring who was coming and going, a second layer of paranoid
patrolling by the crew behind Esther.

Rather than slow her down, the idea that she was being spied on
spurred Esther forward. She took another step toward the conference room, when she recognized Jehn Balajadia—who she'd googled on the way over to Tenth—standing behind Saks a few feet
from the door. Jehn saw her as well, giving her the go-ahead to head
inside. The bodyguards looked her over as well but made no motion
to stop her, and a moment later she was through.

Esther had never been in this room before, and was struck by
the vastness. The room was dominated by a giant table that seemed

like it was nearly fifty feet long, surrounded by plenty of access points for videoconferencing screens and flat-screen monitors. There were chairs on either side and at both heads, but Elon was sitting three chairs in. Esther noticed immediately that it was just Elon—not only was he alone in the room, but there was no laptop in front of him, no computer monitor, no keyboard, not even a notebook. It was just him and his phone, which was in his hands, the screen lighting up his pinpoint eyes.

*The richest dude in the world, alone at a table, checking his phone.*

Esther started toward the other side of the table to sit across from him, when Elon looked up and gave her a friendly smile.

"You don't have to sit all the way over there if you don't want," he said, his slight South African accent bowing his vowels and tightening his consonants. He gestured toward the chair right next to him.

Esther felt her pulse quicken but she headed for the chair, which he pushed out with his foot. Again she was struck by the size difference between the two of them; even sitting, he was going to tower over her, and she was glad she'd worn one of her more aggressive outfits that day—not just the heels, but a lot of black, other than her pink A-line skirt. She was not going to be intimidated by his size, or his status.

His welcome was warm, and from the start he seemed extremely approachable. His sense of humor came out immediately. As she was pulling her laptop out of her bag to show him some of the work she'd been doing, he started right in on shit-talking Twitter 1.0— telling her that Parag and his team were subpar, that they'd made a mess of the company, and that he was going to have a hell of a job ahead of him righting the ship. Although he didn't say anything specifically about what he was about to do, Esther had a feeling her earlier intuitions were correct. If Parag was still in the building, he probably wouldn't be for much longer. The same could probably be said for a lot of the crew hanging out by the elevators. *Dinosaurs, really, just waiting for the comet to hit.*

She turned on her laptop and began walking Elon through some of the products she had been developing in the sphere of creative monetization and payments, but she realized very quickly that Elon didn't have the patience for the details. He'd nod appropriately when she spoke broadly about wanting to harvest the value of the big, creative accounts on the platform and to grow the subscription base, but as soon as she got into the weeds of any product, he completely tuned out. It wasn't that he couldn't follow along; he just seemed instantly uninterested. The more granular she got, the more bored he became. So she quickly adapted, shutting her laptop and focusing on big themes and broad concepts; he seemed pleased, and she could feel their connection—at one point he told her she really "got it" and that he thought they would "work well together." Then he dropped the bombshell.

He told her that he had a very important project that he wanted to get off the ground immediately—a top priority, something that would make a lot of headlines and show the world what Twitter 2.0 was all about—and he wanted her to put together a team and make it happen. She could pull anyone she wanted from the company—engineers, marketing, whatever—and she would answer directly to him. The only catch was, he needed the product ready to launch on Monday.

*Monday—four days away.* It was an insane ask. A project like this would normally have taken months. But it was also thrilling: she'd just met the man, he hadn't even officially taken over the company yet, and he was giving her carte blanche to build a team and ship a product that would dominate the news cycles. It was exactly the sort of challenge that she'd joined Twitter for in the first place—there really was no choice to be made.

She was beaming as she put her laptop back in her bag and rose from the table, just as the door to the conference room opened again. David Sacks swept in with a smirk on his face, heading right toward Elon. If Sacks had even noticed that Esther was in the room, he didn't let on, so she quietly moved around the VC toward the exit.

It wasn't until she'd exited the conference room and navigated past the phalanx of bodyguards and into the no-man's-land between Elon's hangers-on and Twitter 1.0's old guard that she started to breathe again, her pulse still rocketing in her veins. She still couldn't believe what had just happened—not only had she made an impression, but she had leapfrogged to the head of a project that was at the center of Elon's plans for the restructuring of the platform. No doubt Jay would go ballistic, as would many others above her on the food chain, the men and women scurrying around the elevators, who were noticeably avoiding her gaze. But she didn't care; she wasn't doing anything wrong, and she wasn't keeping anything a secret. She was right here, out in front of them, shooting her shot.

Even before she reached the elevators she had her phone out and was constructing an email to Elon, following up on the meeting, outlining what she saw as the first steps to the new project. Then, as an addendum, she added a bit of alpha she thought he might find helpful.

*Hey, you know, if you need a list of the best engineers and innovators at the company, the people you definitely should keep, I've already put one together.* Which she had, because the night before, when she was unable to go back to sleep, she had game-theoried the next steps out. They all knew what was coming, and if they didn't, they could see it in the separation between the two camps—Twitter 1.0 and 2.0—and even in David Sacks's smirk. The knives were about to come out.

Esther felt like she had a unique vantage point; she'd only been at the company a year and a half, and going forward, she didn't believe that the people who had been there a decade or more were necessarily the type of people you wanted to keep. If Elon really wanted to change things up—to *build*—he would want to surround himself with the most innovative of the Tweeps, the most forward-thinking, those willing to take risks.

So Esther had put together a list, knowing full well that the most significant names associated with the PDF she would attach to the email to Elon wouldn't be the engineers and innovators she'd chosen to put on her list—but the ones she'd left off.

A moment later, she was through the gauntlet of pacing dinosaurs and into the solace of the elevator for the short ride down to the street.

---

Esther wasn't in the conference room approximately six hours later, when it became official. But she'd heard about the scene afterward from others who had been in the room, and she could envision exactly how it had gone down. Elon, still sitting a few chairs in from the head of the long table, surrounded by his inner circle: Jehn, Sacks, Calacanis, certainly Spiro in his Miami dress sneakers, and probably even X, somewhere under the table, with wooden blocks.

Apparently Elon had signed the papers with a flourish, and then actually stood up from his chair, raising his hands in the air.

"Fuck Zuck!" he'd shouted suddenly, referring to the Facebook founder and CEO, fellow billionaire and impactor of culture, with whom Elon was now in direct competition.

"Fuck!"

"Zuck!"

Then a moment later, when he'd settled down, maybe it was Spiro, maybe it was Jehn, maybe it was Sacks or Calacanis or even X—

Who

Gave

Him

The

Keys.

## CHAPTER TEN

# October 27, 2022

Jason Calacanis: "Back of the envelope . . .

Twitter revenue per employee: 5B rev/8k employees = 625K
rev per employee.
In 2021 Google revenue per employee 275B rev/135k
employee = 1.9M per employee.
In 2021 Apple revenue per employee 365B rev/154k
employees = 2.37M . . .
Twitter revenue per employee if 3k instead of 8k: 5B rev/3k
employees -= 1.66 m . . ."

Elon Musk: "Insane potential for improvement."

Jason Calacanis: "Sharpen your blades boys."

**A little after 4 p.m.,** and the party was already in full swing.

Jessica concentrated on putting one foot in front of the other as she cut her way through the oddly muted crowd that filled the Commons, the cafeteria/workspace that took up much of the ninth floor of the San Francisco offices and had been transformed into the setting for a company-wide Halloween party. The wide, warehouse-style space was now speckled with jack-o'-lanterns, photo booths, bales of hay, and children's games, crisscrossed by brightly colored tables weighed down by bowls of candy of every discernible size and brand. Hardwood floors culled from the defunct nearby Transbay Terminal were bathed in a swirl of colored lights that cast rainbows to the beat from the kitschy music pumping through the building's PA system.

Jessica had a drink in one hand, something with bubbles and fruit that had been poured for her by a young man she only vaguely recognized, a third-string engineer from one of the company's many IT departments. She'd asked his name at the time but had been unable to hear the answer. Someone had turned up the volume of the music a little too high, either to stifle conversation or to obscure it. Then again, even with a name, she might have had trouble placing the engineer. After all, the company had roughly 7,500 employees, and Jessica's main base of operations was back in New York. Not to mention the fact that the young engineer was dressed as a vampire, complete with fangs and a cape.

Jessica herself had on cat ears and a tail, but the rest of her costume was more superhero than feline. Not Catwoman, exactly; she'd repurposed an old Wonder Woman outfit that hadn't fit her properly since her second child, and added the ears and tail to appeal to her oldest, who at four was obsessed with cats. Her husband had liked the look, too, but she'd left him back in New York with the kids, even though the invitation had been for families. She didn't intend to stay at the party long. Her costume was too tight in the wrong places, and her feet already hurt from the boots she'd found to complete the look. But her physical discomfort paled in comparison to the emotional turmoil that had gripped her, from the minute she'd walked through the office building's glass front entrance.

As she moved deeper into the party, doing her best to smile at the colleagues she recognized, the scene around her felt truly surreal, a Dalí painting come to life. A few hundred of her fellow employees, and in most cases their families, decked out in costumes they had probably planned weeks earlier, before the insanity of the past twenty-four hours had seemed like anything more than a remote possibility.

*A tsunami was terrifying in concept; but no amount of thought could prepare you for the moment when that wave crashed through your front door.*

Through the haze of her thoughts, she noticed a crowd gathered by one of the windows that overlooked Market Street, and started toward them. In the past, the Commons had been one of her favorite places in the San Francisco headquarters; it was one of three cafeterias in the complex—which itself consisted of two buildings connected by an earthquake-resistant, futuristic-looking glass sky bridge. The others included the Perch, and of course the Lodge: two actual, century-old Montana homesteader log cabins purchased on Craigslist when the company had first moved into the headquarters back in 2012, then transported and reconstructed as an employee lounge.

But for Jessica, it wasn't the décor, or the various perks of the complex—a game room! micro-kitchens! neon art installations on nearly every wall!—that made her frequent visits to the San Francisco headquarters over the past decade so special. It was the shared sense of community and purpose, the culture of a place that had begun as a scrappy start-up with a shared ideology, that had always seen itself as an underdog. For as long as she could remember, the company had been at the center of a storm of news, which had kept her and her workmates humble; the values they had started with were pervasive, and every employee seemed to live by them.

But today, for the first time, she felt like that sense of community was about to fracture—or more accurately, *be* fractured, or even swept aside, by a force so powerful, it was almost hard to believe it was wielded by a single, palpably famous man.

Halfway to the crowd by the windows she paused, glancing around. She wasn't sure if *he* was still in the building, or if he'd gone back to the makeshift "war room" he'd set up on the second floor of Tenth. Jessica had spent much time there herself, helping welcome visiting teams from PepsiCo, Wendy's, the NFL, who would gather with brand managers to view the impact of their advertising campaigns, in real time. But as of yesterday, that second floor had been taken over by the billionaire and his team of advisors—a group of powerful men Jessica's colleagues had already taken to calling "his Goons."

No question, Jessica had clearly underestimated Elon's interest in Twitter, back when she'd met with Yoel in New York. The "occupation" had happened fast, and in dramatic fashion. The pictures were already all over the internet—he'd come in yesterday afternoon carrying a white and gleaming porcelain sink, filming himself uttering the words "let that sink in." Shortly after that display, he was being led through the headquarters by Leslie Berland, the chief marketing officer, meeting and greeting the employees as he went. He'd apparently stopped for coffee in the coffee shop, strolled through the Commons, which was already being set up for the Halloween party—#TrickOrTweet, an annual event that employees with kids looked forward to every year—and toured the cafeteria, which was busy preparing Halloween-themed fare: pumpkins spouting spaghetti, blood-red punch galore.

The feel in the office had been a mixture of fear and excitement. Some employees had been terrified, but many were cautiously optimistic. Jessica couldn't deny there was a charisma to the man, the billionaire, an attraction that everyone felt. Despite the rumors, despite the public comments he'd made leading up to the takeover, *people were drawn to him, wanted to be close to him, wanted to hear what he had to say.*

But shortly after his tour of the complex, he'd gone straight to work. Holed up on the second floor of Tenth, bringing in the team leaders and product talent, one after another. The engineers especially: frantically printing out their code to be reviewed and judged. Right away, the rumors had started.

Now, a day later, the rumors were only getting worse. Earlier, in the lunchroom, Jessica's colleagues—dressed up as tigers and Grim Reapers and Jack Sparrows, dining on jack-o'-lantern-vomited spaghetti—began to hear numbers. Twenty-five percent, possibly fifty, affecting every department. In some cases entire teams. From there the rumors turned vicious; the firings would be immediate, before next week's November 1 bonuses kicked in. Jessica doubted that would happen—there were laws in California protecting employees from just such chaos—but she knew heads were about to roll.

She wondered if she herself would soon be tasked with choosing who on her team would be culled, an impossible task. Real people, with real lives, families, personal dramas. *Could she really fire the young woman who sat next to her in New York, six months pregnant and already planning maternity leave? Or the colleague one desk over, who had been diagnosed with cancer two months earlier and was relying on his health benefits to make it through the next year?*

She was shaking her head, barely feeling her feet against the floor, as she finally reached the crowd by the window, then pushing her way through until she was close enough to the glass to see what they were looking at. Down on the street, nine floors below. Another crowd, twice as big as the one around her, had gathered on the sidewalk by the building's entrance. Even from that height, she could see the cameras and microphones, and the half dozen television vans, bristling with satellite dishes and sporting long antennae, parked along the curb.

Word must have gone out that the deal had officially been finalized. "Monster Mash" was on the PA system above her head, blending into "Thriller."

Meanwhile, the billionaire barbarian had officially crashed through the gate.

---

Not two hours later, Jessica witnessed the first of it for herself. Surreal and jarring, like a punch to the stomach, so visceral she had to actually lean against an office door in the hallway where she was standing to keep her knees from going out. Up until that moment, it had all been rumors and secondhand information. Whispered gossip between frightened colleagues, numbers thrown like darts because nobody really knew what was coming.

But now, in front of her, the evidence as to what was coming was unavoidable.

Twenty feet away, Sean Edgett, Twitter's lead legal counsel and part of Parag's leadership team, was being led out of his office by a pair of security guards. He was smiling and waving to colleagues as he went, but it was hard not to see the shell-shocked glaze in his eyes. An assistant trailed a few feet behind with a box of belongings, but Edgett's computer wasn't going with him, nor were any files that pertained to Twitter 1.0 or anything Elon might have defined as proprietary.

In retrospect, Parag, Bret Taylor, and Ned Segal—Twitter's CFO—had read the tea leaves correctly and escaped the humiliation of being duck-walked out of the headquarters, having left the building while the office Halloween party was still in full swing. Jessica had already heard that all three had been fired by email the moment Elon had officially signed the takeover deal, along with a number of other members of the management team. There were rumors that the firings had come laced with a fair amount of vindictiveness—that Elon intended to fire Parag and his team "with cause," which would put their severance packages at risk. From there the rumors got even worse: that Elon was planning a much bigger mass-firing event, to be conducted before November 1, just days away, to cut Tweeps off from their expected bonuses.

Still, there had been no actual official company-wide communication from Elon. Although the billionaire had changed the bio on his Twitter account to read "Chief Twit," for the moment the only messages winding their way down the platform's hierarchy were from what was left of upper management, who were either sending emails suggesting that Tweeps remain calm and continue business as usual, or parroting requests from the cabal of "advisors" that Elon had currently surrounded himself with on the second floor of Tenth. Jessica was only familiar with Elon's "Goons" via Google and the internet: David Sacks; Alex Spiro; Jason Calacanis; Sriram Krishnan, a former Twitter exec and software engineer who worked at the VC firm Andreessen Horowitz; Jared Birchall, Elon's financial guru and current CEO of his brain company Neuralink; and Antonio Gracias, another VC, recently of Tesla's board.

Along with the Goons, Elon had reportedly brought along two of his cousins, Andrew and James; his younger brother Kimbal; and numerous engineers and product people from Tesla and SpaceX, many of whom had filled the parking lot outside with Model 3s, Model Ss, and Model Xs. Though Jessica couldn't know for sure how many advisors and Goons were camping out with Elon in his "war room," she had a pretty good idea what they were there for. Parag, Bret, Ned Segal, and Sean Edgett were only the beginning. With Jessica still in cat makeup and black tights from the company Halloween party, the bloodletting was about to begin.

*Veni, Vidi, Vici,* Jessica assumed, though in this instance it was more *I trolled, I tweeted, I quietly accumulated a large stock position. I flirted with joining the corporate board, I clashed with the CEO, I refused said position. I made an offer that was too good to pass up, I changed my mind, I was sued into reluctantly conquering the company.*

Despite the insanely long lead-up to Elon's acquisition, it was also clear that there was no real plan in place for the transition between Twitter 1.0 and 2.0—just that heads were going to roll. Although Jessica hadn't received any indications yet as to what was going to happen to people like her in Ad Sales and Marketing, she'd been forwarded a bunch of Slack messages that had been sent out to the engineers employed by the company, reportedly scripted by the Goons themselves. As would later be reported by the Verge, apparently the Goons had first demanded that all Twitter engineers, thousands of them, print out "50 pages of code you've done in the last 30 days," to be shown to Musk and his own Tesla and SpaceX engineers—in person.

A frantic scramble had erupted across the company, as engineers—imagining *American Idol*-style judging sessions in front of the billionaire and a bunch of rocket scientists—had begun trying to locate printers (*because who the hell used printers anymore?*). Some even rushed out to the nearest Best Buys and Walmarts with memory cards in hand, until just a few hours later, the Goons rescinded the command, demanding that anyone who had actually printed any code shred it immediately, and instead be ready to show the code—still in person—on their laptops. This command, too, was later rescinded. As far as Jessica knew, no engineers had "auditioned" for Elon yet, but managers were already being asked to put together lists of team members who were absolutely necessary for the functioning of the site.

At the same time, Elon had been making sweeping declarations, both on Twitter and through his Goons, of changes he intended to implement: additions like long-form video, payouts to content creators to compete with YouTube, new payment options—all things that would require engineering talent.

Jessica herself was less concerned about the chaos erupting on engineering teams than she was about how the apparent lack of transitional strategy would affect their advertising clients—and the flow of life-giving advertising dollars. Robin Wheeler, the company's head of ad sales, had hurried back from Orlando, Florida, and she, JP Maheu, VP of global sales, and Sarah Personette, chief customer officer, had been doing their best to assure the teams involved with ad clients that every effort was going to be made to not disrupt the work they'd been doing. Robin had even sent a message via Slack recapping the day, suggesting that Elon had showed "humility" during manager meetings and was asking questions, that he wanted to learn and was "prioritizing product first." Robin would be meeting with Antonio Gracias tomorrow afternoon to give him an overview of their ad business, and she seemed confident that Elon would understand the importance of the relationships they'd built with Madison Avenue, how it was central to keeping Twitter healthy.

In support of that notion, Elon also seemed to recognize Yoel and his work on the safety and moderation front as integral to the platform; he'd even tweeted that he intended to launch "a content moderation council, with widely diverse viewpoints to decide on moderation and account reinstatements." Although Jessica had only texted with Yoel briefly as she'd left the #TrickOrTweet party on her way back to her office, she could tell that Yoel had decided to give Elon a chance. Maybe he felt that it was his duty to try to protect the site through the transition, or perhaps he believed that Elon, as a successful businessman, would understand that no major advertisers would be comfortable spending ad dollars only to have their campaigns appear in a swamp of hate speech and adult content.

But standing in front of her office, watching the company's former head of legal putting up a good front as he was escorted by security out of the building, Jessica had a feeling that none of them could truly predict what Elon was going to do—or what went on in his head. She'd already seen signs of his unpredictability, and worse, hints of paranoia. There was the sudden about-face regarding engineers printing code—although shredding proprietary code could be seen as good business, rather than a sign of paranoia. And Elon's ever-present bodyguards? Well, maybe that was understandable, too, since he was, after all, the richest man in the world.

But along with the strange emails to the engineers, the Goons had also sent word through the company that, beginning immediately, there would be no group meetings of Twitter personnel without management's direct permission. No groups larger than two or three Tweeps would be allowed to assemble.

*Was Elon expecting some sort of mutiny?*

Jessica had no idea; she did know that when Elon's team had been informed that the company would be required to file reports to the Federal Communications Commission surrounding any new products or major changes, Spiro—Elon's legal rep—had responded, according to an internal memo circulating around Twitter: *Elon puts rockets into space—he's not afraid of the FCC.*

Maybe he wasn't afraid of the FCC; but when you escort long-time employees out of your headquarters, ask engineers to shred documents, surround yourself with bodyguards, and ban any impromptu meetings of the Tweeps you haven't fired yet—it sure seems like you are afraid of something.

## CHAPTER ELEVEN

**On any other Thursday night,** the procession would have seemed macabre: a few dozen cars snaking slowly through the open iron gates of one of the oldest cemeteries outside Charlotte, lit from both sides by the flickering orange glow of torches. The air was thick with the scent of burning, the only sound the crunching of gravel under the car tires. Both Mark and his wife, Gina, were dressed head-to-toe in black. Mark wore a cape tied tightly at his neck, while his wife sported a robe of velvet and silk that shimmered down over her stockinged legs.

It was only when he caught a glimpse of the two of them in the rearview mirror that the atmosphere shifted from macabre to absurd; his fake plastic fangs were so long they hung down over his bottom lip, and Gina's pointed black hat was nearly piercing the faux leather upholstery of his Buick's ceiling. Mark smiled as he watched Gina add more green makeup to her cheeks, and then she raised an overly jagged eyebrow at him.

"Ready to party like it's 1699?"

He laughed, shaking his head. As bad as the joke was, the levity was appreciated. Waiting in the line of cars to enter a Halloween party sponsored by a local Charlotte charity—more than twenty minutes now, and they hadn't even arrived at the check-in booth a dozen yards inside the cemetery's dramatic front gate—had actually been the best part of his day. It didn't even matter that his Dracula costume was ridiculously uncomfortable, from the fangs to the sticky pomade plastered to his head forming an obscene widow's peak, to the polyester cape that seemed to trap his body's warmth. He felt like he was lugging around his own personal sauna on an already unseasonably warm October night. He'd still have chosen a two-hour wait in the car with Gina over the day he'd spent corralled in his office, waiting for word from San Francisco.

But as the big moment had finally occurred—Elon signing his deal, officially taking over Twitter—there had been nothing but crickets. No email from the new boss telling his employees how excited he was, no comments about what the plan would be over the next few days or weeks, no comfort in the face of the many rumors that were now flying through the company, via text and tweet and Slack. Nothing but goddamn crickets.

Mark had stayed in touch with his team throughout the afternoon, mostly by Zoom. As the firings of Parag, Bret, and the rest of the top-tier managers had made the news, Mark had done his best to keep his charges calm, explaining that he was in the same boat—and although he'd heard all the same rumors they had, he believed that retaining talented employees would have to be a priority for new management. The goal was to make Twitter better, not tear it apart. When those firings were followed by the odd and confusing messages sent to the thousands of engineers at the company, Mark had only been able to shrug his shoulders, reminding his team that it was just the first few hours of Twitter 2.0, that things would calm down as Elon got his footing.

By the time he'd gotten in touch with his own superior, John Kahill, a senior VP in marketing who worked right below Robin Wheeler, and they'd digested the assurances Robin had posted about Elon seeming to be ready to learn and listen, he'd given up on waiting to hear from the new Chief Twit himself. He turned his attention to his costume and went to work in his office bathroom, applying the pomade to his hair, and adding some of Gina's black eyeliner around his eyes. He wasn't exactly in a partying mood, but they'd had the Halloween shindig on their calendar for months, and they would be meeting up with his brother-in-law after the cemetery for dinner. Besides, the cemetery party doubled as a charity event, sponsored by one of the leading homeless shelters in the city. Covid had canceled the party the year before, so no doubt the party planners would go all out this time around. According to the invitation, which had come in a little embossed plastic coffin, there would be multiple bars, a haunted house, a dance floor, and actors dressed as the historic cemetery's most notable residents.

Mark hadn't had the heart to cancel on Gina, and he never did anything half-assed—not even making himself up as Dracula. Besides, looking over at Gina, even with the green makeup covering her face and her eyebrows penciled into points, she was going to be the hottest-looking witch in the cemetery.

An electronic chime rang out through the car, interrupting his thoughts. He tried not to show his concern as he saw Kahill's name flicker across the screen on his dashboard. It rang again as he located his phone in his pocket, choosing to answer with the device rather than the steering wheel.

From Kahill's rushed tone, it was obvious Mark had made the right decision; it wasn't the sort of conversation Kahill would have felt comfortable having through a speaker.

"I don't have time to explain," Kahill started, without any lead-in or small talk. "We have twenty minutes to make cuts."

Mark blinked, feeling the weight of the phone against his ear.

"What do you mean?"

"You know what I mean. Anyone we want to keep, we need to make a list, with specifics. Why they are good at their job, why their job is critical."

"Like, a spreadsheet?"

There were close to a hundred people on Mark's team. Twenty minutes, to figure out who got to keep their job? Many of his team had been there for years—five, sometimes ten. A few underperformers jumped out at Mark, and one or two others who were hard to justify as being critical to their work. But beyond that . . .

"How deep are we cutting?"

Kahill paused, and when he finally answered it was less than informative. Kahill didn't seem to know how deep, just that every person they wanted to keep, they would have to fight for. But that wasn't even the worst of it.

"Sarah Personette is gone."

Apparently the CCO was resigning, which was a huge blow to the advertising and sales operations of the company. Sarah had been the liaison between the company and many of its biggest advertisers, and was well liked and respected. The news got worse from there; Kahill had spoken in depth to Robin, who had intimated that about a quarter of Twitter's biggest advertising clients were going to put all advertising on pause. With upper management being shredded, and now what appeared to be deep cuts being made, Robin and her team were going to have work miracles to keep the company's revenue from cratering.

Mark could see that Gina was watching him; even though she'd only caught one-half of the conversation, she could tell that their evening was about to go south. Mark's laptop bag was in the trunk, which meant he had everything he needed to put together Kahill's spreadsheet. But he wasn't going to be hitting the dance floor anytime soon.

"Can I send word down to our managers—" he started, but Kahill cut him off.

"You can't say anything, not to anyone. And you're probably not going to hear from me again until we get through this."

Mark was surprised by this. He'd worked with Kahill for ten years, and the idea that they weren't going to talk while all of this was going didn't make sense. Kahill's explanation was cryptic: Parag and his colleagues were getting fired with cause. Kahill was fearful that this could happen to anyone on the executive level, and he wanted to be careful about any conversations he was having that had not been expressly demanded by Elon's team.

Mark felt a little shiver, even in the heat of his cape.

"One more thing," Kahill said. "When we make our cuts—Elon has apparently demanded proof that employees are real people, before they'll be eligible for any bonuses."

"Sorry?"

Kahill repeated himself. Elon had made it clear that he would require proof that those who were fired were human.

"Does he want, like, blood samples?"

Kahill didn't laugh. Apparently Elon was serious about the demand. In fact, he'd given Robert Kaiden, Twitter's chief accounting officer, the job of determining which employees were human, conducting a "payroll audit," cross-checking home addresses, phone numbers—basically, turning Kaiden into a living Captcha. A few days later, Kaiden himself would be walked out of the building by security, but until then, it was his role to make sure every fired employee had an actual pulse.

"This is insane," Mark finally said. "You say we have twenty minutes? Why?"

Even as he asked the question, Mark had an idea as to the answer. During the day, he'd heard the rumor that Elon had wanted all of his firing to happen before November 1—just three days away—which was when employee benefits were meant to kick in. And when the billionaire had been told that this would break several employment laws, leading to fines and lawsuits, he'd responded to the effect that he got sued all the time, and was used to paying fines.

According to Kahill, once Elon had been shown the actual numbers—how many millions, if not billions in fines it was going to cost him to make the sort of cuts he wanted to make before November 1—he'd backed off the request. But apparently he still wanted the knives out and slashing right away: all of those lists of people to keep and to cut, ready by Monday—even though on Monday, according to Kahill, Elon wouldn't even be in San Francisco, because the billionaire was heading to New York at the end of the weekend.

"To meet with advertisers?" Mark asked.

He assumed that Robin and her team would be setting up meetings with the major clients, to try to save the company's lifeblood. People like Roger Goodell at the NFL and Mark Read at WPP, the giant British ad company. Robin would want to get Elon out in front of the biggest clients so that he could personally assuage their concerns about content moderation policies, about the personnel changes that were obviously coming, and about his plans for Twitter's future.

"Yes, that," Kahill said. "But I think he's got other plans, too."

Monday, of course, was Halloween, which meant that while Mark and his counterparts all over the company, all around the world, would be finalizing their spreadsheets, deciding which real, human colleagues they would try to save, and which real, human colleagues they'd have to sacrifice—

Elon would be heading to New York—for a number of reasons, but perhaps, primarily, to go to a party.

## CHAPTER TWELVE

# October 28, 2022

**2:10 a.m.**

A three-story, red-brick mansion tucked into a corner lot on the 2600 block of the exclusive Pacific Heights neighborhood of San Francisco. A dark and quiet third-floor bedroom, spacious and elegant, with high, rounded windows and an adjoining bathroom, steps from an elevator at the end of an interior hallway.

From somewhere downstairs, the sound of breaking glass.

Paul Pelosi, eighty-two years old, father of five and the head of a successful real estate and VC investment firm—who also happened to be married to one of the most powerful women on the planet—stirred beneath a heavy comforter. Paul's eyes were still closed, his mind trapped in that blurry state somewhere between sleep and consciousness. Even dulled, his senses were telling him that something wasn't right; but at his age, and at that hour, his reflexes weren't what they used to be.

It took him a full beat to regain enough control over his muscles to shift to his side, his head still firmly pressed against his pillow. Then another beat, to slowly raise his eyelids. He peered out into the darkness of his bedroom, searching for whatever had pulled him from his sleep—and that's when he saw the shape.

Large, intimidating, looming just a few feet beyond the foot of his bed.

Paul froze, his entire body rigid beneath the covers. He blinked, hard, trying to make sense of what he was seeing—and as the last lingering tendrils of sleep released their grip on his mind, he realized that the shape was a man. Hulking and bearded, *there was a man in his bedroom*, hunched forward as he took another step toward Paul's bed.

Panicking, Paul rocketed to a sitting position. A sudden feeling of vulnerability swept through him—he was alone in the house, an old man in boxer shorts and a buttoned pajama top—but he fought to stay mentally in control. Then his gaze shifted to the stranger's hands. In one, the man held a tangle of what appeared to be white plastic zip ties. In the other—a large, heavy-looking hammer. It was a nightmare come to life, the sort of thing that happened in movies or that you read about in the newspaper—the sort of thing that wasn't supposed to happen in real life. *A stranger, in his bedroom.* A stranger, who had obviously broken into his house in the middle of the night.

Paul had lived in San Francisco his whole life; he knew that the city was growing less safe every year, that even in places like Pacific Heights, car thefts and robberies weren't as uncommon as they had been even a decade earlier. Maybe this was just that—a break-in, a thief looking for valuables, who had put a brick through one of the windows downstairs, hoping for an easy score.

Paul sputtered to find words, but the stranger spoke first.

"Are you Paul Pelosi?"

Paul's stomach dropped, fear chasing the last vestiges of sleep out of his body. *No, this was no random break-in.* Paul stared at the man. Above the beard, the man's face was mostly lost in the shadows, but Paul could make out a high, sloping forehead, mean-looking slits for eyes, and a wild mane of auburn hair. Paul didn't recognize the man, but he had an idea why the man had broken into his house.

"Where's Nancy?" the man suddenly shouted, as he raised the hammer. *"Where's Nancy?"*

By the second mention of Paul's wife's name, the man's pitch was nearly at a screech. Paul's throat went dry, but he fought, with every nerve in his body, to stay as calm as possible. He knew, now, that this wasn't just a nightmare come to life; it was his *worst* nightmare, the worst nightmare of every family member of a modern politician, conjured into reality by the incessant, unavoidable drumbeat of partisan ideology, hatred, and conspiratorial insanity that had gripped America for the past eight years. *Where's Nancy?* This man didn't know Paul, and he didn't know Nancy—what he knew was what had been fed to him by a TV screen, a YouTube channel, a Reddit board, a Facebook post, a Google search, and a Twitter thread.

Suddenly the man came around the side of the bed, still holding the hammer high over his head. Paul put his own hands up, palms out, trying to keep his face and voice calm.

"She's not here," he said. "Nancy's not here."

Which was true. He didn't add that she was in Washington; that if she had been in San Francisco, the house would have been protected—under twenty-four-hour surveillance—by Capitol Police. That in fact, there were cameras watching the house now, but that Nancy's detail would be with her, protecting the Speaker of the House—and unfortunately not her eighty-two-year-old husband.

The man seemed momentarily confused, unsure what to do next. Paul shifted his gaze from the hammer to the zip ties, and a new shiver moved down his spine.

"Get out of bed," the man grunted, still obviously confused. "I'm going to tie you up."

Yes, the man obviously did have a plan, and whatever it was, Paul thanked God his wife wasn't home. But he also knew that he had to think fast, that any minute the man's confusion might shift to frustration, or anger. The hammer looked huge in the dark bedroom, its metallic head the size of a giant fist.

His hands still up, Paul shifted his legs over the side of the bed and rose to a standing position. The man started to fumble with the zip ties, and Paul made a sudden decision—lunging forward toward the door that led out into the hallway and toward the elevator leading down to the first floor. The motion seemed to snap the stranger out of his confusion, and he leapt in front of Paul, stopping him before he exited the bedroom.

"Why do you want to see my wife?" Paul sputtered, breathing hard.

"Well, she's number two from the presidency, right?" the heavy-set man huffed back.

Paul nodded, and the man gave him a terrifying look.

"We've got to take them all out."

Paul panicked, and then said the first thing that came into his mind.

"I need to use the bathroom."

He was surprised when the stranger took a step back, and Paul quickly headed toward a door on the other side of the bedroom. Then the man seemed to think better of it, and was suddenly right behind him.

"Hold on," the stranger growled, but Paul had made it to the bathroom door. Even without turning on the light, he could make out the long counter to his left, where he'd left his phone charging the night before. He made a grab for it, even as he felt the man's warm breath on the back of his neck.

"I said hold on—"

But Paul had already hit the emergency button programmed into the phone's screen. He stopped moving, turning to face the stranger, who stood in front of him. The hammer and zip ties were still in his hand, but for at least the moment, he made no move to use them. He might have had a plan—but it was obvious the man wasn't entirely in his right mind.

There was a click from the phone, then a woman's voice.

Paul lifted the phone to his ear, keeping his eyes on the stranger's face. The man just stared back at him, as if he didn't know quite what he was supposed to do next. Paul knew he needed to be careful. He didn't want to do anything to set the man off, but he might only have one chance—one brief chance—to get help.

"Who is this?" he grunted into the phone, as if he didn't know.

A woman's voice responded, loud enough that it echoed off the marble of the dark bathroom.

"This is the San Francisco Police. Do you need help?"

Paul made his eyes wide, for the benefit of the stranger.

"Oh I guess I, I guess I called by mistake. What is this?"

"This is San Francisco Police," the woman repeated. "Do you need help?"

*Careful, now.*

"Oh, well there's a gentleman, uh, here just waiting for my wife to come back."

Paul paused a moment, swallowing.

"Nancy Pelosi," he added, hoping that the 911 operator could quickly corroborate his phone number, confirm that he wasn't just some crank making a late-night call.

He could tell the stranger was getting uncomfortable, shifting his weight between his feet, but Paul needed more time: he needed to thread a dangerous needle, to get the woman on the other end of the line to understand that he was in mortal danger, without upsetting the man with the hammer.

"He's just waiting for her to come back," he repeated, keeping his voice steady, almost affable. "But she's not going to be here for days, so I guess we'll have to wait."

The stranger seemed okay with this. The hammer was still raised, but his body language didn't change.

"Okay," the woman said. "Do you need police, fire, for medical or anything?"

"Uh . . . I don't think so. I don't think so."

But he knew that if he didn't think quick, the call was going to end and he'd be alone, in the bathroom. With the hammer.

"Is the Capitol Police around?"

"No, this is San Francisco—"

"They are usually here at the house protecting my wife."

There was another pause.

"No. This is San Francisco Police."

Christ, maybe the woman didn't have a way of cross-referencing the call. Maybe she wasn't going to get what was happening.

"I know," Paul stalled. "I understand."

Then he decided to take a chance—held the phone slightly away from his ear and addressed the stranger.

"Okay, well . . . I don't know, what do you think?"

The stranger seemed surprised to be suddenly involved in the conversation. He even smiled a little.

"Everything's good," the stranger said.

"Uh," Paul said into the phone. "He thinks everything's good. I've got a problem, but he thinks everything is good."

But it seemed that wasn't enough. The woman's voice grew a little cold, sending a nervous wave through Paul's body.

"Okay, call us back if you change your mind—"

"No no no," Paul interrupted, losing some of his calm. "This gentleman just came into the house, uh, and wants to wait here for my wife to come home and, so uh anyway—"

"Do you know who the person is?"

Finally he was getting through. He kept his eyes on the stranger's face, which was still mostly impassive.

"No, I don't know who he is—"

But suddenly the man took a step forward. His eyes narrowed, as whatever confusion had clouded his thinking started to recede. He shook his head, violently, mumbling angrily.

"He's telling me not to, uh, he's telling me not to do anything."

"What is your address, sir?"

Paul took a chance, giving his address, and then his name again. This set the man off even more, and he reached for Paul's arm.

"Anyway," Paul said, struggling to keep the phone against his ear. "This gentleman says that, uh, he thinks that I definitely ought to, you know, he's telling me to put the phone down. And just do what he says."

"Okay," the woman responded. "What is the gentleman's name?"

Her question rebounded through the bathroom, causing the stranger to pause. Then the man shrugged his rounded shoulders.

"Dave DePape," he said.

"What's that?" the woman asked.

"My name's David," the man said, loud enough to be heard over the phone.

"The name is David," Paul repeated. At least he had the man's name.

"Okay," the 911 operator responded. "And who is David?"

"I don't know," Paul said, almost through his teeth. Was she finally getting it? Or was this an act, to keep him on the phone while she sent help?

"I'm a friend of theirs," DePape suddenly blurted.

"Yeah," Paul quickly added. "I uh, uh, he says he's a friend but as I said I've never—"

"But you don't," the operator said, clearly getting it now. "You don't know who he is?"

"No, ma'am."

"Okay," she started, but now DePape came toward Paul again, menacing.

"He's telling me I'm being very leading so I gotta stop talking to you, okay?"

"Okay. You sure? I can stay on the phone with you just to make sure everything's okay—"

"No," Paul said. DePape's hand was on his arm again, fingers thick and strong, digging into his skin. "He wants me to get the hell off the phone. Okay?"

"Okay—"

"Thank you—"

A second later, DePape grabbed the phone out of Paul's hand and placed it back on the counter. The heavyset man was so close now Paul could smell his sweat, and there was a moment of silence as they just stood there in the bathroom, almost face-to-face. Paul was a head taller than DePape, and in his younger years he might have been able to do something. But the stranger looked like he had a good twenty to thirty pounds on him, was less than half his age, and was holding a hammer. At eighty-two, Paul didn't stand a chance; his only real hope was that the 911 operator had realized that something horrible was happening at the Pelosi house, and would send help soon enough to make a difference.

Still holding his arm, DePape led Paul out of the bathroom and through the bedroom. He was mumbling as he went, but Paul barely caught any of the words. Perhaps he was talking through his original plan, what he'd intended to do with the zip ties and the hammer, what would have happened if Nancy had been home when this stranger had broken in through the downstairs window and made his way upstairs. How he'd intended to tie Nancy up with the zip ties, then demand that she confess to all manner of conspiracies, to whatever nonsense DePape's frenzied sponge of a brain had been fed by the angry voices he followed on the internet, on cable news, on social media. How if Nancy wouldn't confess, he'd take the hammer and break her kneecaps—*break an eighty-three-year-old woman's kneecaps.*

They entered the hallway that led to the rest of the house. DePape seemed to be trying to decide where to take him, so Paul took the initiative and headed toward the stairs that led down to the first floor. DePape remained a step behind him with the hammer and the zip ties. As they reached the bottom, DePape leaned forward, so close his mouth was almost against Paul's ear.

"I can take you out," he hissed, and it seemed like he was going to say more, when a sudden sound interrupted him. A sound from outside, beyond the front door—a car door closing and footsteps moving up the path.

*The 911 operator. She had understood.*

DePape was looking at the door, and Paul could not begin to imagine what the man was thinking, but for whatever reason, DePape hustled him forward. By the time they reached the door, they were standing right next to each other. Then there was the sound of a fist against the wood, a rapid knocking, the sort of knocking that could only come from law enforcement. DePape mumbled another warning to Paul, but Paul reached for the doorknob, and the hammer was back in the air. Just as Paul opened the door, he put his own hand on the hammer as well, feeling the warm, heavy handle.

Outside, Paul saw two uniformed officers, San Francisco PD, standing on the porch. The bigger of the two peered into the open doorway at the two of them.

"What's going on, man?"

Paul glanced at DePape, who was smiling strangely at the cops. Paul didn't know what to do, so he smiled, too. Both of their hands were still on the hammer.

"Everything's good," DePape said.

A bright light exploded in Paul's face as the officer shined his flashlight directly at them. In that moment, the officer saw the hammer—and changed his voice immediately.

"Drop the hammer!" he shouted.

"Um, nope," DePape grunted.

Then he tried to yank the hammer out of Paul's hand. Paul held on with all of his strength, and the two of them began to wrestle for the heavy weapon.

"What's going on right now?" the cop shouted.

Suddenly Paul felt the handle slip out of his hand. He saw the hammer go up over his head and then it was swinging toward his skull. The cop dove forward, shouting, but it was too late. The hammer came down and there was a loud crack. Paul felt his knees buckle and suddenly he was falling.

He hit the ground on his side, his tall body sprawled against the hardwood floor. He felt a sudden warmth spread down the side of his face. His eyes were open but everything was getting blurry. He could hear a commotion next to him, the officer tackling DePape, and more shouting, the sound of handcuffs. Then he saw a dark shape spreading across the floorboards in front of him, a shimmering pool of liquid, and it took him a beat to realize it was his own blood. Then, a moment later, everything

went

black.

# October 31, 2022

*"Elon!"*

*"Over here!"*

*"Elon!"*

*"This way!"*

Shouting, screaming, frantic voices reaching out like claws as the flashbulbs explode, requests, demands, begging and pleading, TURN THIS WAY, face that way, give me something, say something, do something—but you don't stop and you don't care because you're moving at a million miles per hour down the thick velvet blue carpet, because it's raining and you're outside on a snarled strip of sidewalk on the Lower East Side of Manhattan, and the cars are honking and the photographers are jostling and everyone is grabbing and grasping and finally you're right outside the door, a monument of cinder block taking up the entire corner of the block, and you see the bright purple twists of neon up above—*Moxy*, the name of the hotel, eclectic and torturously chic and so brand spanking new, it hasn't really even opened yet—and the massive, dark-suited security guards and the even more massive, goateed and crew-cutted, jacked-up man with the clipboard, and the screaming only gets louder, so you pause, yes goddammit you *pause*, and you face all the cameras and the flashing lights and the paparazzi—and you give them a pose—you lift your fists in the air and you roar, because WHY NOT? You're dressed in crimson and black, with wrist guards and shoulder pads, something someone picked up for you at a costume shop called Abracadabra NYC, "Devil's Champion-Leather Armor Set," seventy-five hundred dollars, but who gives a shit, because you're the richest fucking man in the world, and you're moving forward again, past the security guards and the goatee with the clipboard, and you only look back for an instant, not at the paparazzi—but at the person directly behind you, breathing hard and laughing into the rain, manicured fingernails digging into your hand as you move—because she's your mother, Maye, a former South African supermodel, and she's dressed as Cruella de Vil, and she looks FANTASTIC at seventy-two, and you have no doubt that the paparazzi would love to know about her morning routine, but you aren't going to stop to tell them because you're already inside—

Moving down, down, down, descending to the basement of the hotel where the party is already in full swing, a sprawling underground space lit by red paper lanterns and decorated to the hilt, skeletons hanging from the ceilings and chains clanging against the walls, faux flames leaping from floor lights and half-naked dancers covered in fake blood, writhing and undulating in white ceramic bathtubs—it's crowded and the lighting is dim and your mother is on your arm, not that she'd care, or not that *you'd* care that *she'd* care, because she's a former SUPERMODEL and goddammit you're the *richest man in the world*—and then you start to recognize people, not because you know them personally, but because EVERYONE knows them impersonally, because EVERYONE who is ANYONE is here:

JULIA FOX who used to fuck KANYE is dressed as a furry animal from *Where the Wild Things Are* and ICE T is Dracula and HEATHER GRAHAM is Cleopatra and DEVIN WAY is the Genie from Aladdin and JONATHAN VAN NESS and MARK LONDON are in drag as the stars of *Absolutely Fabulous* and NIKITA DRAGUN is a Teen Titan and THE BLONDS are Priscilla and Elvis and JEREMY SCOTT is Tim Gunn and DAVID KIRSCH is a Naavi and JUNO BIRCH is an alien and JESSE JAMES KEITEL is a Dalmatian and CHLOE FLOWER is Liberace and NIKEATA THOMPSON is the Statue of Liberty and MODEL ANOK YAI is Blade and MODEL LEOMIE ANDERSON is a sexy clown and MODEL ALISAR AILABOUNI is a vampire and MODEL TONI DREHER-ADENUGA is a bunny and MODEL OLIVIA PONTON is Harley Quinn and MODEL upon MODEL upon MODEL are dancing and laughing and drinking Bailey's cocktails, prosecco, and vodka passed along through the crowd by half-naked waitresses wrapped in surgical bandages and everyone is happy and none of them are real, NOT A GODDAMN ONE OF THEM IS REAL, it's uncanny valley come to life, animatrons conjured by the starving paparazzi outside, bags of flesh and bone powered by neurons powered by algorithms powered by the matrix powered by the simulation, lurching and throbbing and pulsing to the beat cascading from the DJ BOOTH where QUESTLOVE, dressed as an ASTRONAUT, of course, a fucking ASTRONAUT, hovers over the velvet-roped VIP BOOTH, while behind him, lurching and throbbing and pulsing, is the host of the party, the belle of the ball, the QUEEN of HALLOWEEN, HEIDI KLUM herself, dressed as a giant earthworm, a disgusting, squirming, flesh-colored, yellow-eyed, mucus-lipped, phallic-shaped earthworm, hanging from a fishing line held by her husband, not SEAL but the other guy, and she isn't really dancing, because how the hell could she, she's a fucking earthworm, and this is her party, and NONE OF THIS IS REAL.

Then you turn and are heading back up the stairs, faster than you came down, and your mother is right behind you, maybe she's confused, maybe she wants to stay and throb and pulse and writhe with the animatrons, with the worm and the Naavi and the Dalmatian and the MODELS or maybe she understands, because even though she is a SUPERMODEL she is also your mother, and she knows, she knows, and then you are at the top of the stairs and through the door and back outside, and the paparazzi are screaming and shouting.

*"Elon!"*

*"Over here!"*

*"Give us a pose!"*

*"Look this way!"*

And the cameras are flashing and everyone's grabbing and you're being jostled and buffeted as you head toward your car, and your driver, and your bodyguards, but you're only vaguely aware, because you've got your phone out of the pocket of your leather pants, your seventy-five-hundred-dollar Abracadabra Devil's Champion leather armor pants, and you're looking at the screen, and you're seeing the texts, and the emails, and the tweets, yes the tweets, and everyone is angry, and many of them, most of them, seem to be angry at YOU.

Because of something you did, something you said, something you tweeted. And even though you've already erased the tweet, you know it's too late, because the internet isn't written in pencil, it's written in pen, and Twitter isn't written in pen, it's written in fucking NEON, and what you wrote, in the early hours of the day before—

After reading about an eighty-two-year-old man getting his skull—

Cracked open with a hammer—

Was—

*"There is a tiny possibility there might be more to this story than meets the eye."*

Linked to a fringe conspiracy theory from an untrustworthy news source.

In fucking NEON.

For the whole world to read.

And you know, you know, as you head for your car, that this is going to be a problem, a HUGE FUCKING PROBLEM, because even if none of this is real—you aren't just the *richest man in the world*, but you're also supposed to be one of the *smartest*.

## CHAPTER FOURTEEN

# November 3, 2022

**There was something** vaguely comforting about being the least important person in the room. Although it went against everything in Jessica's typically outgoing nature, she had entered the conference room on the second floor of Tenth quietly, like a bit of dust floating in through a poorly designed ventilation duct. She drifted past the various Goons she recognized from Google—Jared Birchall, David Sacks, Jason Calacanis—and the remaining Twitter faithful she didn't, executives who only a day ago would have been separated from a moment like this by at least two levels of management. Now they huddled as far as they could get from the central characters seated at the obscenely long table that bisected the room. Jessica also chose a metal-framed chair as distant from the action as was professionally possible, a spot where she was mostly hidden behind a pyramid of boxed spring water and a tangle of laptop computer cords.

That she didn't recognize many of the Tweeps in the room was not surprising, considering the extent of the bloodletting that had already hit the C-suite. Beyond Parag, Bret, Ned, Vijaya, and Sean, in Jessica's own sphere of Marketing and Sales, the bodies had begun to pile up. Sarah Personette was a terrible loss, whether she'd resigned, as had been widely reported by the press, or fired, as was the scuttle spreading through the company. Either way, she'd apparently had all of her access abruptly cut off by the end of Elon's first full day, which had sent shock waves through the advertising community. In short order, Sarah's "vanishing" had been followed by the loss of Leslie Berland; the happy face she'd put on when Elon had first walked his way through the San Francisco headquarters had been replaced at 5:01 p.m. on Tuesday, November 1, by a tweet consisting of a blue heart—the only real announcement that she, too, had just been *vanished*. Sarah's and Leslie's loss had left an advertising abyss, but it had quickly been filled by JP Maheu, global VP of ad sales.

It was JP who had guided Elon through a wild twelve hours of meetings in New York, which had been brainstormed and choreographed by both JP and Robin Wheeler. Although Robin, who was a force of nature when it came to the complex art of managing advertising clients, had couched it in more optimistic terms, Jessica knew New York was a last-ditch, emergency strategy to stop what seemed inevitable: the full collapse of Twitter advertising.

The frantic dash through New York had gone surprisingly well—but not for JP Maheu. Just yesterday, shortly after Elon had been spirited back to his private jet for the return flight to the San Francisco headquarters, JP had been walked out of the New York offices. Robin had been coming out of a meeting when she, along with many of her team, had gotten a text directly from the Global VP as he was escorted through the halls, simply saying: "Bye, friends."

It hit as another total shock. Jessica had been in Robin's office with Robin and a few high-level managers shortly after the firing.

"What the hell just happened?" Robin had asked the room.

Someone had responded, "Calm down, take a breath."

"Don't tell me to take a breath," Robin had shot back. "We just lost both of our biggest connections to Madison Avenue, discarded like it's no big deal."

Then she'd added, "I don't think I can stay. This is insane. They are firing people for no reason."

Robin grew teary-eyed, and Jessica herself had struggled to hold back her own emotions. There was hugging in the room. If there were two people Twitter couldn't afford to lose, it was Sarah and JP. Sarah was one of the most beloved people in advertising sales, and JP's connections were unparalleled.

If Robin left as well, Jessica didn't see how Twitter's ad sales business would survive.

Calmer minds were trying to convince Robin that she should at least wait around until the end of the week—hopefully then there would be more clarity about employee bonuses—when a phone in Robin's office began to ring. It was Antonio Gracias, one of Elon's most hands-on Goons. Robin had balked, but someone told her to answer—because Antonio was probably calling to ask her to run everything now that JP and Sarah were gone.

That's exactly why Antonio had been calling: "Hey, Robin, JP is no longer here, and I want you to run Sales and Marketing." And the first thing he wanted done? "I need you to put together a list of the people we are going to cut and I need this by tomorrow."

Robin's fingers had whitened against the phone.

"Listen," she'd responded, curtly. "You just got rid of the two people closest to Madison Avenue. If you want me to do this—"

*What two people?* Antonio had interrupted. *We didn't fire Sarah, she resigned.*

"The point is," Robin had continued, "we've lost two people imperative to this business. If we're going to survive, we need to get in front of our clients at scale—with Elon. And we need to do this—*immediately.*"

So now here they were, barely two days later, in the conference room in Tenth, Jessica hiding at the far end of the table, and twenty feet away, facing a teleconference camera, side by side—Robin and Elon. Elon was in a black, short-sleeved T-shirt and sporting some sort of chain necklace, like he'd stepped off the set of a hip-hop video; Robin was also in black, her long blond hair framing high cheekbones and a serious expression. And why shouldn't she look serious? She was now in charge of everything, standing ankle-deep in the blood of her former superiors.

For both of them—Robin and Jessica—this was their first time meeting Elon in person. When Elon had first walked into the room and sat down next to Robin, Robin had given him a brief smile, saying simply, "Hello, boss."

Elon had paused, then charmingly smiled back.

"Boss. I like that."

A bit of the tension was broken, but Jessica knew the few remaining Tweeps in the room were as nervous as she was. Not only for their own jobs, but for Twitter itself. It wasn't just the firings—the loss of people who seemed integral to Twitter's way forward. There were also rapidly aggregating self-inflicted wounds. Tweets were spreading throughout the platform that Elon was planning some sort of amnesty for banned accounts—people who had been kicked off the platform for posting racism, antisemitism, and hate speech from both sides of the political aisle. There were even hints that he intended to bring back Trump, who was still banned from every social media platform—Twitter, Facebook, Instagram (probably even Myspace and Friendster). Then the most self-destructive incident of all, Elon's tweet, right before Halloween, about the brutal assault on the husband of the Speaker of the House: *"There is a tiny possibility there might be more to this story than meets the eye."*

Elon Musk wasn't some conspiracy theorist sitting in a dark corner of the internet. He was the new CEO of Twitter. When gently approached about the inappropriate nature of the tweet, he'd responded that although he was the head of Twitter, he wasn't going to stop tweeting as himself—Elon Musk, the person, not the CEO. Jessica knew this was an impossible stance. To the general public, he was now the face of Twitter. To advertisers, this was even more of a cemented truth.

JP and Robin's frantic work on setting up those meetings in New York had been about exactly that, an effort to reassure advertisers that the new face of Twitter wasn't the guy who tweeted conspiracy theories about Paul Pelosi, but the guy who had built SpaceX and Tesla into billion—and trillion—dollar companies. And from all accounts Jessica had heard, Elon had performed exceptionally well, saying all the right things as he charmed the CEOs and ad reps in one-on-one meetings throughout his time in New York.

Today's virtual meeting would be an exclamation point for the statement Elon had been making in person. The quarterly meeting of Twitter's Influencers Council was arguably the platform's most important method of outreach to Madison Avenue, as the audience consisted of up to a hundred of the biggest names in the ad business. This would be Elon's chance to reassure the community en masse that he was moving Twitter in the right direction, despite what they might have perceived as stumbles in his first few days at the helm.

Robin would be running the meeting from her seat next to the billionaire. Yoel was in and out of the room as well, representing Safety and Moderation. In the days since the takeover, Elon had elevated Yoel's front-facing profile both privately and publicly—and for good reason.

On top of the firings and Elon's erratic tweeting, news stories had now proliferated throughout the mainstream media, responding to what appeared to be a sudden surge of hate speech overwhelming the platform since the takeover. Although theories in the press abounded—that Elon had already tweaked the moderation algorithms to allow more "free speech" on the platform, resulting in a storm of antisemitism, racism, and personal attacks; or that people with bad intentions were "testing" the platform during the chaotic changeover of leadership—the truth turned out to be something much more sinister.

Beginning almost immediately after Elon had signed the papers to take over Twitter, the platform had been the victim of a coordinated troll attack. According to the Trust and Safety Council's own investigation, over three hundred fake accounts had spewed over fifty thousand racist, antisemitic, and violent tweets across the site in a period of a few hours—the biggest spike of hate speech Twitter had ever seen.

As Yoel had explained to Elon when Elon had first returned to the headquarters, the moderators had gone into full battle mode, and had successfully stifled the surge in less than a day. Recognizing the attack for what it was—most likely a paid trolling assault, conducted by a troll farm overseas—they had quickly banned the fake accounts and erased the hate tweets. In fact, they had done such a thorough job of combating the troll attack that the total incidence of hate speech on the platform was now below the base level of inappropriate messaging from *before* Elon had taken over.

Elon had remained surprisingly nonplussed as he'd listened to Yoel's account of the troll attack; it was almost as though he had fully expected something of the sort to happen, and Jessica couldn't help wondering if the trolling simply validated the inclinations of paranoia she had already sensed from the billionaire. To be fair, the fact that he was paranoid didn't mean someone *wasn't* out to get him. Surely Elon had enemies; he had just fired almost all of Twitter's previous management and eliminated the company's board of directors. He was taking aim at Facebook—and Zuckerberg wasn't known for playing nice with competitors—and there were always hedge fund activists, competing car companies, even the Tesla faithful, who were upset at Elon's diverging interests, some even calling for his ouster as the head of the car company. Who knows, maybe Elon even believed it was his sometime nemesis Bill Gates, creeping around in the middle of the night with what amounted to a virtual hammer? Once you started down the rabbit hole, every shadow you saw looked like a rabbit.

But the relatively good news was that the enforcement strategy Twitter already had in place had been successful; they had policed the surge of hate speech, and taken down the troll attack.

In that spirit, the Influencers' video chat began on a high note: Robin's brief introductions, then reassurances to the ad execs that Twitter and Elon remained committed to the safety of the site. Even from the start, Jessica could see that Elon knew how to talk to an audience of suits; he came off as charming and attuned to their concerns, stating that brand safety was a top priority. That freedom of speech was primary, but freedom of speech didn't equate to freedom of reach, and that he was going to put even more resources into the work Yoel and his team were doing to keep hate tweets off the platform. With Robin's help, he was able to dodge the more pointed questions about his recently deleted Pelosi tweet, and what he explained was necessary, cost-cutting employment restructuring.

The site, according to a tweet Elon would post the next day, was suffering *"a massive drop in revenue," "losing four million dollars a day,"* and now that as much as 50 percent of the biggest advertisers had either paused their ad buying or threatened to do so, the losses were only going to accumulate. Still, in the Influencers meeting, he avoided getting adversarial, even though he would likewise soon be tweeting about the "activist groups" that were trying to get advertisers to boycott the platform, what he called "unamerican" activity. This boycott, called for in an open letter by forty activist organizations—including the NAACP and GLAAD—coincided with the troll attack that had hit the site during Elon's first twenty-four hours at the helm, painting an ugly picture of Twitter's advertising landscape. Yet somehow, Elon remained optimistic throughout the video call, and by the time the tech crew was shutting down the ring lights and severing the conferencing connection, Jessica felt some of her concerns allayed.

Elon wasn't a monster, nor was he unreasonable. With Robin by his side, he looked and sounded like a CEO, and if the adults in the room could continue to keep him, his paranoia, and his Goons in check, perhaps things would not turn out as bleak as she'd previously feared.

------

Jessica didn't see the email until a little after midnight, Thursday turning into Friday. She was sitting at a desk that was only slightly bigger than her laptop, kitty-corner to the queen-sized bed that took up most of the hotel room in San Francisco she had been calling home ever since Elon had walked through Twitter's front doors.

She had been planning to Zoom with her family, until she'd realized how late it had gotten. Although Elon had swept out of the conference room and into the waiting arms of his Goon squad as soon as the video call had ended, Jessica had spent the rest of the afternoon and well into the evening huddled with Robin and the other remaining marketing and sales reps. Jessica's job during that extended session was to make follow-up calls to clients; but it had been almost impossible to concentrate on being bubbly and reassuring on the phone, while across the room Robin and her colleagues were hovering over spreadsheets filled with employee names and their respective accomplishments—turning the spreadsheets into lists that Jessica knew had only one, macabre purpose.

Jessica had finally settled down at the desk in the hotel room with an open demi bottle of something red from the nearby minibar—no nearby wineglass, because the room hadn't come with any and it seemed too late to call down to room service (besides, it was a *demi* bottle, which somehow sounded both classy and the slightest bit illicit). Before long she was surfing emails, and those lists began to really hit home, erasing any last licks of the optimism that she'd felt in the conference room before Elon had exited with his Goons.

*Team:*

> *In an effort to place Twitter on a healthy path, we will go through the difficult process of reducing our global workforce on Friday. We recognize that this will impact a number of individuals who have made valuable contributions to Twitter, but this action is unfortunately necessary to ensure the company's success moving forward. . . .*

After nearly a week of total silence, it was the first company-wide missive: an email informing the Tweeps that the rumors they had heard were true. Mass firings would be taking place—but, as the email continued, not in person, not during business hours, not in any organized fashion that one might expect from a billion-dollar company in the business of social media.

*Given the nature of our distributed workforce and our desire to inform impacted individuals as quickly as possible, communications for this process will take place via email. By 9AM PST on Friday, Nov 4th, everyone will receive an individual email with the subject line: Your Role At Twitter. . . .*

No visit from HR, no face-to-face with management, no personal calls from a direct superior. Tweeps, many who had been with the company for a decade or more, many who had been integral to building Twitter from a bootstrapped start-up into a global town hall, would wake up tomorrow morning to find out that they no longer had jobs. More than that, they would immediately lose all access to their Twitter accounts, their Twitter emails, the company Slack.

*To help insure the safety of each employee as well as Twitter systems and customer data, our offices will be temporarily closed and all badge access will be suspended. If you are in an office or on your way to an office, please return home.*

Jessica stared at the email, before reaching for the wine bottle with trembling fingers. She'd never been fired from a job before, but she couldn't imagine that this was normal. She had the sudden thought that perhaps the reason there wouldn't be any calls from HR was that there wouldn't be anyone left in HR.

She would find out after the fact that the chaos would extend far beyond HR; that so many of her fellow Tweeps would be fired by morning, whole systems within the company would stop working. In various headquarters, the Wi-Fi would go out, because the IT personnel had been locked out of their accounts. Whole teams would vanish—but since the company directory had gone offline (and, reportedly, the IT engineer who knew the directory's password had been fired along with his office-mates), it would be impossible to know what core products would be affected, or who was left to take over for those who were suddenly gone.

Opening up her Slack and Twitter that night, Jessica watched the sudden chaos and confusion in real time. Even though the email had informed the Tweeps that they would find out their fates by nine a.m. the next morning, the knives began slashing almost immediately. One by one, Jessica watched as colleagues posted blue hearts or the salute emoji on their Slack account—only to have the account vanish a moment later, a silent parade of doomed souls. One by one, people she had worked with for years suddenly found themselves locked out of their emails and unable to turn on their laptops—learning their fates with the click of a finger.

Dawn was just clawing at the edges of the drawn window shades on the other side of the hotel room by the time Jessica closed her laptop and rested her head against its cold aluminum case, the now-empty demi bottle just inches from her heavy-lidded eyes. She still had access to her email and her Slack—for now—as did most of her team, as far she could tell. Robin was still emailing reassurances to the marketing department, and Yoel was still in his office, striking down the hate-spewing troll accounts as quickly as they appeared.

But even as she nodded off toward sleep, she could still see that never-ending parade of blue hearts and tiny, saluting emojis. The final gasps of Twitter 1.0, *#lovewhereyouwork*, the sparkly, glittery company of Tweeps she'd known and loved.

By morning, half of Twitter's roughly 7,500 employees would be gone. And that, Jessica would soon find out, was only the beginning.

**Esther Crawford**
@esthercrawford

When your team is pushing round the clock to make deadlines sometimes you
#SleepWhereYouWork

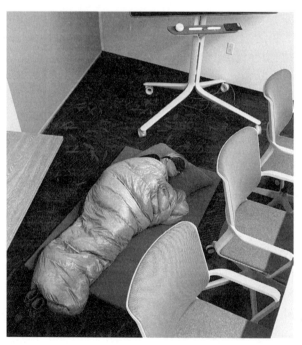

3:34 AM Nov 2, 2022

## CHAPTER FIFTEEN

# November 9, 2022

**If Esther had a chance** to go back in time and do it again, she might not have hit send; but then again, everyone who tweeted had a tweet he or she regretted, and hey, it wasn't every day you turned into a meme.

Admittedly, it had been 3:34 in the morning on a Wednesday, and she'd been going hardcore for four straight days; she hadn't left the office—not even for a meal—since Saturday morning. It hadn't even been Esther who had taken the photo. One of her product managers had done the honors, after Esther had cocooned herself for a brief nap between product sessions. He'd obviously thought it was funny, maybe even an homage to their new boss, who was famous for sleeping at Tesla and had recently been sequestering himself on a couch in the library.

Yet while Esther hadn't taken the picture or posted the original tweet, she had retweeted it. She had fully expected the tweet to go viral, but she hadn't counted on the amount of vitriol that had come her way. She would be the first to admit she might have read the room wrong, and the timing was—well, unfortunate. This tweet came on the heels of Elon's Pelosi tweet, the layoffs of top management, and the sudden exodus of advertising clients. It had been getting viral numbers almost right away, and then had truly gone stratospheric the next night—Thursday—in the midst of the mass firings.

It was the media that had put the two themes together: Esther "simping" for the impetuous billionaire while he shredded Twitter. Suddenly she was being portrayed as *glorifying* "hustle culture" while Elon was haphazardly firing Tweeps who had been with the company for a decade, cutting the company so deep to the bone that internal systems were threatening to collapse. But Esther saw the image of her, in her sleeping bag, on the floor of a conference room, as a badge of honor. When she had launched her first start-up in her early twenties, fresh out of a cult and barely getting by on welfare, she had worked round the clock, forgoing meals and sleep for days on end. This wasn't late-stage capitalism at its worst, or Elon enslaving employees for his own bank account—this was Esther, leading by example, trying to elevate her new team to achieve something for the greater good.

Angry, laid-off Tweeps could call it hustle culture, but Esther was just out there shooting her shot; she'd survived the first round of layoffs because she'd made herself indispensable, and now she was one of the few Tweeps left working face-to-face with Elon, building Twitter 2.0.

The grind had begun almost immediately on Saturday morning, before Elon had left for New York. It was Sriram Krishnan, the former Twitter engineer, VC investor, and podcaster—and perhaps, to Esther, the least objectionable of Elon's Goons—who had initiated the top-priority project that Elon had personally tapped Esther to run. Sriram called Esther at 9:30 a.m. with the details on Elon's new mandate. Although she'd developed a social relationship with Sriram before he'd been ousted by Parag in Sriram's previous incarnation as a Tweep, in Esther's entire history at Twitter she'd never been called on a Saturday before, certainly not about work. "What are you doing right now?" Sriram had started the call.

"Eating cereal?" Esther had responded.

"Elon wants to see how soon you can be here."

With that, the next phase of Esther's life had launched like a rocket. She'd arrived at headquarters thirty minutes later, walking into the conference room on Tenth to find Elon once again seated at the long table, but this time, not alone. Sriram was next to him, as well as two engineers—one of whom Esther vaguely recognized, an impressive Tweep named Vrijay, and another she'd never seen before. Jehn was also at the table, taking notes on her laptop. Jason Calacanis and David Sacks came in and out, as well as various other people from Elon's inner circle. It was obvious as Esther walked into the room that the group had been conferring for some time before she'd arrived, but she still had no clue as to what she was doing there.

Elon welcomed her with a nod, and was already midsentence before she found a seat on the other side of the table. She only caught part of what he was saying, but it was about money. He was expounding on how absolutely terrible Twitter's financial situation was, how the company was heading breakneck toward bankruptcy. The numbers were frightening—before Elon had taken over, the company had about four and a half billion in revenues and almost the same in costs: running basically at breakeven, like a not-for-profit endeavor. Now Elon had added on one and a half billion in debt financing, and revenues were taking a hit. Doing the math, Twitter would soon be at a deficit of $3 billion a year—or more. That gave the company about four months of runway until destruction. Putting aside the fact that much of this financial despair was self-inflicted, it was a tough pill, and Elon was nervous about Twitter finding a way to survive, let alone reach profitability.

From there he shifted directly to subscriptions: Twitter, he told the room, needed a real subscriber base. His intention was that 50 percent of Twitter's revenue would come from subscribers.

There was already a subscription option on Twitter—a product called Twitter Blue, which had launched in the summer of 2021, originally at a cost of $2.99 a month, then jumping to $4.99 a month. Esther had worked on it personally though it hadn't gained much traction, and by rough estimates was only bringing in $100 million a year, barely a punctuation mark on Twitter's bottom line. This was primarily for two reasons. First, people simply didn't want to pay for social media. Facebook, Instagram, and Twitter (and before them Myspace) had always been free, and the world had grown accustomed to getting things on the internet for free. Second, and more specifically, if people were going to pay for a social media site, there had to be a very good reason—features that seemed worth paying for.

Twitter Blue, in its current incarnation, offered a handful of features: the ability to "undo" tweets for up to thirty seconds after writing them, as well as access to some customizable changes to the app: color themes, icons, bookmark folders. Most users were happy to forgo these superficial benefits in exchange for free Twitter.

Elon, it seemed, intended to up the ante. Although customizing the app and undoing tweets were too trivial to get anyone's attention, there was one valuable commodity that Twitter did have at its disposal: the famed "Blue Check." This was the symbol that Twitter doled out to verified celebrities, journalists, politicians, and notable figures. It not only increased a user's visibility on the site, but marked them as "more reliable," and in some people's views, "special."

It was no secret that Elon had major issues with the "class system" that the Blue Check had, perhaps unintentionally, created. The sometimes shadowy process by which the Blue Checks had been handed out only made the system seem even more unfair. Rumors abounded, as of yet unproven, that in the past, Tweeps had sold Blue Checks for as much as thirty thousand dollars to wannabe notables— and there were many true celebrities, journalists, and the like who spent years trying to attain the elusive mark, both for ego and for real, potential gain. The value of the Blue Check wasn't simply that it was hard to get; the Blue Check, no matter its provenance, meant the user had been verified as someone both real, and at least relatively, important.

Most people understood that the Blue Check system, though certainly flawed, added immense value to the Twitter experience. All tweets were created equal, but some tweets were invariably more equal than others. An update on the war in the Ukraine, for example, coming from an anonymous user, versus an update from a Blue Checked reporter from Reuters, with a bio that put him or her on the ground in Kiev, could be read differently. If you were looking for information on something medically related, or political, or in the entertainment field, it was usually preferable to read tweets from people who had credentials and were verified as members of those particular communities.

But Elon had a different view, whether it truly came from some notion of egalitarianism, or was an ideology motivated by profit, or instigated by an urge for revenge on the various Blue Check journalists and pundits who had attacked Tesla, and Elon, over the years. Elon intended to restructure the Blue Check system, melding Twitter Blue with the uber-valuable mark of importance. People, he told the room, wouldn't pay to undo an errant tweet, but they *would* pay for a Blue Check.

Esther didn't immediately hate the idea; she had always believed that verification was valuable, and that if there was a way to do it, at scale, that might be something people would pay for. But it was immediately obvious, at least to her, that paying for Blue Checks was not the same thing as paying for verification. To verify people—effectively—would involve more than a payment system. They would probably need to employ a third-party vendor with the ability to make sure people were, indeed, who they said they were.

From the outset of the meeting, it was clear that Elon saw this as a business opportunity that was also a "general good." Likewise, as Elon spoke, Esther could see the change in the other people's posture in the room; nobody was going to risk pushing back, even if they disagreed. Calacanis, for one, was cheerleading Elon's idea like a hyped-up teenager. Sacks, too, was throwing out wilder and wilder ideas, as good an acolyte as any billionaire could hope to have. Vrijay and the other engineer were mostly silent, but nodding in tune to Sacks and Calacanis, as Jehn steadily typed into her laptop.

Esther considered going along with the rest of them, but that wasn't her personality. And since meeting Elon, she had done a fair amount of research on the billionaire. She knew that he expected loyalty, but he also respected people who knew their shit. There were stories of Elon walking the Tesla factory, asking random employees what a nearby tool was for—and firing the employee if he didn't get it right.

Esther was in the room, which meant she needed to add value.

She started by agreeing. She told Elon, and the room, that there was a way to make this work, that verification was valuable, that Twitter Blue had always been priced too low, and that there were applications that could be added to make it worth double what they were already charging. But—here she treaded carefully, but remained assertive—the Blue Check needed to come with real verification, because otherwise it could be disastrous.

Elon did not seem upset at her pushback; quite the contrary, he half-smiled at her, seeming to ponder what she was saying. But then he launched into a thirty-minute monologue about how users paying for a Blue Check would transform the business, and perhaps social media in general. How Twitter would make money in an entirely new way and free itself from the shackles of advertising. How this was really all about free speech—FREE SPEECH—and that for FREE SPEECH to be real, unfettered, and accessible to everyone, you had to change the way Twitter earned its revenue.

He turned directly to Esther as he finished speaking, and reiterated that he wanted her to lead this project; that he wanted to launch on Monday, and that he wanted to do a kickoff with the team that would develop the new Twitter Blue in one hour.

*One hour.*

Esther's heart skipped. Elon wanted to do a *kickoff* with the *team* in one hour? There literally was no fucking team. There were Jehn's notes, Calacanis and Sacks's crazy cheers, and two competent engineers.

But she could tell—this wasn't the moment to push back again.

As the meeting ended, she hurried across the hall to a smaller conference room with Vrijay and his counterpart, shutting the door behind her. As the two engineers looked at her, bewildered, she suddenly felt the energy rising up her spine. This was insane—but this was her moment.

"Okay, we have one fucking hour. I can think of a few people off the top of my head who could do this. I'm sure you two have lists as well. We need engineers, designers, product people, sales."

They looked at her, still deer in the headlights. Deer who had probably graduated at the top of their classes at MIT or Stanford, and could outprogram half of Silicon Valley in the back of a Tesla speeding through a Boring Company tunnel.

"Let's do this."

Immediately, the three of them began making calls.

---

An hour later, they were back in the main conference room across the hall, again at the long table, but now the table was cluttered with open laptops, all filled with the tic-tac-toe of a virtual conference call in full swing. Esther's heart was still beating fast as she sat by Elon's side; there had never been a moment like this at Twitter 1.0, and before today she wouldn't have thought it was possible. She and the two engineers had pulled together a killer team, to try to build the ultimate, killer product: a new Twitter Blue that would enable anyone, anywhere, to buy a vaunted Blue Check.

Elon had given Esther the entirety of Twitter—or what remained of it—to build her team, and the result was a hodgepodge of experts from various departments. There were twenty engineers on the call, as well as people from marketing, sales, and design. Of the previous people she'd worked with, she'd pulled only the engineers she believed would be hungry enough to try to do this. She'd caught one engineer on his way to the airport, about to fly home to New York because he'd assumed he would soon be out of a job. And a designer, also in an Uber on the way home—Esther had the young Tweep turn the Uber right around and deposit her somewhere she would have access to good internet for the call.

"This is an Elon Project." Those turned out to be the magic words that got people to drop everything, change their plans, get back into the game. *This is an Elon Project.* No matter what anyone was feeling about Twitter now that Elon was running things, no matter how scared they were of the Chief Twit, how much they disagreed with his trolling or his politics—*This is an Elon Project* had them head down and fingers coding. This was how Elon had built

Tesla, SpaceX, and his reputation. People, deep down, wanted to be part of an Elon Project.

From then on, Esther was given free rein of the second-floor conference space. It became her own, independent war room. And in that war room, Esther and her team had total and complete tunnel vision. Outside, Twitter was lurching through a sea of bad media—Elon's awful tweet, advertisers leaving, the mass firings— but Esther didn't have time for any of that. From that moment on she #sleptwheresheworked, and all that mattered was that work.

The moments when she did come up for air, checked her texts and her tweets from family, friends, former colleagues, she remained mostly objective. She didn't blame Elon for the firings. She knew that Parag had his own lists already drawn up and had only postponed a mass layoff because Elon had moved into the picture. Nor did she blame her former colleagues. Twitter was going through financial difficulties, which meant people, even good people, were going to lose their jobs. But she was disturbed, like most people, by the way the firings had happened. The impersonal email, the sudden cutting off of access, the seemingly harsh way in which longtime employees were being treated.

At the same time, she felt vindicated by her own actions, her own intuition. Thousands were being fired, but she was leading something cool and real, had leapfrogged up the chain of command, and was now one of the few people working with Elon face-to-face.

When, one day before her own fateful tweet, on Wednesday, November 1—at three a.m.!—Elon's team had sent out an email ending remote work, except under extreme conditions, pretty much demanding that people return to their offices the next day— Thursday!—she'd certainly balked at the suddenness of the demand.

By now many Tweeps didn't live anywhere near an office, and all of them had been promised that remote work would be a part of the Twitter landscape forever. But still, Esther herself couldn't really complain; by that point she was imbedded so deep in the office working on Twitter Blue, she was about to become a *meme.*

Of course, Elon's original goal of having Twitter Blue built by Monday (also Halloween) had been an impossible goal; he'd replaced that with the following Monday—November 7. Although Esther had seen that as a technically possible goal from an engineering standpoint, she'd had a very different, more important concern.

"Elon," she'd told her boss, "do you really want to be personally blamed for the outcome of the biggest democracy on Earth's elections because you screwed with the Twitter algorithm the day before the midterms?"

Elon had reacted with a raised eyebrow.

"When are the midterms?"

November 8, Esther had explained, exasperated.

"Ah, okay, that makes sense," Elon had thankfully responded. "You can launch it afterwards."

After the fact, media would gleefully report that the launch was delayed, to which Esther had responded, in a closed meeting with her team, "Fuck, they're shitting on us and I'm over here trying to save democracy?"

The longer timeline to launch, however, did not address the central issue that Esther had tried to bring up in that initial meeting: that the Blue Check needed to mean *actual* verification to be valuable. But it was obvious from every subsequent conversation she had with Elon on the point that he held the belief that *payment* represented verification—something he repeated like it was a mantra, as if just repeating it made it true.

Esther had worked in payments all her career, and she knew full well that payment was not verification. Anyone could buy a prepaid debit card, and there were numerous ways to disguise oneself, both legally and illegally, when making virtual payments.

As the launch date grew closer, Esther brought the point up again and again, and she hadn't just been speaking for herself. She had gained the reputation of being the one person who could push back on Elon without meeting total disaster, so often private meetings would end with *let's have Esther tell him,* or *maybe Esther can bring this up,* or even *this seems like an Esther job.*

Frankly, she didn't mind. She liked that Elon took her seriously, and there was a rush to having that sort of power, the ability to go to him, face-to-face. She also had begun to think of her role as being an adult in the room; as Jehn had told Esther, when Jehn had taken her aside before one of Esther's meetings with Elon, Elon was *special.* A genius, surely, but he could also be difficult, humorous, and yes, often immature. Esther believed Elon needed an adult in the room, and his Goons were anything but. At best, they were his yes men; at worst, they were there to rile him up, pushing him further down dangerous pathways than he might have gone on his own.

But no matter how much power she felt she had to really push back, on the issue of payment as verification, she continued to hit a brick wall. At one point, at the end of a particularly intense meeting where she laid out her evidence that allowing anyone to buy Blue Checks, and pretend that meant they were verified, would end in a bad, potentially dangerous product, Elon had come frighteningly close to blowing up at her. Although he didn't yell (he never yelled), he made his views extremely clear.

"There's only one product manager at this company, and IT'S ME."

Esther got the picture. Even if she believed they were on the verge of releasing a potentially bad product, she had no choice but to continue forward. Still, it was hard to stifle what she believed were very real concerns.

During a meeting on one of the first nights, she'd been in the war room with two of Elon's less front-facing Goons. One was Steve Davis, the president of Elon's Boring Company, who had degrees in aerospace engineering, particle physics, and economics. Davis had once owned a yogurt shop that gave rebates to customers who dressed like Bjorn Borg or could answer trivia about *Seinfeld*. Also present was Jared Birchall, Elon's main moneyman, fixer, and the CEO of his Neuralink company. Birchall was a devout Mormon who dressed conservatively and whom Esther found immediately disarming, intelligent, and even friendly. These two men knew Elon better than she ever would.

So she'd asked them, "I'm leading this thing—how do I not fuck it up?"

Davis—smart, but extremely high-strung, as if every cell in his body was moving even when he was standing still—had explained that at Elon's other companies, they gave the billionaire daily updates, each with a countdown embedded in the document, leading up to the moment of a product launch.

Esther had taken this advice literally; from then on, she'd started giving Elon twelve-hour updates with a countdown in one corner: "120 hours to launch. 100 hours to launch. 90 hours to launch." The idea was then copied by others on her team, becoming the format to keep Elon apprised of their progress: "60 hours to launch. 40 hours to launch"—

—leading right up the very morning of the launch itself.

@ElonMusk

Please note that Twitter will do lots of dumb things in
the coming months.

We will keep what works & change what doesn't.

-11:44 AM 11/9/22

The dust was still settling after Twitter 2.0's first, and thankfully mostly uneventful, first US election, when Esther entered Twitter headquarters, on the night her life had been building toward since that first meeting with Elon in his war room in Tenth.

Surprisingly, the first person who greeted her as she came through the lobby was a two-foot-tall ball of energy—X, pirouetting through the mostly empty hallway with a rocket-shaped wooden block in his hands, followed by one of Elon's bodyguards. The kid saw her and paused, smiling, so Esther smiled back.

"Hey, buddy."

X looked at her intently. Then he showed her the block, and his little voice rang out, so loud it hurt her ears.

"Fucking nine!" X shouted. "Fucking nine!"

Esther looked around, wondering what she was supposed to say in response, when the bodyguard loudly corrected: "Falcon Nine. *Falcon* Nine."

X grinned, spun on his heels, and raced back down the hall.

Esther laughed, admittedly unnerved, and continued to the elevators.

She continued on to the conference room she and her team had taken over on the tenth floor. It was called Caracara, named for a particularly territorial tropical bird of prey, mainly indigenous to South and Central America, because it was big enough for all of her engineers and had what was arguably the best views in the building, its windows overlooking the San Francisco City Hall and the city beyond.

Esther had learned a lot about the billionaire in the week leading up to the Twitter Blue launch. He was intense, brilliant, spontaneous, and, above all, completely unpredictable. Although he had left Esther and her engineers alone for much of the technical development of the project, he had been extremely involved when it came to the big-picture questions—most notably, there had been numerous meetings about the price point—how much, exactly, Elon intended to charge people for the previously lauded "Blue Check."

Initially, Elon had settled on a price of twenty dollars a month; he'd made it clear that he hated prices that ended in .99, such as 9.99 or 19.99—and liked the feel of a round number like twenty dollars. Esther had always believed that Twitter Blue had been priced too low, but twenty seemed high to her. Also, she'd had to explain to Elon that Apple, through which the majority of Twitter users accessed their accounts, always priced things at increments of .99. Leaving that aside, Elon had suggested that all subscribers should be forced to purchase their subscriptions for a year up front. Esther had balked at the notion. Two hundred and forty dollars for a platform that most people currently got for free seemed extreme, but when she tried to explain this to Elon, he'd laughed at her. Anyone who has an iPhone, he exclaimed, can easily afford two hundred and forty dollars for a year of Twitter. In his mind, having an iPhone equaled having disposable income.

Esther had grown up poor, and had experienced tough economic circumstances many times since she'd reached adulthood. Having a phone, she tried to argue, didn't mean someone was wealthy. The average person didn't have tons of savings or extra income lying around for another subscription service. Try as she might, she couldn't get Elon to connect with that reality. It wasn't until he tested the price point on Twitter—and received an instant response in the form of a tweet from a famed horror author:

> @Stephen King
> $20 a month to keep my blue check? Fuck that, they should pay me. If that gets instituted, I'm gone like Enron.

Then Elon seemed to get the message:

> @Elon Musk
> We need to pay the bills somehow! Twitter cannot rely entirely on advertisers. How about $8?

Just like that, Twitter Blue's price shifted from twenty dollars a month to eight—which became 7.99 because of the Apple App Store.

Though Elon had reacted to Stephen King's dismay at the twenty-dollar price point by shifting gears, he had still notably ignored the larger sentiment of King's tweet: that King, like most legacy Blue Checks, did not seem to understand why Elon believed he could charge celebrities and notables for their Blue Checks, when from their point of view, they were providing Twitter with the content that brought people to the platform in the first place. Sentiment across Twitter from the legacy Blues seemed to rally around King's tweet—and it seemed likely that most would not pay for something they'd formerly gotten for free.

Esther was less concerned about potential backlash—perhaps even an exodus of celebrities and notables from the site—than she was with Elon's continued belief that payment itself equated to verification. Not to mention what she expected would likely happen the minute the switches were flicked, and people were able to buy Blue Checks just by entering credit card information.

The day before the launch, Esther had gathered her nerve and hit Elon with her concerns one last time—and made the mistake of bringing up the issue in front of people: her entire team.

"There's a good chance this isn't going to go well," she'd warned Elon, while he was checking his phone from his seat at the end of the conference table. "We don't really have impersonation security in place for a launch at this scale. We don't have real verification. I think you need to know this is likely to go sideways."

When he finally looked up from his phone, she'd started to walk him through the potential scenarios—but trailed off as a big grin had broken across his face.

"Sounds like Esther is talking out of fear," he said to the room. "I don't make decisions out of fear."

He was mocking her, openly, and she'd had no choice but to accept it and move on. It helped to know that she wasn't alone in her concerns; the same day, Elon had received a seven-page report from Yoel Roth and his team at Trust and Safety detailing exactly why the launch was likely to go badly, spelling out everything that Esther had just tried to tell Elon in explicit terms. As far as she could tell, Elon respected Yoel, and had presented Yoel to the public and to advertisers as someone who was going to be an important part of Twitter 2.0's future. Although the diverse "Moderation Council" that Elon had promised to build in order to aid Yoel had yet to come into existence, Elon seemed to understand that Yoel was extremely good at his job, and had been in the trenches long enough to know how the platform was likely to respond to a new product such as this. Yoel was one of the few people from Twitter 1.0 that Elon had publicly defended: tweeting, after some of Yoel's earlier left-leaning tweets had surfaced, *"We've all made some questionable tweets, me more than most, but I want to be clear that I support Yoel. My sense is that he has high integrity, and we are all entitled to our political beliefs."*

But Yoel's seven-page report landed just about as forcefully as Esther's protestations; Elon had rolled his eyes at both of them, and the countdown had continued unimpeded. The only concession he made was that he, at least initially, agreed that a separate gray badge signifying an account's "official" status—as, say, a corporate or government entity—would be added to some legacy tweeters.

Now, a day later, Esther was a bundle of nerves as she swept into Caracara. Her team was already gathered around the conference table, ready (if noticeably reluctant) to hit those switches that would launch the new Twitter Blue out into the world. To Esther's surprise, Elon was already in the vicinity. She certainly hadn't expected the billionaire to accept her offer when she'd invited him to watch the launch with her team, but, it had turned out, he had spent the night before on a couch in the library, so had elected to cancel all of his plans for the morning to watch along with the rest of them.

He came into the room with a bit of troubling news, however; for whatever reason, he'd decided to scrap the idea of adding an "official" badge to *any* of the newly purchased Blue Checks. He wanted it to be a completely level playing field—no special treatment, no caste system, nothing but equal Twitter for all.

As noble as it might have seemed on paper, the idea of Twitter as an equal playing field—notables, companies, politicians treated just like everyone else, with accounts that looked just like everyone else's—gave Esther a queasy feeling. But she knew she didn't have much of a choice. She wasn't driving, she was sitting in the back of the car—or the Tesla, speeding down a highway at a hundred miles per hour, praying that the AI behind the wheel had a good grip on the steering wheel.

She took her seat next to Elon, gave the nod to her engineers—
and the new Twitter Blue went live.

---

It wasn't long before everything went sideways. Maybe two, three
hours; by midafternoon, for sure, it was obvious to everyone in the
room that the project was a complete and utter disaster. All of
Esther's (and Yoel's) concerns had come true, in vivid, almost Hollywood fashion. Not only had people happily paid eight dollars for a
chance to impersonate celebrities, professional athletes, political
figures, and the accounts of major companies—they'd gotten
impressively *creative* about it.

Some of the impersonations were clearly comedy: a Nintendo
corporate account tweeting a picture of Mario giving the middle
finger, a tweet from a fake Tesla corporate account, *"Our cars do not
respect school zone speed limits. Fuck them kids"*; a tweet from Nestlé,

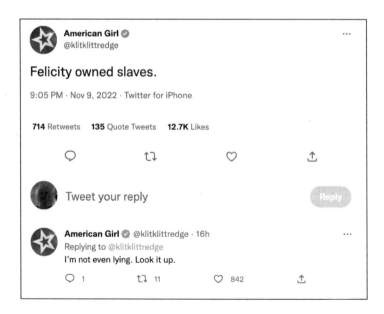

*"We steal your water and sell it back to you lol"*; a tweet from Coca-Cola, *"If this gets 1000 retweets we will put cocaine back in Coca-Cola."* Other tweets skewed more malicious. A fake account appearing to be the account of former president George W. Bush tweeted *"I miss killing Iraqis"* and was quickly retweeted by a fake Tony Blair *"Same tbh."* A fake American Girl account tweeted: *"Felicity owned slaves."* A fake Lockheed Martin went political: *"We will begin halting all weapons sales to Saudi Arabia, Israel, and the United States until further investigation into their record of human rights abuses."* And perhaps most notably, a fake Eli Lilly pharmaceutical company informed: *"We are excited to announce insulin is free now."*

Because the purchased Blue Checks were indistinguishable from vetted, legacy checks, the fake accounts were likewise indistinguishable from the verified, real corporate and celebrity accounts—which meant that anyone who happened to be browsing Twitter that afternoon and into the evening hours could easily stumble upon Senator Ted Cruz tweeting *"I am pro-life because I feast on neglected babies. Nine months after prom night I wander the streets and check the dumpsters for dinner, and you will not believe how fresh, and how sweet, the meat is."* Or Rudy Giuliani tweeting: *"I stand with Kyrie Irving and Kanye West because George Soros once pushed me down in the street and I was stuck on my back like a turtle for several minutes."*

To Esther's surprise, Elon, next to her in the conference room, was laughing, sometimes uproariously, as he scrolled from tweet to tweet. When he got to the Nintendo account—Mario and his extended finger—Elon nearly fell out of his chair. When he got to Eli Lilly, he exclaimed, "Well, insulin should be zero. Maybe this will pressure them to do the right thing," and then, "People shouldn't take their brands so seriously." When someone mentioned that Eli

Lilly's stock price was taking a hit because of the impersonation, Elon thought it was hilarious."

"

To Esther, none of this was funny. She felt responsible, not just for what was now an obvious, and easily predictable fuckup, but for the loss of revenue that she knew Twitter was about to experience. If advertisers had been scared away from Twitter because of Elon's Pelosi tweet, *what were they going to think of this*?

As things were going poorly with the launch, both Robin and Yoel had tried to convince Elon to amend the new Blue Check protocol. They encouraged him to at least reconsider adding an "official badge" to corporate accounts. But Elon had refused, playing the growing disaster off like it wasn't a big deal.

Yet later, at some point during the afternoon, Elon had received enough frantic calls from Marketing, Sales, and anyone involved with advertisers that he'd finally given the order to shut down the revamped Twitter Blue, pausing all new accounts, instructing mods to weed out and suspend all the imposters. Yet even as he flicked the off switch, Elon did so with a smile on his face. To him, this was an amusing failure: a badly launched product, but somehow, to him, not a refutation of what he still believed was the future of Twitter Blue—and the Blue Check.

It soon became clear that others didn't feel the same.

Shortly after the newly launched Blue Check unraveled in historic fashion, Elon took part in a Twitter Spaces hosted by Robin Wheeler and Yoel Roth, an open version of the advertising influencers call of the week before. Though the Spaces had gone fairly smoothly—Robin and Yoel doing their best to keep Elon tethered, like they were guiding a helium balloon—there was obvious tension moving through Twitter headquarters. Soon word began circulating that a number of senior Tweeps were planning to resign—most notably Yoel Roth.

Later, Yoel would tell Kara Swisher that it was a combination of things that had made him leave Twitter, comparing it to "the experience of being a frog in a pot of boiling water"—that leaving was akin to protecting himself from being "boiled alive." He added that if Twitter was "ruled by dictatorial edict" then there was no need for him at the company. The fact that the "Content Moderation Council" Elon had promised had never materialized was one component of his decision, but it seemed the Blue Check fiasco was Yoel's final straw. Elon had launched the new Blue Check despite Yoel's specific warning that it would be a disaster, and it had failed "exactly" as Yoel had predicted it would.

Yoel's resignation immediately put pressure on Robin, as she was now the most senior front-facing person on the advertising side, and over the next day she indicated that she, too, was planning to leave. But multiple frantic calls from Elon's circle soon led her to a bout of introspection; maybe she wasn't ready to go, and she did still feel she could make a difference. She had one foot out the door, but somehow Elon convinced her to keep the other foot inside the building.

In the hours after Elon's Spaces and the disaster that had been the new Twitter Blue's launch, Esther did her best to put as good a spin on the situation as she could, telling her team that they had done everything Elon had asked; they had built the product exactly as their boss had specified in the allotted time, and the Blue Check's embarrassing failure had been predictable, unavoidable, and entirely not their fault. But it still hurt. Esther had pushed back as hard as she had thought she'd been able to, but it simply hadn't been enough. And though Elon had laughed through much of the day and night, when he'd been given the news that Yoel had resigned, his amusement had vanished. For the first time since Esther had started working one-on-one with the billionaire, she'd seen him truly upset, an emotion that only grew in intensity when, a week later, Yoel published an op-ed in the *New York Times* outlining why he had left, and the perils he saw in Twitter's future.

As the news of Yoel's leaving sunk in, Elon didn't yell, he didn't curse, he didn't even raise his voice. But he was seething, pacing the conference room as his Goons walked him through the ramifications. More than that, he seemed genuinely surprised. It occurred to

Esther that not many people quit on Elon. Over his career, he'd fired thousands, probably thousands upon thousands—but those few he'd chosen to carry his mission forward were usually thrilled to toil in his presence, to simply be part of whatever it was he was trying to build.

Yoel's resignation was something new. Esther didn't entirely understand; she knew that if Elon had felt the urge to fire Yoel, the billionaire would have done so without a second thought, probably by email. But Yoel hadn't been fired; he had chosen to leave. And that, to Elon, wasn't simply a business decision.

*It was a betrayal.*

## CHAPTER SIXTEEN

# November 16, 2022

*Elon Musk 12:00 AM*

*To Team:*

*Going forward, to build a breakthrough Twitter 2.0 and succeed in an increasingly competitive world, we will need to be extremely hardcore. This will mean working long hours at high intensity. Only exceptional performance will constitute a passing grade.*

*Twitter will also be much more engineering-driven. Design and product management will still be very important and report to me, but those writing great code will constitute the majority of our team and have the greatest sway. At its heart, Twitter is a software and servers company, so I think this makes sense.*

*If you are sure that you want to be part of the new Twitter, please click yes on the link below:*

*Anyone who has not done so by 5pm ET tomorrow (Thursday) will receive three months of severance.*

*Whatever decision you make, thank you for your efforts to make Twitter successful.*

**Mark shook his head** as he reread the email for what had to be the hundredth time, his phone flat on the table in front of him, nestled between a ceramic bowl half-filled with rice and a plate containing the remains of what had once been an Instagram-worthy pyramid of soup dumplings. The private dining room spread out before him was now empty. He'd excused his team as he'd sent for the check, because he knew they had a difficult rest of the day ahead of them and would need time to themselves, to digest not the food, which barely any of them had touched, but the decision each one now had only a few more hours to make.

The dining room was snug; barely a nook nestled in the back of the Jade Dragon, a cheap, trendy Chinese dive with a flickering neon-red sign out front, tucked in an alley in downtown Charlotte. The walls were rugged, the long wooden table in front of Mark lacking any flashy décor other than an unshuffled deck of bamboo placemats and a pile of chopsticks, many of them still unused. The chairs were a mismatched collection of worn and weathered, some with threadbare cushions, others with peeling vinyl. A few frayed lanterns hung overhead.

Mark had chosen the Dragon, and its back room, because of its gritty appeal, which seemed perfect for the impromptu meeting, which he had called together just a few hours earlier. Since most of his team were spread out across the country, it had only been about a dozen physical bodies along one edge of the table—but nearly five times that in Zoom windows on his phone and on his laptop, both positioned on the opposite side of the table for the benefit of the rest of the group.

As Mark had expected, the feeling in the room had been as grim as the décor. Though his team had gotten through the initial round of bloodletting relatively intact—shrinking its head count from around a hundred to seventy-four—they had not been insulated from the general state of panic that had gripped the company in the past few days. Mark had witnessed, like everybody else on the marketing and advertising side, the complete chaos of the failed Twitter Blue launch, and he'd had an inside track into some of the aftermath, via a call from John Kahill and Robin Wheeler.

To Mark's surprise, that call had started off well. Robin had described a meeting that had taken place after the Blue Check debacle, in Caracara—it seemed Elon had taken over the conference room for the Twitter Blue launch and had since decided it would be his new command center going forward. There marketing had been able to walk Elon (in person and not via a square on a screen) through all of the ad-side concerns. Elon had been receptive; he'd fully admitted that the Twitter Blue launch had been a disaster; had committed to being more careful going forward; and agreed to take time to consider Twitter's clients and advertisers before launching anything new. The billionaire had apologized to the room, owning his mistakes. Robin had pushed even harder—asking that Elon face the company (what was left of the company, anyway) in an all-hands as soon as possible. To her shock, Elon had immediately agreed.

Not only did Elon promise to do a scheduled, in-person all-hands event at headquarters, but he called for a sudden, informal company chat the very next evening, November 10—giving only twenty minutes' notice to anyone who happened to be in the building, or anyone who wanted to attend online. Throughout the hour-long meeting, he'd been incredibly direct and open, explaining why he believed Twitter could someday have as many as a billion users. He pointed out how he'd sold Tesla stock to save Twitter, but that he felt the job cuts had been necessary—and that in his mind, Twitter was still overstaffed. When pushed on the subject of remote work, he'd been even more direct: "Let me be crystal clear. If people do not return to the office when they are able to return to the office, they cannot remain at the company. End of story." He'd further told his audience that "bankruptcy is not out of the question."

Despite that direct expression of the challenges facing them, to Robin, Kahill, and Mark, Elon's willingness to address the company honestly was a welcome change. And, Robin had added, the Chief Twit had been so nice and amiable during her face-to-face meeting that after the event had ended, she'd stayed behind to apologize to Elon personally for nearly resigning along with Yoel Roth. Elon had responded well: "No problem, I would probably have done the same thing if I'd had the information you'd had."

As Robin had turned to leave, Elon had stood up from his chair, raising his hands in the air in an enthusiastic fist pump, awkwardly shouting, "Let's kill it! Let's fucking GO!"

Robin had left the meeting optimistic, if a little unnerved. Between that meeting and the company talk the next day, Elon had talked her off the ledge, and both she and Kahill had made Mark believe that despite the rocky beginnings of Elon's takeover, things might finally get back on track. Twitter Blue had been mothballed, for the time being. The round of cuts, though painful, impersonal, and deep, had probably been necessary—and the company, now down to around 3,500 employees, was lean but, in Mark's opinion, still mainly functional. Mark's job going forward would be tricky—everyone on the marketing side would have their work cut out for them to bring back advertisers after the Blue Check fiasco, but eventually Madison Avenue would want to put its money to work.

And then—the email.

Mark shook his head again as he looked down at his phone. It wasn't the sort of thing you expected in your inbox at midnight, but that's exactly when Elon had sent the thing, and not just to Mark, but to everyone left at the company. An ultimatum, asking employees to decide, by 5 p.m. that day, whether they were "hard-core" enough to remain at Twitter.

Elon had just fired between 25 and 50 percent of Mark's colleagues, and now he was demanding some bizarre pledge of loyalty from the remaining Tweeps: a promise that they were ready to work long hours (under what sounded like extreme conditions) or take three months of severance.

The minute Mark received the email, he knew how it would go down. People were already raw and upset at how impersonal the firings had been; this email was going to push a lot of them off the ledge. Sure enough, by morning Mark had already seen dozens of angry posts spreading through Slack and Twitter. He knew that a large number of Tweeps had already decided that the email was the last straw. They were ready to resign.

When Mark had called together his team for the impromptu lunch, he hadn't been sure what, exactly, he was going to say to them—but once he'd seen the faces of his team, their concerned, frustrated, and in some cases outright angry expressions, both in person and online, his thoughts had coalesced into what he now felt was one of the best speeches he'd ever given.

"I'm not going to hard-sell any of you," he'd started. "If you feel you need to go, I understand. But I want you to know that I've decided to stay."

The truth was, he hadn't actually decided until he'd said the words, just as a waitress had placed a giant plate of dumplings in front of him, the steam swirling up in twists toward the lanterns dangling from the ceiling.

"A lot of us have been here for many years, and we've been through a lot together. I want to stick around—because of all of you. And frankly, I want to see what happens. Hell, who knows, it might be fun."

A lot of what Mark had begun to hate about Twitter had been wiped away, obliterated in Elon's first two weeks. Nobody was arguing about a smoothie bar or extra personal days anymore; everyone was focused on survival. Seeing people fired had been hard, emotionally, but much of the restructuring had been necessary.

"I guess I am willing to be hardcore," he'd finished, laughing, and some of his teammates had laughed with him. It was an absurd choice of words, and he hated the idea of having to sign some sort of loyalty pledge, marking a box on a Google note board that would be filed away somewhere, or shared between Elon's Goons, or, who knows, maybe posted on the wall of the billionaire's bathroom. But, yeah, Mark was willing to be hardcore, if it meant Twitter was going to survive and grow.

Now that his team had left the restaurant, and Mark had gone through the letter one last time, he clicked open the link and punched in his response. He had no idea how many members of his team would do the same, or how many would take this opportunity to throw in the towel, get away from the madness, earn that severance. Odds were likely that a lot of people were going to leave, and those who stayed behind were going to be picking up the pieces for some time—

His thoughts were interrupted, because right under his thumb, his phone was vibrating, an incoming call. As usual, it was Kahill.

To Mark's surprise, Kahill wasn't calling to tell him more war stories from headquarters.

"You still with us?" Kahill started.

"As hardcore as they come," Mark joked.

"Good, because I've got a job for you. And Mark—word is, it's an Elon Project."

Mark raised his eyebrows.

"If he needs a new rocket, he's gonna want someone from engineering."

"Not a rocket. He needs slides. Good ones, lots of them."

Mark nodded, understanding. The all-hands he'd promised Robin was not intended to be some sparsely attended, last-minute company call, but a real, in-person rap session. The new boss's first real face-to-face event with Twitter. After the past two weeks, and the midnight email, he'd want to make a good impression. So of course, he wanted slides.

Slides, Mark could do. But if the mood at the all-hands was going to be anything like when Mark's team first sat down in the back room of the Dragon, Elon might have been better off hitting Engineering up for a big, flashy, and really fast rocket.

## CHAPTER SEVENTEEN

# November 21, 2022

**The Halloween decorations** were long gone. No more pumpkins vomiting spaghetti or dry ice spitting fog above the hardwood
floor, no more bats hanging from the ceiling rafters—just the huge
Twitter bird affixed to the back wall and a dense crowd of Tweeps,
seated in Twitter Blue cafeteria chairs or standing shoulder to shoulder beneath the exposed beams that braced the ceiling of the cavernous Commons. Even the open, second-floor balcony of the
cafeteria/open workspace was filled with employees, everyone cran-
ing to get a good view of the raised stage at the front of the usually
airy room. Most of the other furniture had been moved aside for the
all-hands. The tables, desks, couches, and even many of the potted
plants were pushed into the corners to make room for the sort of
crowd that Twitter headquarters hadn't seen since well before the
pandemic—perhaps the biggest gathering of Tweeps, in person,
since the last OneTeam off-site, so many years ago.

Jessica stood near the back of the room, in between a young
woman from Sales and a middle-aged engineer, who both looked as
grim as Jessica felt. To describe the morale as low would have been

the understatement of the year. Although everyone in the Commons had presumably responded to Elon's hardcore letter by pledging to be "part of the new Twitter," with its "long hours" and "high intensity," if the missive had been meant to be some sort of motivational tool, it had clearly missed its mark. From what Jessica had heard, a full half of Twitter's remaining employees had opted to resign and receive the three months of severance rather than be trapped under the boot of the new regime. So many employees had opted to quit that apparently now some managers had been tasked with trying to rehire people the company had previously fired, to keep the platform functional. In one comical instance, Twitter's own user handle had gone dark on the platform, because the only person who had access to its password was no longer employed by the company.

Jessica herself had spent the entire day struggling with her own decision whether or not to stay, and had only been swayed by assurances from higher-ups in Marketing that Elon had learned something from the mess of the Twitter Blue launch. She'd waited until the last minute—just before 5 p.m. Thursday—before she'd clicked through to the link, and it wasn't until the next day that she'd found out that the regime she'd bowed to had struck hard, again, disabusing her of any notion that things were going to get better anytime soon.

Friday morning, after the hardcore letter had been put to bed, and what was left of Twitter was sleeping off what felt like the mother of all hangovers, Robin Wheeler had received a call from Elon. After the positive conversation she'd had just days earlier—him raising his fists into the air, "Let's go!"—she'd expected to be going over strategies to bring the advertisers back to the platform. Over 50 percent of the company's advertisers had now paused their ad buys, cutting revenues nearly in half. Even before the Twitter Blue fiasco,

Elon had alienated many of their larger clients—not only with his Pelosi tweet and his continued threats to bring back banned and controversial users to the platform. In even more personal terms: back on November 4, right after the successful dog-and-pony show of the Influencers Council call and his meetings on Madison Avenue, the billionaire had responded to a tweet by conservative politico Mike Davis pointing out that Elon had *"nearly 114,000,000 Twitter followers,"* and that the billionaire should *"name and shame the advertisers who are succumbing to the advertiser boycotts. So we can counter-boycott them."* Elon countered with another ultimatum: *"A thermonuclear name & shame is exactly what will happen if this continues."* In Robin's experience, nuclear threats didn't go over any better with the suits on Madison Avenue than they did with getting employees to be happy about "long hours" and "high intensity."

But Elon hadn't been calling Robin on the morning after the hardcore email to talk through ways of mollifying the advertising community. He'd called to tell her that Twitter needed to make more cuts. That he needed her to cull more people from her already depleted departments, and that he needed more lists, more spreadsheets, of people to let go.

Robin had instantly balked at the request. "Damn," she'd said, "you've already asked people to stay if they wanted to stay, to commit to being hardcore, to working long hours under high intensity. And over the past twenty-four hours, my managers and I have been trying to explain to our teams how we are going to make this work, move forward, build a better Twitter. And you want to cut more people?"

She'd paused—and then she'd refused. She simply couldn't put more people out of work, not without a better understanding of a future landscape, or some promise that this wasn't going to happen over and over again. She needed some indication that this wasn't just a whim, some decision by a billionaire to make a balance sheet look a little better. She needed to believe this was something that would be good for the future of Twitter.

Elon had been polite and calm, and hadn't raised his voice. He'd simply fired her, effective immediately.

Jessica had been shocked by the news. Elon had fired Robin for refusing to fire any more of her team; it was almost poetic. Shortly afterward, Jessica had gotten word that Elon had closed the company headquarters for the weekend, sending everyone home and locking the front doors. She assumed this was a reaction to the poor response he'd gotten for the "hardcore" email. For some reason, Elon had expected people to rally around him, to be excited to go hardcore—maybe pulling up sleeping bags next to the billionaire and his newest acolyte, Esther Crawford. Just like he'd expected Robin to happily fire more of her team at his sudden request, people with families and mortgages and health issues and babies on the way, just fire them, right after they'd pledged to stay.

Now, three days later, here he was, in front of the entire company—who knows how many people in the Commons, hundreds more watching online, but just a skeleton of the vibrant, #lovewhereyouwork Twitter 1.0—up on the stage, flanked by his two enormous bodyguards. Dressed entirely in black: black pants, black boots, a black T-shirt emblazoned with the words "I love Twitter"— also in another shade of black. Cameras bristled around the stage for the video audience, and perhaps Elon could see himself reflected in their lenses, cutting a striking, defiant figure in front of what he must have realized was a mostly hostile audience. But still, somehow he was smiling, and as he began talking, Jessica realized that she was witnessing a total disconnect. Somehow, Elon seemed to believe that he continued to be the charismatic celebrity who had first strolled through Twitter's front doors carrying that sink. That the

Tweeps now gathered around him, terrified, traumatized, and many of them angry, were still the same fawning and awed NPCs who had followed in him through the halls that first morning.

He spoke directly, as usual, launching the all-hands with his signature, slightly awkward charm. *Hey, really excited to be here, it was tough making these decisions but it had to be done—now we are done with layoffs.* At this, there was a ripple of applause, maybe a sigh of relief. Then he went right into a series of slides that had been prepared for him by Creative: big, colorful slides that seemed to illustrate aspects of the business going in the right direction. One showed a decline in hate speech, after a spike during Elon's first few days. Another documented an increase of time spent on Twitter by users. With each slide, Elon seemed to become less interested. By the fourth, he was speaking faster and waving his hands around as if he was in some sort of rush. It was some sort of graph labeled MDAU—Monetizable Daily Users—and it seemed that Elon had no idea what the letters stood for. He just looked at the slide, said, "Yeah, yeah. See, even MDAU is going up," and then waved them to the next.

By the end of the slides, he was hitting the same notes that the audience was all too familiar with: how Twitter would grow to a billion users, become the free speech global town hall at the center of the world's conversation, a platform to host text, video, powered in part by subscription, that would eventually morph into some sort of everything app.

But it was clear, as the all-hands shifted from Elon's presentation to Q&A, that the gathered Tweeps were less concerned about Twitter's future than they were about their own present. They were still focused on what had happened over the past few days, and the sudden changes to the company culture that seemed only to be getting worse.

Three days before, after he'd fired Robin Wheeler, closed the Twitter offices, and lost half of the remaining Twitter employees to his hardcore email, he'd tweeted a poll:

Reinstate former President Trump

Yes

No

Followed by:

Vox Populi, Vox Dei

By Saturday night and the poll's closing, over fifteen million people had voted, choosing "yes" by a close margin of 52 percent. To Jessica, the poll, timed as it was—headquarters closed, its employees reeling, half of Twitter's advertisers gone—had almost seemed like a slap in the face of Twitter 1.0. The old ways of running the platform were clearly done; there would be no consulting a moderation council (if one actually existed) or talking things through with Marketing, or Sales, or even Site Safety—as most of those departments were shells of their former selves. This wasn't even a decision by fiat; this was a poll, of Elon's followers, who clearly fell to right of center.

But during the Q&A, in response to a question about what appeared to be a shift in Twitter's character, Elon only responded curtly: "This isn't a right-wing takeover of Twitter. It's a moderate-wing takeover of Twitter."

From there, the all-hands spiraled downward. His answers became terse, sudden, often with waves of his hand, as if he were swatting away Tweeps' concerns, or maybe the Tweeps themselves. It was about the fourth question when things really went off the rails; a young Tweep with a work and life background in China had stood up, first thanking Elon for his time, and with all respect asked about a comparison that had been made between Elon's vision of Twitter as an everything app and China's WeChat, pointing out that WeChat was essentially government run, and gave the Chinese government the ability to take people's data and follow them.

While the kid was speaking, Elon's entire demeanor changed. His face went red, and he suddenly interrupted: "You just don't get it!"

The interruption had been so abrupt that the kid lurched back, nearly hitting one of the cameras stationed right behind him to capture the moment for the online audience.

"You don't understand," Elon continued, growing visibly angrier. "I didn't say we are building WeChat. I said WeChat provides a lot of utility and we need that! We're not building freaking WeChat!"

Elon threw his hands up in the air in exasperation.

"Next question!"

Jessica felt the air in the room snap, like a leather belt pulled tight. The kid was nearly in tears, and the people around him inched away, like he'd become radioactive. Jessica made a mental note to go check on the Tweep after the all-hands, to make sure he was all right. But then the all-hands got even worse—Elon telling the audience, as the Verge would later report, "I don't think about competitors."

"I don't care what Facebook, YouTube, or what anyone else is doing. Couldn't give a damn."

"We just need to make Twitter as goddamn amazing as possible."

By the end of the session, all of the awkward charm was gone. To Jessica, Elon seemed visibly upset, as if he wanted nothing more to do with the gathered audience. As he was led off stage by his bodyguards, the murmur in the crowd was audible; instead of assuaging anyone's nerves, the all-hands had only added to the sense of fear, and impending doom.

What struck Jessica most was how surprised Elon had seemed at the questions—shocked even, to be in front of an audience that wasn't brimming with praise and accolades, that wasn't there to clap hands and call him a genius. He'd fired half the company, and disrespected another contingent with a single email (enough to make them want to quit); he'd torched the ad side of the business and embarrassed the platform with Twitter Blue; he'd gotten rid of almost all of management, and was now bringing back Donald Trump, who many of Jessica's colleagues believed to be the single most visible purveyor of hate speech—on a global scale—in Twitter's history. Yet somehow he still expected to be positively received, to be praised, perhaps even, to be loved.

As Elon swept by, nearly carried forward by the sheer size of his dark-suited bodyguards, she could see something in his eyes—he didn't seem just shocked and angry. There was something dark, there. Perhaps that paranoia again, but now Elon had evidence that it wasn't in his head: the Tweeps had turned on him, just as he had expected they would.

This feeling she got, watching Elon exit the Common, scared Jessica more than anything else that had happened so far. He did not strike her as the sort of man who took betrayal well.

## CHAPTER EIGHTEEN

# December 11, 2022

**There are very few emotions** as pure and primal as fear.

Yoel Roth's heart was pounding so hard it felt like it was about to shatter through his rib cage. He dragged an overstuffed suitcase across the bedroom of his modest two-bedroom home in the suburban enclave of El Cerrito, just north of Berkeley. He had tried to gather only the essentials—a few changes of clothes, bathroom necessities, a handful of books—but the uncertainty of how long he'd be gone gnawed at him, making every decision feel heavy, dense, and onerous, pressing down against his trembling shoulders.

The shades of his bedroom were drawn, the lights off, and he could hear his partner, Nicholas, ten years his senior, somewhere in the nearby kitchen. Nicholas was filling shopping bags with food from the refrigerator, and rummaging through shelves high and low, collecting silverware and cooking utensils from the drawers. Nicholas, too, was working in the dark, but his movements seemed steadier, his demeanor calmer.

Despite Yoel's anxiety, the irony of the moment was not lost on him. He had spent most of his adult life battling hate speech on the internet—and now, suddenly, he found his life overwhelmed by its wrath. The commentary directed toward him had begun slowly, like dark, wispy clouds in the distance—something he could mostly ignore—abstract and almost academic in nature. After all, he had been dealing with hate speech as part of his job for more than a decade, had written papers on the subject and built a team dedicated to identifying, policing, and moderating its most vitriolic forms.

But over the days and weeks since he'd resigned from the company and handed the duties of his team off to whoever was left behind, the dark clouds had become a tempest, the vitriol twisting and mutating into an all-consuming force. Now, finally, it had shifted from abstract to something very real: threats of actual, physical violence that had him packing up his house in the middle of the night.

Yoel was well aware that his resignation from Twitter, coming on the heels of the Twitter Blue launch, had upset his former boss. He'd heard through the Tweep grapevine that his op-ed in the *New York Times* had caused even more distress to Elon, often visible to those who worked in close proximity to the billionaire. But he could never have imagined that Elon would react so viciously, transforming what had been a manageable, ignorable rumble of online animosity into something far more sinister and unrelenting.

It had begun with a sudden tweet just yesterday, out of the blue and in the middle of the afternoon. Elon had actually been responding to a run-of-the-mill bit of digital hate. One of the billionaires' many followers posted one of Yoel's own ancient tweets from November 2010, well before Yoel had gone to work for the platform:

> Can high school students ever meaningfully consent
> to sex with their teachers?

Yoel's tweet had included a link to an article written by somebody else, discussing the controversial subject. It had been the sort of edgy tweet that had been fairly common before the era of MeToo and cancel culture, one that Yoel would probably have avoided posting in the current age. Even so, dredged up, on its own, the tweet probably would have made little more than a ripple—had not Elon Musk, with his hundred and twenty million followers—not responded:

This explains a lot.

Then the billionaire had gone much further, following up with a tweet of his own, sharp as a dagger:

Looks like Yoel is arguing in favor of children being
able to access adult internet services in his PhD thesis.

The tweet had continued with an image of a paragraph from a three-hundred-page thesis Yoel had written as a student at the University of Pennsylvania. The subject of the paragraph had been an analysis of how young, gay teenagers made up a subset of the user base of queer-oriented sites like the dating app Grindr. In the piece, Yoel had surmised that sites like Grindr, though too "lewd" and "hook-up-oriented" to be "a safe and age-appropriate resource for teenagers," were indeed places where many kids under the age of eighteen gathered. Thus, Yoel had concluded, "we can't readily dismiss these platforms out of hand as loci for queer youth culture. Rather than merely trying to absolve themselves of legal responsibility or, worse, trying to drive out teenagers entirely, service providers should instead focus on crafting safety strategies that can accommodate a wide variety of use case. . . ."

On its own, the paragraph was moderately controversial; as part of a three-hundred-page thesis, it was an out-of-context, minor point. But in the form of a tweet, by Elon Musk, with the sort of right-of-center following that he had gathered in the month and a half since he'd taken over Twitter, it was an *accusation.*

When he'd initially read the tweet, Yoel had been stunned, and terrified. It was exactly the sort of post that Yoel and his team at Trust and Safety might have moderated—perhaps stifled, or muffled, or silenced. But Elon, being Elon, had done the exact opposite. He'd given the tweet the biggest megaphone on the entire platform, his own user stream, immediately sending the worst of his followers into motion.

The storm of hate Yoel experienced afterward had been beyond extreme. Ugly comments had quickly morphed into actual threats, and then moved well beyond Twitter to Yoel's email, his voice mail, and then out of the meta and into the real.

The feeling of being "doxed"—having your private, identifying information published on the internet, for anyone to find—was uniquely violating. The idea that anonymous, hateful people, the sort of trolls who inhabited the dark corners of social media, were now sharing details of Yoel's life, his personal information, even his *address*, was chilling.

Despite his outsized role at Twitter, Yoel had always been an extremely private person. His footprint on the internet had, up until recently, been incredibly small.

When Elon had first taken over Twitter, Yoel's name had only emerged because of his role in Trust and Safety. When old tweets of Yoel's had surfaced, indicating his fiercely liberal political views, Elon had actually stood up for him, suggesting that Yoel's personal opinions hadn't factored into the responsible way he'd done his job.

But since Yoel's resignation, his notoriety had grown, especially since the release of Elon's most recent of projects, which the billionaire had first teased on November 28:

The Twitter Files on free speech suppression soon to
be published on Twitter itself. The public deserves to
know what really happened. . . .

Followed by:

This is a battle for the future of civilization. If free
speech is lost even in America, tyranny is all that
lies ahead.

The Twitter Files, a series of tweet-threads filled with data, messages, emails, and dramatic postulation, all derived from Twitter's internal communication channels, were eventually curated and posted by a rogues' gallery of well-known conservative and libertarian journalists, including Matt Taibbi, Bari Weiss, Lee Fang, Michael Shellenberger, David Zweig, and Alex Berenson. The Files, dropped almost at random over the next few weeks, offered a deep look into Twitter 1.0's inner workings. Specifically, the decision-making around some of its more controversial bans, shadow bans, and outright account suspensions—including the deliberations that had resulted in the silencing of the *New York Post*'s Hunter Biden Laptop story and the ban of President Trump. The Twitter Files revealed the platform's relationship with national intelligence agencies such as the FBI, as well as individual political heavyweights, who had, depending on how you looked at it, either pressured Twitter or made requests of Twitter—for information, account bans, and the elimination of individual tweets.

Though released with a fair amount of fanfare, the Twitter Files hadn't made much of a mark in mainstream media, likely for a couple of reasons. For one, they hadn't seemed to reveal anything that people didn't already suspect—namely, that politicians, corporate interests, and protective agencies such as the FBI and Department of Homeland Security kept an eye on social media and made requests when they felt dangerous content was being disseminated. From the Files themselves, it was clear that the company didn't always succumb to those external demands, and that Yoel's Trust and Safety team had deliberated intensely before making any decision involving moderation.

More than anything, the Twitter Files seemed to showcase the immense effort that went into running a site as vast and complex as Twitter. They revealed that mistakes were made, that people both inside and outside of the platform regretted certain decisions, and that they tried to correct them.

But it was also clear, especially to critics from the right, that typically Twitter's moderation seemed to fall in the direction of liberal bias. And to those critics even farther to the right, it seemed that something much more subversive had been going on: that intelligence agencies and politicians had pushed Twitter to ban users and silence posts for entirely political purposes.

Elon himself had put the view succinctly, on December 10, just two days before:

> Twitter is both a social media company and
> a crime scene.

As head of Trust and Safety, Yoel's name had been all over the Files, and now he didn't have Elon to come to his rescue. Instead, the billionaire himself had come after Yoel in the most vicious of ways.

Shortly after resigning, Yoel had actually stood up for Elon's character, telling Kara Swisher, "I think one of the things that is tricky about Elon, in particular, is that people really want him to be the villain of the story, and they want him to be unequivocally wrong and bad, and everything he says is duplicitous. I have to say . . . that wasn't my experience with him."

But now Yoel was seeing a different side to the billionaire, who had chosen to strike out at him in the most public way imaginable.

In the rational portions of Yoel's brain, he could understand some of Elon's motivation. The billionaire was under immense pressure, and, according to Yoel's friends back at Twitter, had been looking more frazzled, despondent, and cornered every day. And Yoel made an easy target, since his name was already being bandied about by Elon's followers. Still, this felt particularly personal.

The accusation he'd made of Yoel—and that's really what it was, the dog whistles of pedophilia and grooming were undeniable—had instantly turned a growing stream of anger, aimed at Yoel by the Twitter Files, into a waterfall of hate that had now breached the fragile barrier between the virtual and the actual.

What had once seemed theoretical and impersonal was now a real-world nightmare, haunting the corners of his El Cerrito home.

His jaw tightened as he pulled the suitcase behind him, hoping his partner was already ahead of him, on his way toward the front door. Because the threats Yoel had now received told him, in no uncertain terms, that the anonymous users, the shadow banned, the voices filled with hate had moved out of the dark corners of the internet—and into Yoel's life.

They knew his name.

They knew his face.

They knew where he lived.

And he had no choice but to run.

# PART THREE

"The future of humanity is going to bifurcate in two directions: Either it's going to become multi-planetary, or it's going to remain confined to one planet and eventually there's going to be an extinction event." —ELON MUSK

"Failure is an option here. If things are not failing, you are not innovating enough." —ELON MUSK

"I would like to die on Mars. Just not on impact."

—ELON MUSK

## CHAPTER NINETEEN

# December 11, 2022

**Sunday night,** a little after ten p.m.

Yoel Roth and his partner were still in the midst of fleeing their home, suitcases in tow and their emails besieged with vitriolic, homophobic messages, their cell phones buzzing with unknown callers and anonymous, virulent texts, their lives upended by hate: hate speech, hate tweets, hate texts, hate calls, hate upon hate upon hate . . .

While Elon Musk stood in the wings of a massive stage at the front of an even more massive arena, waiting for his cue, bouncing from one foot to the other as the noise from a raucous crowd crashed over him in wave after wave after wave.

It was the hottest ticket in town. The Chase Center, corner of Third Street and Sixteenth in the Mission Bay neighborhood of San Francisco. A comedy show starring Chris Rock and headliner Dave Chappelle, two of the top comedians in the country, sharing the stage in front of a sold-out crowd.

Rock had already finished his set, a fiery mix of controversial takes and knives-out comedy, one of the first shows in which he talked about Will Smith and the slap heard round the world. Now

Chappelle was about to close out the night, pacing the stage with a mike in one hand and a drink in the other.

For Elon, it was exactly the sort of respite that he needed, after the sort of weekend he'd just endured. Not just the massive amount of hours he'd put in after the Twitter Blue launch and the loss of high-level managers and advertiser favorites, like Roth and Robin Wheeler (all while running Tesla, SpaceX, and all of their derivatives), but navigating the media firestorm that had engulfed him over the past forty-eight hours. Yet he had only himself to blame— as usual, he'd set the fire himself—and nothing he'd said was particularly out of character. He'd always been one of Twitter's premier trolls; it just so happened that he was now also Twitter's CEO, so his posts had taken on a level of gravitas that made them even more ignitable.

He'd followed his Saturday attack on Yoel Roth's decade-old thesis with an even more incendiary post:

*My pronouns are Prosecute/Fauci*

In follow-up tweets and responses, he intimated that he'd found evidence in the Twitter Files implicating Dr. Anthony Fauci—the chief medical advisor to the president and the de facto head of the White House's Covid response—in a Covid-information-related social media cover-up. He also elaborated on his attack of the practice of employing "pronouns," a firebrand issue involving the trans community. Predictably, Elon's tweet was met with thousands upon thousands of replies on either side of both issues, many of which bordered on what Yoel Roth's team would have once defined as hate speech.

When confronted by numerous notables, such as Scott Kelly, NASA astronaut:

*Elon, please don't mock and promote hate toward already marginalized and at-risk-of-violence members of the #LGBTQ+ community. They are real people with real feelings. Furthermore, Dr. Fauci is a dedicated public servant whose sole motivation was saving lives.*

Elon had fired back:

*I strongly disagree. Forcing your pronouns upon others when they didn't ask, and implicitly ostracizing those who don't, is neither good nor kind to anyone.*

*As for Fauci, he lied to Congress and funded gain-of-function research that killed millions of people. Not awesome IMO.*

Had Yoel Roth and Robin Wheeler not already been fired, it was the sort of tweet that might have had both of them running for the hills. In many ways, the post was a work of troll art: a heady blend of dog whistle, straw man, and conspiracy theory that would have made the highest-paid troll farm operators in Eastern Europe proud. But this tweet hadn't come from some warehouse in Azerbaijan, it had come from Twitter's own CEO.

No wonder Elon had chosen to blow off steam in a real-life dark corner, surrounded by eighteen thousand people who obviously had a sense of humor. Elon loved comedy, and the more puerile, the better. He'd promised to remove the *w* from Twitter's name even before he'd taken over the company, and he'd even hosted *Saturday Night Live* in May 2021, when taking Twitter wasn't even a passing thought in his mind. The reviews, as they usually did, tended negative, but the live audience had loved him, and why shouldn't they? He'd been self-deprecating—telling the crowd he was on the spectrum—and up for anything, playing characters as diverse as Nintendo's Wario and a Gen Z doctor. More than anything, he'd been himself: the charming, amusing, brilliant billionaire who was trying to make the world a better place.

*Beloved, praised, applauded.*

Who cared what the major media was now saying about him or the continuous stream of angry tweets being spewed at him from left-of-center pundits, journalists, and celebrities; couldn't any of them take a damn joke? In real life, did it matter what a bunch of failing newspaper boomer pundits thought of him? IRL, he was still Elon Musk.

*Beloved, praised, applauded—*

His thoughts were interrupted by a voice from the stage, reverberating even louder than the noise from the audience. Dave Chappelle, speaking into that microphone.

"Ladies and gentlemen, make some noise for the richest man in the world!"

Suddenly Elon swept forward onto the stage. Black Twitter T-shirt, black jeans, black boots, hands in the air, and a grin on his face. He was up there, the bright spots in his eyes and Chappelle pacing toward him with a wide smile and the crowd exploding in shouts and applause and—

*boos.*

Louder and louder, boos. At first contained by the applause, but then rising in volume and intensity, a wave of boos, thousands thick. Billowing down from the balcony and up from the floor seats, bouncing off the walls and bounding down from the ceiling.

A cascade of fucking boos.

Elon's hands were still in the air but his face changed, a stunned look flashing across his features. Chappelle, too, was uncharacteristically nonplussed. Chappelle looked at Elon. Elon looked at Chappelle.

"Hey, Dave," Elon finally sputtered.

"Controversy, buddy," Chappelle responded, finding his voice.

Elon chuckled nervously, as the boos continued to descend on him.

"You weren't expecting this, were you?"

Then Chappelle found his footing.

"Sounds like some of the people you fired are in the audience."

Elon laughed at that. Chappelle might have been right. It was San Francisco. The most progressive city in the country, and the home of Twitter's headquarters. But it was also a Chappelle audience. Not exactly a bastion of card-carrying liberals.

"Tough love in here," Chappelle continued, into the microphone, "all those people who are booing—and I'm just pointing out the obvious, you have terrible seats."

He tried a few more jokes, as Elon wandered awkwardly around the stage, not quite sure what to do. The boos hadn't stopped; if anything, they'd gotten louder.

"Dave, what shall I say?" he finally asked.

"Don't say nothing. It'll only spoil the moment. Do you hear that sound, Elon? That's the sound of pending civil unrest. I can't wait to see what store you decimate next, motherfucker. You shut the fuck up."

Elon chuckled again, but he looked even more awkward, shoulders slumped, arms bouncing at his sides. As both he and Chappelle continued to pace, Chris Rock bounced onto the stage as well. Then Rock was prodding the group, bringing up one of Chappelle's most famous catchphrases, which Elon duly parroted into the mike.

"I'm rich, bitch!"

But he was nearly drowned out by the boos.

He shook his head, clearly bewildered.

"Times like this," he finally said, low. "I think we're in a simulation. Like, how can this be real?"

And then: "Thanks for letting me onstage."

Chappelle seemed almost relieved it was ending.

"I wouldn't miss this opportunity," the comedian responded. "The first comedy club on Mars, that should be mine. A deal is a deal, Musk."

Then Musk was off that stage, awkward and fast, as the show lurched toward a close.

---

It wasn't until 9:13 the next morning, after a sea of brutal tweets reconstructed the disastrous evening in vivid detail, turning it into one of the biggest trending news stories on the platform, that Musk finally felt the need to respond:

> Technically, it was 90% cheers & 10% boos (except
> during quiet periods), but, still, that's a lot of boos,
> which is a first for me in real life (frequent on Twitter).
> It's almost as if I've offended SF's unhinged
> leftists . . . but nahhh.

As tweets went, it was almost as awkward as Elon had been onstage next to Chappelle, as the boos had rained down upon him. No doubt, the experience was an awakening, a hit to his esteem that would be hard for anyone to shake off—up until two months ago, nearly every sentence that had described him, in media and online, had contained the words *genius, inspirational,* and *entrepreneur.*

Now he was being booed out of the Chase Center, in the home-town of his newly acquired company, a company that was shedding revenue

almost as fast

as it was

employees.

## CHAPTER TWENTY

# December 12, 2022

**A Monday morning** that started with a whimper, not a bang, and Esther couldn't have been more relieved. It had been a month since she'd watched the Blue Check fiasco alongside Elon and her team, and now here she was back in Caracara, where she had just flipped the switches launching a revamped, resurrected Twitter Blue to little fanfare, with mostly muted expectations. It wasn't a soft launch, exactly, but it also wasn't a nuclear bomb going off outside her window. Although people were still able to buy the previously vaunted Blue Check for eight dollars (eleven, if they made the purchase via the Apple App Store), this time around, Elon had allowed her team to include a modicum of review to each customer before the check was emblazoned next to their profile. Further, there was now also the addition of color coding—gold for companies, gray for governments—that would endow a little more security to the system at large.

If Esther had been able to convince Elon to make these concessions a month ago, perhaps she could have saved the company from days of viral embarrassment, not to mention countless millions in advertising. In retrospect, perhaps she'd been too timid around the billionaire—not a description she would ever have imagined anyone leveling in her direction, since she was usually the first person in the room to say exactly what she was thinking. But in the days and weeks that had followed, she'd learned a lot about Elon, and how to best steer him away from those ledges he was so keen on dancing toward.

To Elon's credit, he'd taken full responsibility for the original launch of Twitter Blue and the mess that had ensued—but he'd only become more convinced that subscription, and the selling of Blue Checks as a form of verification, was the necessary way forward. People were going to pay eight dollars for their checks whether they liked it or not. In Elon's mind, that was Twitter's future: a revenue stream that didn't depend on advertisers, and a user experience that was more equal, more verified, and by ideological edict—more free. He'd also promised, in various Spaces and advertising calls, that Twitter 2.0 would also be more fun, though from what Esther was seeing, it didn't appear the billionaire himself was still enjoying himself the way he had when he'd first taken over. The Elon who had laughed his way through the first launch of Twitter Blue had been replaced by someone who seemed more morose and serious; he still engaged with the world through memes and humor, but there was almost always an edge to the jokes, an undercurrent of what seemed like real anger.

No doubt the man was exhausted. He'd been working round the clock, still sleeping at the San Francisco office when he wasn't on his plane or at Tesla or SpaceX. But he was also clearly feeling the effects of the constant barrage of bad mojo that was being hurled at him. His onstage treatment at the Chappelle show the night before was something nobody was speaking about in the hallways of Twitter, but it was on everybody's mind. Although the venue had done its best to keep people from accessing their cell phones and recording devices during the show, dozens of videos had already leaked online, percolating through the Twitter platform at breakneck speed.

The incident concerned Esther, as she nursed a latte at the head of the long conference table. She didn't think it meant anything significant about what Elon was doing with Twitter—it was like eggs and omelets: you couldn't expect the eggs to applaud the chef as they sizzled in the pan—but there was no way to know how Elon was going to *react*. Yoel Roth's "betrayal" had sent him on a vindictive Twitter rant, and Elon hadn't stopped there. Nearly simultaneous to the quiet relaunch of Twitter Blue, the billionaire had dissolved Yoel's Trust and Safety Council, through an email. It had been sent (around the same time Elon had been tweeting that only 10 percent of the 18,000 audience members were booing him) to whoever was left of Yoel's colleagues, per the Daily Beast:

> *Dear Trust and Safety Council Members:*
>
> *As Twitter moves into a new phase, we are reevaluating how best to bring external insights into our product and policy department work. As part of this process we have decided that the Trust and Safety Council is not the best structure to do this.*
>
> *Our work to make Twitter a safe, informative place will be moving faster and more aggressively than ever before and we will continue to welcome your ideas going forward about how to achieve this goal. . . .*

The move would surely put another nail in the coffin of Twitter's ad sales business. But, as Esther had learned over the past month, Elon was more often motivated by instinct and intuition than she would have expected from the most successful businessman alive.

As she'd worked with the billionaire, she'd seen her role shift: from being the adult in the room to attempting to be the angel on Elon's shoulder, pulling him back from the various dangers, real or imagined, that she knew might set him off.

The War with Apple that hadn't been might have been her greatest accomplishment in this regard. Not only had she been the only remaining Tweep from Twitter 1.0 who had his ear, but she was also the only person left in products who was actually talking to Apple execs on a daily basis, due to her role in payments and the developing project, Twitter Blue.

Elon had started down the path toward war because he didn't understand the byzantine structure of in-app purchases and had been under the illusion that you could set up a payment system for something like Twitter Blue that sent subscribers into your own, custom platform. Esther, on the other hand, literally had sections of the app store regulations memorized. She knew that in-app payments were Apple's bread and butter, and they wouldn't ever back down from their 30 percent tithe.

Once she'd calmed Elon to the point where he was no longer planning to rally a hundred million Twitter followers to show up at Apple's headquarters with picket signs and pitchforks, she'd been able to suggest a tête-à-tête with her counterparts in payments, to which Elon had first readily agreed. But then the billionaire had done her one better; he'd canceled the meeting with Apple's payment wonks and had instead told her he wanted to meet with Tim Cook himself: the Apple CEO and the Twitter Chief Twit, face-to-face, to hash things out.

So Elon had gotten on his jet and headed to Cupertino. The billionaire had strolled into the massive, $5 billion, UFO-shaped headquarters of the biggest company in the world. He paused at the reflecting pool in the center of the environmentally friendly grounds that filled the donut hole inside the 1.2-million-square-foot, mostly glass building housing twelve thousand of Apple's employees, long enough to snap a photo with his phone and tweet it to his followers—*"Thanks @tim_cook for taking me around Apple's beautiful HQ."*

When he'd returned to Twitter headquarters, Elon had been all smiles. He had gone from (a day earlier) accusing Apple of threatening to toss Twitter off its App Store, calling Apple un-American and dangerous, threatening to sue them in court, create his own smartphone, or rally together a protest at Apple's front door, to working everything out in a single afternoon, two masters of the universe chatting in front of a glorified duck pond.

From Esther's point of view, it was a classic Elon moment; he'd charmed Tim, and Tim had charmed him right back. Now Tim was a Friend of Elon, and Elon didn't go to war with his friends.

But Esther also knew it was a tenuous and temporary form of loyalty that could turn on a dime. Yoel Roth had once been a Friend of Elon. Now Yoel was hiding in some hotel, fearing for his life. In a larger sense, the outside world—the mainstream media, the late-night comics, the business journalists, the media pundits, the regular people in the regular world—used to all, for the most part, be Friends of Elon. Now at least "10 percent" of them were booing him onstage, and a much larger portion "during the quiet moments" seemed to be mocking and taunting and hating him.

Even Elon's own inner circle had seemed to be backing off, though it was unclear why. It could have been self-motivated, to protect their own image as Twitter 2.0 was more and more under attack from the major media outlets, or simply because they didn't have the bandwidth to run their podcasts and their VC investments while hanging around a building South of Market that no longer even had a smoothie bar, or it could have been Elon who had asked them to take a step back. It had been reported that Musk had even had issues with Calacanis, after the most visible of his "Goons" had tweeted a little too often about the changes occurring on the platform.

Esther was running into the Goons less and less as the weeks progressed. Sriram was gone entirely, having left around the time of the failed Twitter Blue launch, and Sacks was basically now a non-presence. Steve Davis was around the offices more than most—which had set the outside world tittering (and Twittering)—that perhaps the Boring Company exec was being groomed as a potential Twitter CEO if Elon ever decided to step down.

Esther's run-ins with Davis hadn't all been pleasant, though she believed the exec respected her work. One incident stood out. Davis had texted her out of the blue, stating that he had an expert in payments he wanted Esther to meet with, as she worked on the Twitter Blue launch—a guy the overly kinetic Davis described as someone "who really makes shit happen."

Davis had then introduced her to his "expert," who turned out to be a low-level employee at the Boring Company. This person was in charge of selling random merchandise such as the Boring Company's "Not a Flamethrower" (which was actually a portable, personal flamethrower) and the same company's upcoming cologne (Burnt Hair). The man's expertise, as far as Esther could tell, was that he'd figured out how to put a "buy" button on their Shopify page. *You mean you turned a toggle on?* Esther had shouted, inwardly. Then, outwardly, she'd marched right into Davis's makeshift office at Twitter and laid down the law.

"Do not ever insult me like that again. This is a fucking waste of my time—my time is valuable, I'm trying to get shit launched for Elon and you have me talking to this guy? By the way, does Elon know that you fired half the engineers we need to get Twitter Blue off the ground?"

In retrospect, she'd probably come in a little hot—but Davis had looked terrified, and had seemed to have gotten the message. Jared Birchall, who had been in the room the whole time, had looked up at her with an expression bordering on awe.

"Who are you?" he'd exclaimed, and when she'd told him, it had been the beginning of a solid business relationship.

But neither Jared nor Steve was there to coax Elon away from his self-destructive instincts; Jared was his consigliere and his money guy, and Steve was an acolyte and potential choice for CEO. That left Esther, in her mind, as the only person who could nudge Elon back onto the right, safe path.

She'd succeeded in forestalling the War with Apple, and now she'd managed a softer, quieter, more responsible launch of Twitter Blue. But she could see from the weekend of Elon's tweets and his reaction to the incident at the Chappelle show that things had gotten much more serious, and dangerous—and that it was only going to get worse. The Yoel Roth accusations, the Fauci-pronouns instigation, the elimination of Trust and Safety: it seemed like Elon was on a frightening path. The world—formerly a Friend of Elon—seemed like it was turning against the billionaire. If Elon had ever needed an angel on his shoulder, it was probably now.

Sitting at the conference table, staring up into the frosted glass, she thought back to a moment from just before the weekend, when she'd wandered into the bathroom just outside Caracara. She had found Jehn, Elon's right-hand woman, at the mirrors, curling her hair. It ended up being the longest conversation she'd had with the attractive, competent businesswoman, much more in depth than when Jehn had taken her aside to give her the rules of how one talked to Elon. In the bathroom, Jehn told her about the one-year-old she had at home in Austin, whom she barely saw, now that she was at Twitter. How she hadn't planned on being in San Francisco, how the takeover had been a surprise, but that was how it worked with Elon if you happened to be in his orbit. If he needed you, then you were along for the ride.

She struck Esther as someone who was smart and beautiful who had placed herself in this arguably diminutive role. Was she Elon's assistant? Was she a confidante? Was she an executive?

At the time, Esther had decided to try to open up to Jehn. She'd told Jehn how she saw herself as being in a position to influence Elon in a good direction. How sometimes he'd been about to tweet something crazy, and she'd tell him, *No, no matter what you do, do not tweet that*, and he'd actually listen, especially when she'd couch it in humorous terms: *I'm your official advisor, Elon, and I'm advising you not to tweet that.*

But now, Esther had told Jehn, she was scared. It was getting harder and harder to push Elon in the right way. She had asked Jehn to help: *help me influence him.* Jehn had paused, still looking in the mirror, then had turned toward Esther. She had spoken quietly, but forcefully.

"I don't influence him. That's not why I'm here."

And then: "My job is to help him achieve his goals."

She'd turned back to the mirror, back to curling her hair.

Lost in the frosted glass of the conference room, Esther understood. Jehn wasn't at Twitter to stand up to the billionaire, or to be an angel on his shoulder. She was a beautiful and competent implement, like a high-quality torque wrench or an elegantly tuned slide rule. That was why she was an integral part of Elon's inner circle, a perpetual Friend of Elon.

Esther knew she could never be a torque wrench. It just wasn't in her nature. She had no choice but to continue trying to influence the billionaire, to be the adult in the room, to be the angel on his shoulder. She would strive to remain as useful as she could, a Friend.

But she was aware that the events of the past few days and weeks—Twitter Blue, Apple, Elon's tweets, the world's reaction—were building toward something ominous. From Esther's perspective, Elon seemed, more than anything, like a spring wound tight.

She doubted it would take much to trigger him. Then, well, Esther would be diving for cover along with everyone else, because she had a feeling it would be like a torque wrench hurled through a pane of frosted glass.

## CHAPTER TWENTY-ONE

# December 13, 2022

**Somewhere between** nine and ten p.m., a crisp and clear California night. A stretch of the 110 leading into South Pasadena, a suburb of Los Angeles. The rumble of cars racing down the highway, headlights and taillights blurring into a vivid streak of never-ending color.

A car slid in and out of the traffic, sleek, dark, and glistening, like a water snake just beneath the surface of a stream. The driver skilled, professional; in the backseat, the most precious of cargo: Elon Musk's two-year-old son, X.

Maybe the driver was chatting with the toddler, maybe he was checking the GPS or the time, but eventually he cast a glance at the rearview mirror and noticed the other car. It looked like a Hyundai, beige and boxy and mildly insectlike. Weaving in and out of traffic behind them, matching their speed, sometimes hanging back, sometimes moving what appeared to be too close.

A coincidence—but then, maybe not.

The car carrying X shifted lanes; the Hyundai followed suit. Worried now, X's driver exited the highway, and the Hyundai followed. Minutes later, around 9:45 p.m., both cars were parked in an Arco station off the highway.

The beige Hyundai—and it was, indeed, a Hyundai—with the passenger-side window down, was tucked away in a spot right up next to the gas station, a place normally reserved for the attendants and the manager. There was a man behind the wheel, dressed entirely in shades of black; thick, long-sleeved hoodie pulled down almost to his eyes, gloved left hand on the steering wheel, mask over his nose and mouth. The *Washington Post* would later report that the man's name was Brandon Collado; that he'd rented the Hyundai via the car-sharing app Turo; that he was an Uber Eats delivery driver; that he believed X's mother, the pop star known as Grimes, had been communicating with him through coded messages in her Instagram; that Elon Musk was "monitoring his real-time location"; and that Musk was able to "control Uber Eats to block him from receiving delivery orders."

X's driver, mostly in the shadows, approached the half-open window of the Hyundai, his own car parked a few spots away. Both men had their phones out, the modern equivalent of a feudal-era duel, cameras capturing each other in cones of flickering light, as their heated conversation rose up into the LA air . . .

---

A short time later, Elon Musk was sitting in a dark conference room at Twitter headquarters, staring at his phone.

Having just taken the sort of call that would leave any parent shaking, gripped by fear, anger, maybe even impotence, Elon was now in a nightmare, exaggerated by his circumstance and standing, by the sheer nature of being not just one of the wealthiest men on Earth but one of the most famous.

He wasn't in LA, and he wasn't dancing through the shadows of that gas station parking lot, and he hadn't been behind the wheel of X's car, and he couldn't, in that moment, grab his son and hug him and hold him and make sure he's safe, but what Elon could do was try to make sure this would *never happen again.*

Elon seemed sure that the man in the Hyundai wasn't just some stranger in a black hood and mask; his actions had been intentional. If Elon's suspicions were right, Collado had been led to the car by information he'd gleaned online. Perhaps on Twitter itself—and Collado hadn't been tracking X, a helpless two-year-old child: *Collado had been trying to get to Elon.* It was impossible to know for sure what led Collado to that gas station, and he would deny accusations of stalking; but Elon didn't like it either way.

Elon had been a rich celebrity for a long time; but things felt different now. People thought he was paranoid because he banned group meetings at Twitter headquarters and locked employees out of the office over random weekends and sauntered the halls trailing a pair of giant bodyguards—but why shouldn't he be paranoid? He had released the Twitter Files, showing at the very least the hint of "deep state" fingers finding their way into Twitter 1.0's pie. He had activist groups lobbying advertisers to sink his efforts at financing the company, while troll farms lobbed hate speech attacks all over the platform. He was fighting a war against a "woke virus," battling for freedom of speech, for transparency of the algorithm, while disloyal Tweeps betrayed him at every turn.

When he'd first taken Twitter, he'd defined freedom of speech as "when someone you don't like says something you don't like." Although he'd been called thin-skinned by the press, he'd had no issue with people trolling him on the platform, had taken no steps to ban accounts for simply being mean. He'd gone even further, publicly allowing an account that had been a thorn in his side for some time to remain, alive and unfettered; an account dedicated to tracking Elon's private jet called @ElonJet, run by a Florida college kid named Jack Sweeney. Shortly after taking over Twitter, Elon had tweeted:

> My commitment to free speech extends even to not banning the account following my plane, even though that is a direct personal safety risk.

The truth was, although Elon hadn't banned it, he had contacted Sweeney personally to try to get him to drop the @ElonJet Twitter account: "Can you take this down? I don't love the idea of being shot by a nutcase?" He offered the college student five thousand dollars. Sweeney had responded: "Any chance to up that to $50K? It would be great support in college and would possibly allow me to get a car, maybe even a Model 3." Their communication had ended there.

Sweeney had posted a Twitter thread on December 10, just a few days before, claiming that a member of Twitter's Trust and Safety Council, Ella Irwin, had been tasked with shadow-banning his account—removing his account from search functions, using the algorithm to make sure his tweets weren't seen, liked, or retweeted—an obvious example that Elon had embraced the strategy of Freedom of Speech, not Freedom of Reach. Upon Elon's dissolution of the Trust and Safety team, Sweeney's accounts had returned to normal engagement.

But it was obvious Elon was now having second thoughts; accounts like @ElonJet lived in the virtual, online world, but they had downstream effects in the real, physical world of freeways and Hyundais and Arco parking lots.

The gray line between the virtual and the real was growing more frayed by the day. And though Elon would always be a target, that didn't mean he had to be an easy one.

Still, it wasn't until the next night, December 14, 7:48 p.m., that he tweeted:

> Any account doxing real-time location info of anyone
> will be suspended, as it is a physical safety violation.
> This includes posting links to sites with real-time
> location info.
> Posting locations someone traveled to on a slightly
> delayed basis isn't a safety problem, so is ok.

Followed by a tweet that seemed to come straight from his soul:

> Last night, car carrying lil X in LA was followed by
> crazy stalker (thinking it was me), who later blocked
> car from moving & climbed onto hood.
> Legal action is being taken against Sweeney &
> organizations who supported harm to my family.

But he wasn't finished yet, adding:

> Anyone recognize this person or car?

Attached to the tweet was a ten-second video showing the black-clad "assailant" in his Hyundai, presumably taken by X's driver at the Arco station.

Maybe Elon recognized the hypocrisy of the series of tweets: in one tweet, outlawing "doxing" on the site, making it the capital of capital crimes; and in the next, posting a video of the man his security had told him had accosted X's car, asking his hundred and twenty million followers to dox the man, en masse.

But the contradiction went even deeper than his tweets. Elon had been motivated to buy Twitter by an ideology. His goal had been to ensure unfettered free speech because free speech was a necessary component of his comprehensive strategy to save the human race. He had promised the Twitterverse that moderation would no longer be mysterious or heavy-handed; that he'd bring back banned accounts and open-source the algorithm.

*Speech*, he'd exclaimed, like a Founding Father reincarnated in a black T-shirt, black jeans, and black boots, *would henceforth be free*.

But, damn it—they hadn't just come after him.

They'd come after his *son*.

What did free speech mean in the parking lot of an Arco station off the 110?

What was ideology, really, *when they came after your family*?

---

It started with the kid.

Shortly after Elon posted video of the alleged assailant involved in the stalking incident in LA, he began making his demands. Although Trust and Safety had been dissolved, Ellen Irwin immediately raced into action, lest she herself become another victim of what eventually evolved into Twitter's version of the Night of the Long Knives.

Jack Sweeney's @ElonJet was the first to feel the blade; the account was suspended, followed by Sweeney's personal account. As the @ElonJet suspension was reported by journalists from numerous mainstream outlets, the carnage began to spread. Any reporting on the incident—which usually included a link to Sweeney's web presence—led to another beheading, as journalist after journalist found themselves suspended from the platform.

By Thursday evening, twenty-four hours later, Elon had frozen the Twitter accounts of the *New York Times'* tech journalist Ryan Mac, CNN reporter Donie O'Sullivan, Voice of America writer Steve Herman, mega-pundit Keith Olbermann, *Washington Post* writer Drew Harwell, Business Insider's Linette Lopez, and Mashable's Matt Binder, among dozens and dozens (one count put it at over *nine hundred*) of other lesser-known journalists from every legacy media company across the globe.

The suspensions happened without warning, possibly ordered directly by Elon—not by a committee reviewing tweets, or by some newly formed moderation council, but potentially Elon himself, who had presumably spent part of the night scrolling through Twitter and passing accounts over to Irwin and her team for immediate action. According to insiders, at certain points during the night he'd literally texted Irwin names of journalists, reportedly telling her that if her team couldn't remove the names as fast as Elon was sending them to her, she would be out of a job. It was a scene of total chaos, spurred in equal parts by a sense of anger and of panic.

In many cases, it appeared that the journalists who were suspended had only been reporting on Elon's new anti-doxing policy, without conducting any doxing themselves. One thing the vast majority of the suspended journalists had in common was that they had, for some time now, been reporting negatively on Elon's takeover of Twitter.

Although Elon surely could have expected the response that followed, even he had to be struck by the universality of the condemnation.

As reported by *Politico*, on Friday, December 16, Anthony Romero, the director of the American Civil Liberties Union, commented: "It's impossible to square Twitter's free speech aspirations with the purging of critical journalists' accounts. The First

Amendment protects Musk's right to do this, but it's a terrible deci-sion." Likewise, the *New York Times* saw the suspensions as "ques-tionable and unfortunate." CNN added "impulsive and unjustified." The *Washington Post* stated that the action "directly undermines Elon Musk's claim that he intends to run a platform dedicated to free speech." Melissa Fleming, the UN undersecretary-general for global communication, put it succinctly: "Media freedom is not a toy. A free press is the cornerstone of democratic societies and a key tool in the fight against harmful disinformation."

By Thursday evening, Elon had his back up against the wall, posting gamely into the fury coming at him from all sides:

> Same doxing rules apply to journalists as to
> everyone else.

Followed by:

> They posted my exact real-time location, basically
> assassination coordinates, in (obvious) direct
> violation of Twitter terms of service.

Despite Elon's purposefully inflammatory language—*assassi-nation coordinates*—it was obvious by Friday morning that his explanations were falling mostly on deaf ears. Even Bari Weiss, one of the journalists he'd handpicked to release a portion of the Twitter Files, came after him in a post that gained over nine million views:

> The old regime at Twitter governed by its own whim
> and biases and it sure looks like the new regime has
> the same problem. I oppose it in both cases. And I

think those journalists who were reporting on a story
of public importance should be reinstated.

Out of all the responses that had been flung at Elon in the day
and a half since he'd begun suspending journalists, this seemed to
hit him the hardest, causing him to publicly respond:

What should the consequences of doxing someone's
real-time, exact location be? Assume your child is at
that location, as mine was.

The emotion in his response was palpable; he wasn't just against
the wall, he was hurting.

When Weiss didn't immediately respond, Elon couldn't let it go:

Bari, this is a real question, not rhetorical. What is
your opinion?

Which was then followed by a personal attack:

Rather than rigorously pursuing truth, you are virtue-
signaling to show that you are "good" in the eyes of
media elite to keep one foot in both worlds.

More raw emotion, displayed publicly, to millions upon millions across the platform. *They had come after his son.* And they
were upset with him? For temporarily throwing a few dozen journalists off a social media platform?

Yet, at some point over the next few hours, the hypocrisy of the
moment must have dawned on Elon; hadn't he bought Twitter over

this precise issue? Wasn't the loss of freedom of speech on a social media platform supposed to be a danger great enough to imperil his mission to keep humanity moving forward?

By 10:56 p.m. that same evening, he'd calmed himself enough to post a poll on the platform:

> Unsuspend accounts who doxed my exact location in
> real-time
> Now
> Tomorrow
> 7 days from now
> Longer

Perhaps recognizing that his emotional state made him momentarily ideologically unreliable, he would leave it up to the people.

---

By twenty minutes after midnight the next evening, he had his answer. A majority of the poll's voters had asked that the journalists accounts be unsuspended immediately, and Elon tweeted, as promised:

> The people have spoken. Accounts who doxed my
> location will have their suspension lifted now.

With that, the Night of the Long Knives ended; the majority of the suspensions were revoked. But it was obvious, even from the tenor of Elon's tweet, that something inside of him had changed.

This wasn't funny anymore, and this wasn't a game. This wasn't a time for memes, or for Elon's signature sense of humor. The poll had been another surprise, like being booed onstage at the Chase Center. He had likely assumed—like he'd always been able to assume—that the majority of people were on his side.

He had been wrong. The people had spoken, and he had, reluctantly, listened.

But a dark cloud was building around Elon, obvious to anyone who was too slow to avoid his presence as he stalked Twitter's headquarters that weekend. His son was safe, and he'd stepped back from the brink of treating Twitter like his personal fiefdom, where he could ban accounts that displeased him at will. But the emotional effects of what had happened on that freeway and in that gas station parking lot wouldn't simply dissipate; they would linger, malignant, like a vile tweet in a thread of similar tweets that just seemed to get longer, and longer, and longer . . .

Life might very well have been a simulation, a virtuality populated by NPCs—but to Elon, the simulation had never felt so real.

## CHAPTER TWENTY-TWO

# December 17, 2022

**"You sure about this?** I mean, it doesn't look like you're pulling any punches."

Esther stared down at her laptop, which was propped up in front of her on the bed. Her husband was next to her, close enough to have read the title of the email Esther had just written, more than enough to inspire the look of concern that had spread across his face. She shrugged, but paused a moment, wondering if maybe he was right. Rarely did she write emails that she didn't send; she was a direct person, who usually didn't fear confrontation. And in the month and a half since Elon had taken over Twitter and her own status had skyrocketed at the company, she'd lost count of the number of confrontations she'd had with the Chief Twit.

But like everyone else who worked with the billionaire, she could sense that things had changed; especially over the past few days, he'd become visibly morose, quick to anger. She didn't entirely blame Elon for the events that had occurred since Wednesday, when the car carrying his kid was allegedly stopped by some sort of deranged stalker—she might have reacted similarly, if she'd been in charge of Twitter. He'd walked back most of his missteps, reinstating the banished journalists. But more worrying was the shift in Elon's mood and, along with it, the way he was now making his decisions. He'd always worked on instinct more than calculation, but now he seemed to be acting out of pure emotion.

Thursday night, in the midst of his campaign against the mainstream journalists on Twitter, Esther had listened in on a live Spaces conversation that had been broadcast on the platform to what ended up being hundreds of thousands of listeners. It had originally been a conversation organized by journalists with large Twitter presences to discuss the sudden suspensions, and Elon had joined the fray unexpectedly. At first he had seemed quite willing to have the sort of dialogue that usually brought out the best in him.

But things hadn't gone as planned. After a few softball questions thrown at the entrepreneur, at around 11:30 p.m. Elon had found himself confronted by one of the journalists he'd banned from the platform—Drew Harwell, of the *Washington Post*, who had questioned Elon on his banning @ElonJet and any journalist who reported on @ElonJet.

Elon had sounded calm and logical at the beginning of his response, pointing out that doxing was an unpleasant experience, but his tone had quickly become harsher, his words tumbling out faster and faster.

"There is not going to be any distinction in the future between journalists, simple journalists, and regular people," he said. "Everyone is going to be treated the same. They're not special because you're a journalist. You're just, you're Twitter—you're just, you're a citizen. . . . You dox, you get suspended, end of story."

His vehemence ratcheted up from there, as he realized that he was talking to a reporter who was supposed to be blocked from the platform. A reporter he had waved away from Twitter by fiat, an *unperson* who shouldn't have been able to be on the Spaces in the first place.

"And ban evasion or like trying to be *clever* about it, like oh, I posted a link to the real-time information is obviously, that is obviously someone trying to evade the meaning, that is no different from pen and paste than actually sharing real-time information."

Harwell tried to push back on the idea that the journalists had posted real-time information—that they'd just reported on the news, showing the links to the suspended accounts as a matter of proper reportage—and had pointed out that Elon had responded by using the same tools the billionaire had railed against Twitter 1.0 using in response to issues like the Hunter Biden laptop.

Elon had mumbled a bit, then shot back, disdainful and seething at the same time: "You dox, you get suspended. End of story. That's it."

Then he'd abruptly left the Spaces. Not only that, but a short time later, the entire Spaces application went down across the platform. Twitter later reported that they had taken the chat service down to fix a technical bug—which, it was also later reported, was the ability for banned account users to access Spaces—and, presumably, confront Elon in unpleasant ways.

Whatever this was, it clearly wasn't freedom of speech.

Esther wasn't an ideologue, and she didn't feel a need to hold Elon to some high philosophical standard as he worked through what was obviously a personally painful event. She was more concerned that Elon seemed to be making more and more mistakes as he responded to his emotions. He hadn't yet seemed to understand that running a social media site was harder than building a rocket.

Issues surrounding freedom of speech weren't something that you could calculate, like the burn rate of an engine. Freedom of speech was messy and dirty, and any business built around monetizing conversation was going to face a unique set of problems, which could quickly compound and lead to disaster.

Still, staring down at the title of the email she was about to send, she wondered if this was as much an existential moment for herself as she felt it could be for the company she loved.

*Twitter is in a death spiral.*

Her husband was right: she wasn't pulling punches. The body of the email was as direct as the title; in multiple paragraphs, Esther laid out why she believed Twitter was on the verge of collapsing. In her estimation, the company had around six weeks of runway before the spiral would be irreversible. Unless Elon acted quickly to fix what he'd broken, though the platform might continue to function, it would be like a terminal patient in a surgical OR, slowly bleeding out on the table.

In the email, she'd broken Twitter's illness out into three categories: Revenue, User Engagement, and Employee Morale. It might have been possible to massage the numbers for public consumption enough for an all-hands presentation or an advertising Spaces. Internally it was common knowledge that in these three areas, Twitter was well beyond the brink.

Esther knew that the prudent thing would have been to keep her head down and her mouth shut—especially in light of Elon's current mood, which was darker than she'd ever seen before. But she still believed she was in a unique position to reach Elon with her concerns—which also meant she had a unique responsibility to speak up. Even if it meant her job.

Elon had enough people around him whose only mandate seemed to be to prop up whatever strategy, decision, or whim Elon brought forward. People like Calacanis, or his cousin James, or Steve Davis—men who seemed to worship Elon, who might very well have jumped off the tenth floor of headquarters if Elon had only asked. It wasn't merely a brain trust. It was, in Esther's opinion, very much like a cult—of personality, of shared ideology, of aligned interests. And cults were something Esther intuitively understood, in a way that most people could not.

In Esther's mind, what Elon really needed right now, more than a thousand sycophants, was a single voice willing to say "no."

With little more than another shrug toward her husband, she decided against the prudent thing, and hit send.

Esther didn't have to wait long for Elon's response—which her husband read right along with her, his eyes widening in tune with her own. As often happened with Elon, the billionaire had either ignored most of what she'd written, or had digested her thoughts and decided to take the conversation in an entirely spontaneous direction anyway.

Not two hours after she'd sent her missive, "Twitter Is in a Death Spiral," he'd come back with two sentences:

*The economy is about to experience cardiac arrest, but almost no one understands this yet. Twitter will need to drop to the absolute minimum number of employees.*

Esther read through Elon's response twice, shaking her head. She wanted to talk about sushi, but he was complaining about the price of tires. She knew that if she was going to get anywhere, she was going to need to do this face-to-face.

---

The conversation took place in their usual spot: Caracara, behind the wall of frosted glass, the hulking gargoyles waiting outside. Elon, alone at the conference table, checking his phone.

This time it was Esther sweeping into the room, not the billionaire, and she moved with as much self-confidence as she could muster. She was nervous, but not jittery or frightened—she and Elon had worked together nearly every day for more than a month now, and she felt she'd built up credibility, and maybe even a level of real respect. She knew, from her dealings with the Goons, that it would take years to build the sort of two-way loyalty that his inner circle enjoyed, but she was pretty sure Twitter didn't have years.

Sitting next to him at the table, she opened her laptop and started with the most basic, general premise: Elon needed to take immediate steps to fix each part of Twitter. From the very beginning, he tried to change the subject to the broader economy. He reiterated what he'd said in his response to her email, that the entire economy was about to collapse, that all advertising was probably going to zero anyway, but she wasn't going to let him wriggle out of taking responsibility by blaming it on outside forces.

For the first half hour of their conversation, she argued her point over and over: "I can't leave this room until you understand the state of the business, because nobody else here will tell you the truth."

As she spoke, she felt herself getting fired up, more determined each time he tried to wave off her critiques as "sky-is-falling" exaggerations or biased opinions based on flawed, media-derived data. In that moment, she believed it was not only her responsibility to be the voice of reason—it was her *calling*.

In fact, her name—Esther—had come from scripture. In the story of Purim, from the book bearing Esther's name, Esther was a beautiful woman who worked her way into the court of a Persian king, becoming his wife and using her position to save her people from catastrophe at the hands of an evil advisor. Esther had always taken her name to heart, had even gotten it tattooed on her body, and in that moment she couldn't help feeling that perhaps she, too, had been put in this position—in the court of a modern-day king—to say the hard things that needed to be said.

Yes, Elon had a tendency to lash out, especially when there were more than two people in the room. Esther had seen it happen in numerous meetings. During product development on Twitter Blue: engineers were called idiots to their faces, people got fired right in the middle of an argument.

But Esther didn't believe that would happen to her, certainly not when it was just the two of them, alone in Caracara. So she barreled forward, refusing to back down. She told him that advertising had cratered, taking Twitter's revenue stream with it. She told him that user engagement was rapidly descending, despite what he had been saying on Twitter and elsewhere. Sure, there had been a peak in user minutes directly after his acquisition, but engagement had been spiraling downward ever since. Most important, she told him that you can't build a company with people who don't trust you, and vice versa. There was zero internal communication; just fear, backstabbing, and loathing. Eighty percent of the people who still remained at Twitter were interviewing elsewhere.

Toward the end, she was almost on her feet.

"There's only one person who has gotten us to this place—but there's one person who can turn it all around. And I believe in you," she said.

Esther knew it was the sort of statement that Elon tended to respond to: direct, but bookended by praise. And, after a brief pause, he seemed to hear her. For a brief moment his dark mood cleared, and he even smiled at her. He told her that she'd made some good points, that he would think about what he could do better, and that he accepted responsibility for the mistakes that had already been made.

When she left the conference room, she felt optimistic that she'd reached him. At the very least, she'd told him, face-to-face, things that nobody else would.

Passing by the bodyguards outside, she threw a last glance back at Elon, alone in Caracara, sitting in the center of that huge conference table, once again scrolling his phone. He was hunched forward, shoulders rolled, and the smile he'd displayed just moments earlier was gone.

He looked almost, *despondent.*

All that money, and power, and all those people who circled around him—yet he seemed so completely alone in that big glass conference room, with just his phone as company.

She thought back to a conversation they'd had a few weeks earlier, in the heat of restructuring Twitter Blue. It had just been the two of them, and they had been talking about family, about how they'd both gone to Burning Man and it had made them think hard about their place in the world, and where they came from. Elon had told her that his older kids, his teenagers, didn't like to hang out with him. Although she was very close to her own kids, she knew that teenagers could be difficult. But this was Elon Musk, a man who made self-driving cars and rocket ships and flamethrowers, who dug tunnels under Las Vegas and was going to put a man on Mars. *What teenager wouldn't want to hang out with a man like that?* She'd felt bad for him at the time, and she felt bad for him now.

She had the sense that it wasn't just Twitter in a downward spiral.

Elon seemed to be spiraling, too.

## CHAPTER TWENTY-THREE

# December 18, 2022

**Close your eyes** in a conference room on the tenth floor of an office building in San Francisco, then open them a day later and you're halfway around the world, a place where the sun is as bright as a nuclear bomb in the sky above your head, and the breeze is laced with salt and sand, so much sand that sometimes it burns to breathe, but you're smiling, *yeah you are*, because you're surrounded by people, so many people, tens of thousands of them, shouting and cheering and screaming, an entire stadium full of people rising up in the middle of a goddamn desert, like something out of mythology, like something *biblical*, even spiritual, and all around you, all you can see are jerseys, stripes of blue and white and darker navy, blending together into something vibrant and powerful and ALIVE.

Elon shivered, in the center of it all, smiling despite the press of the crowd and the feeling that so many of the people around him were looking at HIM and not the field down below, watching him and not the players racing down the pitch.

Of course, he wasn't actually *surrounded* by the mass of humanity, as much as he was *suspended* above them. He was in a multilevel luxury box near the top of the massive, elliptical-shaped Lusail Stadium, in the city of Lusail, Qatar, twelve miles north of Doha. The private box offered a view over at the packed bleachers below, where more than eighty thousand rabid football fans had gathered for the biggest sporting event in the world: the finals of the World Cup, a knockdown affair between Argentina and France that was being broadcast to more than one and a half billion households around the globe.

The luxury box wasn't overcrowded, but Elon certainly wasn't alone in the rarified space. Nearby stood the CEO of Qatar's sovereign wealth fund—the Qatar Investment Authority—Mansoor Bin Ebrahim Al-Mahmoud, who also happened to be an investor in Elon's takeover of Twitter, to the tune of $375 million. Alongside Al-Mahmoud were a number of men dressed in traditional Middle Eastern garb, white flowing robes and head coverings; the luxury box was one of the few places in the stadium that weren't a blur of different shades of blue. Elon himself was wearing a hunter-green T-shirt and dark pants, helping him stand out from his Qatari counterparts, though he wasn't the only foreigner in the box. To his left sat Jared Kushner, the ex-president's son-in-law, with his narrow jaw and close-set eyes. Jared had his own massive financial relationships in the Middle East, both with Qatar and nearby Saudi Arabia. A few seats over from Jared was Indian billionaire Lakshmi Mittal, head of the world's second-biggest steel manufacturer. Turkish president Recep Tayyip Erdogan was likely also nearby, as he'd been seen shaking hands with Elon earlier in the day. And of course Nusret Gokce, aka Salt Bae, a man famous for throwing salt at meat—which wasn't a euphemism—who had over fifty million followers on Instagram. By the end of the game, Nusret would reportedly get himself banned from some future FIFA events for taking too many pictures with Messi, the Argentinian soccer star, and the World Cup trophy and posting them to his Instagram, though to be fair, the entire event—from its pageant-filled introductory ceremony to the number of celebrities in the luxury boxes and stands—seemed designed to be displayed on social media.

Elon had certainly been doing his part, in that regard. Beginning the evening before, when he'd tweeted

> First World Cup match on sunday!
> Watch on Twitter for best coverage & real-time commentary

before hopping on his jet for the eight-thousand-mile trip (no doubt, tracked by the newly resuscitated @ElonJet, though the information would now be reported on delay), and he'd followed that up with a relative tweetstorm from the very moment he'd walked into the stadium.

At 9:53 a.m., he'd begun, *"At World Cup right now,"* attaching a video of the pitch engulfed in the opening ceremonies, lit up by a raucous fireworks display, between undulating French and Argentinian flags.

At 10:27 a.m. he'd tweeted, *"Great goal by Argentina! (three Argentinian flag icons),"* along with a video, followed forty minutes later by

> Super exciting World Cup!
> ▨ ahead 2-0 at halftime.
> Can ▮ ▮ come back?

Seeing that tweet reach over thirty-eight million views, he'd continued his livestream at 11:54 a.m.:

*Well done France!* ▌▐▌▐▌▐▌
*Evenly matched game!!*

Then, a minute later:

24,400 tweets per second for France's goal, highest
ever for World Cup!

And they were saying engagement was down? *24,400 tweets per second.* Inspired, Elon could only continue, at 12:39 p.m., "3-3 *WOW!!!*"

Finally, at 1:02 p.m., at the close of the game, when Argentina took the victory in a nail-biting penalty-shooting competition:

Duel in the Desert.
Couldn't ask for a better game. Incredible
play by ▭ ▌▐ !!!

There in that luxury box, surrounded by the beautiful and the wealthy, live-tweeting the biggest sporting event of the year to his 120-plus million followers, Elon felt better than he had in days, maybe weeks, maybe months.

It must have been the perfect salve for the harsh reality he'd recently experienced, a sense of pure *surreality.* The algorithm behind the simulation had reworked itself around its main player, and now the NPCs were shifting back into their proper roles. Every face turned toward him was beaming—even the Qataris, the billionaires, the Kushners, filled with awe and respect and yes, he could think it, love.

Elon felt their love balloon inside him, lifting him up, and then he was leaning over the balcony of the luxury box and he was shaking hands with the fans in their jerseys of blue and blue. He was shaking and hugging and loving the strangers, the fans, the Qataris, the Kushners.

It was a reset, a reawakening. He was away from San Francisco and those dark headquarters and the Tweeps who hated and feared him, who conspired behind the frosted glass. Away from the journalists who wanted to dox him and the mainstream media who wanted to destroy him.

They were all so shortsighted. *24,400 tweets per second.* Adoring fans. The simulation was back on track.

---

It wasn't until after the nuclear sun had slipped beneath the horizon and Elon was back in the cool leather comfort of his private jet, arcing back over the curve of the world, that he made a decision, and crafted a tweet. Whether it was partially motivated by a conversation he'd had with a Qatari royal or an Indian billionaire or even a Kushner, or whether it was just a momentary whim, he crafted a tweet. Not just a tweet, a poll. Because he wanted to know what he believed he already knew—that everything that had felt wrong was now right, that everything that had gone dark was now light:

> Should I step down as head of Twitter?
> I will abide by the results of this poll.

His poll had gone out at 2:20 a.m., Qatari time (6:20 p.m. Twitter time), but it wasn't long, maybe a matter of minutes, as the votes poured in by the thousands upon thousands, that Elon realized that he had misjudged the moment. That he had been *caught up* in the moment. That he had been *fooled* by the moment.

Refreshing and refreshing, the numbers grew worse and worse. And worse.

Even as his private jet rose high above the Earth, in its leather-lined belly Elon was descending, spiraling, plummeting.

Down, down, down.

*Vox Populi, Vox Dei.*

## CHAPTER TWENTY-FOUR

# December 20, 2022

As the saying goes, be careful what you wish, as you
might get it.

@Elonmusk 6:43 p.m. 12/18/22

**Jessica could tell** that something was wrong the minute she
stepped off the elevator onto the tenth floor. Turning a corner into
the open workspace that bordered Caracara, she could see small
groups of Tweeps in the far reaches of the room, trying to look
inconspicuous as they eyed the bodyguards by the conference room
door. There was no longer much furniture to hide behind: no water
coolers, no potted plants. Four days earlier, before Elon had left for
Qatar and the World Cup, Twitter had held a "swag selloff," a sort of
garage sale for Twitter employees, where Jessica's fellow Tweeps had
been encouraged to buy items as diverse as office supplies, T-shirts,
and the indoor shrubbery, most of it emblazoned with the Twitter
logo. Everything had been priced to sell—two bucks a pop for most
of the items—and the sale had raised around eleven thousand dollars, which probably hadn't done much for Elon's bottom line. But

selling the potted plants had an added advantage; they needed to go because there was no longer any staff still employed in the building to water them.

At the moment, the tenth floor could have benefited from some greenery, since the atmosphere felt so devoid of life. The Tweeps, gathered in twos and sometimes threes despite Elon's mandate against roving cabals and covens, were speaking in hushed tones, perfect for a funeral. The bodyguards, chiseled from stone, weren't speaking at all.

> No one wants the job who can actually keep Twitter
> alive. There is no successor.
> @Elonmusk 7:04 p.m. 12/18/22

Jessica moved quietly through the workspace, winding between the open desks and cubicles, dodging spaghetti curls of extension cords that had once been hidden by elaborate ferns. Slipping past a programmer's workstation—a bleary-eyed young man she didn't recognize, head down over a laptop, fingers furiously attacking a keyboard (perhaps undoing one of management's more recent blunders, the banning of posts promoting competing social media networks, something Elon had already apologized for)—she caught sight of two women she recognized from the former Trust and Safety team, who were still involved in some level of moderation. She headed toward them, her feet gliding over the hardwood floor.

> I will resign as CEO as soon as I find someone
> foolish enough to take the job! After that, I will just
> run the software & servers teams.
> @Elonmusk  8:20 p.m. 12/20/22

Even before she reached the pair of Tweeps, she could tell they were talking about *him*. Between words, they took turns casting furtive glances toward the frosted glass wall that separated Caracara from the rest of the floor.

Rumor was, he'd been there all day. Alone, the door guarded by his stone-faced bodyguards. From Jessica's vantage point, it looked like the lights behind the glass were either off, or dimmed down low. He might have been at the table, but it was hard to tell. It was tough to see anything beyond shadowy shapes that could have been furniture, a now-privatized potted plant, or maybe a despondent billionaire, reacting to what might be one of the biggest emotional blows he'd ever received.

Jessica had seen the poll when Elon had first tweeted it out, and had checked and rechecked it again and again for the next twenty-four hours until it had closed. She had not been surprised by the outcome, but she had balked when she'd seen the engagement numbers. Seventeen and a half million people had voted in the poll—already a huge number, but nothing compared to the *three hundred and sixty-three million people* who had viewed the tweet. That was more views than there were people in the US, a testament to Twitter's international imprint, and to Elon, to the platform's continued ability to engage its user base. The billionaire had shown, once again, that Twitter really could be an online version of a global town hall.

Now the people had spoken, and the results of the poll were indisputable. Fifty-seven percent of the votes had landed in the yes column—nearly ten million people—that Elon should, indeed, step down as head of Twitter. Elon hadn't needed to wait for the poll to close, twenty-four hours after he'd posted it, to know the direction the wind was blowing. He'd known almost immediately; he'd tweeted a couple of times in the few hours after he'd posted the poll, and then he'd gone dark, silent, for nearly a day. It might have been the longest he'd gone without tweeting in years, certainly the longest since he'd taken over Twitter.

Jessica had heard that when he'd arrived at headquarters after he'd returned from Qatar, he'd barely spoken a word to anyone, moving through the halls with his head down and his shoulders hunched. Even his own bodyguards had remained an extra few feet behind him as he'd moved, and if any of his Goons were in the building, they'd hidden themselves from view.

Things had only gotten worse since he'd shuttered himself in the tenth-floor conference room. The few attempts by Tweeps to get his attention about company business had been rebuffed by the bodyguards, who had been given orders not to allow Elon to be disturbed. Nobody had even seen Jehn—usually, Elon's constant liaison to the outside world—and as far as anyone could tell, he had remained sequestered, alone and mostly in the dark, for hours.

The texts Jessica had received from colleagues throughout the San Francisco headquarters had ranged across the board, from frightened—what happens to a company when the CEO has an emotional breakdown because millions of people just told him they wanted him to resign?—to amused—live by the tweet, die by the tweet—to genuinely confused—how had Elon shattered his own reputation so thoroughly, in such a short amount of time, and still not realized that he wasn't perceived as the same infallible genius by the world outside his inner circle? But she, herself, had felt conflicted by the turn of events. She hadn't voted in Elon's poll, but she wasn't sure she'd have piled on the billionaire after the week he'd just endured. She had kids of her own, and she didn't blame Elon for overreacting when his son's car was allegedly accosted. He had made many mistakes at the helm of Twitter, but she still hoped he could see reason, and realize that running a social media company wasn't the same as building a rocket. It wasn't just math and science, action and reaction; it wasn't always rational, because it was a business built around people, full of emotion.

She was two steps away from the women of Trust and Safety when she finally caught some of the words they were using. It wasn't just concern for what would happen next with Twitter: whether Elon would really step down as CEO, ignore the poll, or continue lashing out (as he had at advertisers, at journalists, at Tweeps who had questioned him at the all-hands, or on Spaces, or on Twitter itself, at Yoel Roth, at Robin Wheeler, at almost everyone who had ever stood up to him)—it was actual, real concern for Elon himself.

Jessica might have heard the words "wellness check" and believed, with a start, that the two women were actually considering calling San Francisco law enforcement to ask for a *wellness check*.

On Elon Musk.

Elon had cut himself off from the rest of the company so thoroughly that the only way these two employees thought they could make sure he was okay was to call 911.

Jessica felt her cheeks burning. She didn't see either of the women reaching for their phones, but even so, it was enough that they were even considering it. Jessica *had* come to the tenth floor with the intention of talking to Elon. Of actually walking right up to the billionaire and trying to reach him, not as an employee, not as a critic, not as someone who wanted something from him or even someone who wanted him gone. She had intended to talk to him as a person, a fellow human, a parent, someone who cared about the world, just as he did, and wanted to make it better, just as he did.

But standing there, listening to her fellow Tweeps talking about a wellness check, looking at the bodyguards, the frosted glass—it had become too much. It was all just too much.

She turned, and headed back toward the elevator.

———————

Twenty minutes later Jessica was standing outside on the corner of Market and Tenth, the breeze pulling at her laptop bag, as she waited for the Uber that would take her back to her hotel. The laptop bag was light, barely more than the material it was made of; she'd left her computer on the desk she'd been using since she'd changed her travel plans to remain in San Francisco after Elon had taken over the company. She doubted it would take longer than a half hour to pack up her hotel room, and then she'd be on her way to the airport and the red-eye back to New York, where her husband and kids would be waiting.

She hadn't officially resigned yet—she would wait until she was on board the flight to write the email—but she already felt the weight of the past two months lifting from her shoulders. She didn't know what was next, but she hoped she would one day find another community as uplifting, connected, and well-intentioned as the family of Tweeps with whom she'd helped build Twitter 1.0. Maybe she'd reconnect with some of them wherever she landed next; after all, the vast majority no longer called the art deco warehouse looming up behind her home.

She fought the urge to glance back at the headquarters. If she had, she wondered if she'd see his silhouette, hovering behind the windowpanes that stretched around the tenth floor. She hadn't heard any sirens—there were no signs of police or fire rescue—so she assumed the Tweeps outside Caracara had already deescalated their concerns.

Elon, no doubt, would eventually recover from the slight to his ego. Already, on Twitter he had begun to wriggle out from under the impact of the CEO poll. One of his preferred followers—an outspoken internet entrepreneur, activist, hacker (and, once upon a time, fugitive, charged with computer fraud and data espionage crimes, who had long been fighting extradition to the United States, where he faced additional charges of money laundering, racketeering, and wire fraud), Kim Dotcom had tweeted:

> Hey @elonmusk, it's unwise to run a poll like this when you are now deep state enemy #1. They have the biggest bot army on Twitter. They have 100k "analysts" with 30-40 accounts all voting against you. Let's clean up and then run this poll again. The majority has faith in you.

He followed up with a tweet musing that perhaps Elon had only posted the poll as a "honeypot" to catch the bots. At that point, Elon had broken his silence to respond:

> Interesting.

When later, another follower had suggested that

> Blue subscribers should be the only one that can vote in policy related polls. We actually have skin in the game.

Elon had rallied to the idea:

> Good point. Twitter will make that change.

Whether it was a coping mechanism to get past the idea that the majority of people wanted him out, or he truly bought into the idea that the poll's results were suspect, it was clear that Elon wasn't going to simply take the poll for what it was, and step down. Not immediately, anyway. But he couldn't pretend, now, that his actions at Twitter hadn't colored the way the world saw him—that his take-over of the platform hadn't damaged his reputation in ways that would reverberate significantly.

He wouldn't leave right away; apparently, even *Vox Populi, Vox Dei* had its limitations.

It seemed his ego and thin skin and primal need to win wouldn't allow it. More likely, he would spend enough time at the helm of the platform to save face before finding a way to try to resurrect his reputation on a wider scale.

But none of that mattered to Jessica anymore. She had seen the effect of the poll herself, had known how hard it had hit the billionaire, and she had no doubt that whenever he finally stepped out of that conference room on Tenth and began roaming the halls of Twitter again, firing out proclamations, firing more Tweeps, and tinkering with the platform until it was unrecognizable, he would not be the same Elon who had walked through those front doors carrying a sink.

The way Jessica saw it, Elon Musk didn't break Twitter.

Twitter broke Elon Musk.

She wasn't going to wait around for the billionaire, or what was left of the platform, to pick up the pieces.

## CHAPTER TWENTY-FIVE

# February 13, 2023

**Mark had an oversized** Hefty bag in one hand and his cell phone in the other as he stumbled through his dark living room, halfway into a scavenger hunt that was being replicated in households all across the country. The TV was still on at the head of the room, though the postgame interviews and touchdown replays had long been replaced by local programming. There was some sort of talk show/infomercial chittering on, hosted by pretty people who were way too chipper for two in the morning, as Mark used the light from his phone to navigate an obstacle course of temporarily rearranged furniture, searching out half-empty beer cans and paper plates still weighed down by pizza grease, pausing every few feet to wipe Cheetos dust from a couch cushion or pick up a pretzel from the floor.

Mark did his best to move quietly, for the same reason that he hadn't turned on the living room's overhead lights to make his work easier. An open floor plan was perfect for a Super Bowl party for sixteen of your closest friends, but decidedly less so when you were cleaning up while trying not to wake your newly pregnant wife.

Though Gina was only six weeks along, she was already feeling the effects of the growing life inside her. Crazy, how quickly life could change; it seemed like yesterday, he'd been in that Chinese restaurant, rallying what was left of his team after Elon's "hardcore" email. By Christmas, barely a month and a half later, he'd put a down payment on a house, and on New Year's, he'd found out he was going to be a dad.

They'd only moved in a week ago, and other than the living room, the place was mostly still unfurnished—which made the cleanup that much easier. Whenever the light from his phone played over something that looked like it might be a stain, Mark fought both his training and type-A personality and left it alone.

The phone wasn't just a makeshift flashlight; it was open to Twitter. Not only because Mark's whole life still revolved around the platform, as he and his skeletal team (now down to a sleek and harried thirty-four creatives) struggled along with the rest of his Ad Sales colleagues to rebuild whatever they could of the company's advertising roster. Although in public, Elon had made comments alluding to the fact that most advertisers were returning to the platform, the truth was more "nuanced." Apple was back, but many of Twitter's big-name clients were still on pause, including AT&T, Mars, and Volkswagen. Coca-Cola and Unilever were no longer top spenders on the site, and overall, ad revenues were now a pale shadow of what they'd been before Elon had taken over.

But Mark's phone had been open to Twitter most of the night for the sheer fact that nothing went better with the Super Bowl than Twitter. The Kansas City Chiefs and the Philadelphia Eagles were battling it out on the field, but on Twitter it had mostly been about bad ref calls, the commercials in between the action on the grid, and Rihanna's halftime show—and Mark had been there for all of it, reading comments, laughing at memes, posting when he had something to add, and scrolling whenever there was a lull in the game.

It was what Twitter was best at: real-time conversation, opinion, and news, shared instantly and globally, often with takes from people who were right in the middle of the action.

It had been six weeks since the World Cup. Elon himself had resumed much of his Twitter personality, after his brief and uncharacteristic silence following the chastisement of his CEO poll. There had been engineering issues, partial outages, continual complaints about a rise in hate speech, ever lowering engagement, and often confusing tweaks to the user experience—but Twitter, as a platform, was still humming along.

Still, to Mark, the Chief Twit seemed different; there were no more stories of him strolling Twitter headquarters, his Goons and bodyguards in tow, making proclamations about free speech and asking for hardcore fealty oaths. Now the stories were more chaotic: Elon's underlings pinging engineers at random, demanding sudden changes or new products (that seemed to have grown out of some equally random Twitter conversation Elon had engaged in)—usually in the middle of the night—and always, with a threat of a firing attached.

As much as Mark had been disturbed by the snowflake culture of Twitter 1.0, he had to admit that along with the snowflakes, at this point Twitter had lost much of its vibrancy. A year ago, he'd have surfed the company Slack, finding channels brimming with ideas, debates, passionate arguments, and collaboration. Now Slack was always eerily quiet, bubbling with an undercurrent of fear and uncertainty.

Skirting around one of the beanbag chairs to collect a paper plate that had lodged beneath the couches, he used his thumb to shift over to the site; unlike in the old days, when he'd have Slack open next to Twitter for much of the night, he barely ever checked the messaging board anymore, and he expected little more than the usual ghost town.

To his surprise, he was immediately greeted by a notice indicating that a message had just been posted to anyone and everyone who might happen to be online. Even more surprising, the message had been posted by James Musk, Elon's cousin and one of the handful of Goons who still roamed the halls in San Francisco. Not only that, it was a matter of "high urgency" demanding immediate response. James, it seemed, was looking for engineers and programmers to "debug" an "issue with engagement across the platform"—and whatever the problem was, it couldn't wait until morning.

Shocked at the emergency coding of the missive, Mark sat hard onto a corner of the couch. He checked the time: 2:40 a.m. Insane, this deep into the night of the Super Bowl, and James was running around headquarters like a chicken with his head cut off, screaming for engineers. No doubt it was some sort of Elon Project.

It wasn't until the next day that Mark would find out all the details of what had spurred the early morning panic session—when the event was covered by tech journalists Zoe Schiffer and Casey Newton of Platformer. Apparently the emergency that had sent James Musk into a tizzy had to do with a tweet that Elon had sent during the game, supporting the Eagles. Elon's tweet had generated 9.1 million impressions; this might have seemed a healthy number— but a tweet by President Biden, sent during the same game and offering support for his wife, who was also a fan of the Eagles, had garnered twenty-nine million impressions.

This had not sat well with Elon, who had immediately deleted his own tweet, hopped on his private jet, and flown directly to San Francisco.

According to Platformer, James and Elon frantically gathered eighty engineers—in the middle of the night—to fix this "issue with engagement across the platform," meaning, the fact that Elon's tweet had gotten less engagement than a tweet by the president of the United States. The engineers were told, in no uncertain terms, that if they didn't succeed they would all be fired.

By the next afternoon, the problem would indeed be solved, in a particularly blunt manner. The engineers would rewrite Twitter's code to emphasize any tweets by Elon Musk. Twitter's vaunted "algorithm" would reportedly magnify tweets by Elon by "a factor of 1,000," something Platformer would report was called "a power user multiplier" that "only applies to Elon Musk."

Sitting on the edge of his couch in his darkened living room, staring at James Musk's urgent Slack message, Mark could only shake his head.

This wasn't the Elon he had seen on that screen in Houston, years ago, charming and galvanizing the crowd of Tweeps, moving even the snowflakes to applaud. This wasn't about Free Speech or a Global Town Hall or a Level Playing Field or Truth or Mars or some Existential Human Condition or whatever the hell Elon actually believed.

This was just chaos. A foundering ship helmed by a captain too preoccupied with his own whims to steer it to safety.

Yet Mark knew he wasn't going anywhere, not yet. He had a new mortgage, a pregnant wife. His team, what was left of them—relied upon him. More than that, he still believed in *Twitter.*

And part of him still believed in Elon—not the Elon who fired engineers in the middle of the night, but the Elon he'd seen in Houston, the Elon of rocket ships and electric cars.

He hit the button on the side of his phone, shutting down the screen, and let himself sink back into the couch, the only sound in the darkness the garbage bag at his feet, settling to the floor.

## CHAPTER TWENTY-SIX

# February 25, 2023

**Although she hadn't checked** the GPS on her phone, Esther was fairly certain she was somewhere between the fifth and sixth circle of hell, slouched in a beach chair of questionable structural integrity, wedged between a lazy river filled with sunscreen-slathered cherubs and an incessant, four-piece steel drum cover band set up in the shadow of a massive faux tree house, its limbs spewing forth a torrent of chlorinated tears.

Certainly, Dante had nothing on the sprawling, aquatic dystopia that was Great Wolf Lodge just outside of San Francisco. The northwoods-themed, kitschy hellscape was a Huckleberry Finn–inspired water park fever dream; surrounding Esther marched a procession of damp, bedraggled children clinging to soggy inner tubes like shipwreck survivors, amid cannonball splashes and high-pitched laughter, while a veritable mosh pit of beleaguered parents struggled to discern between genuine cries of distress and simple whines for more overpriced chicken fingers.

Esther had already spent a day and a half navigating the labyrinth of gift shops, swamplike humidity, and the barrage of piercing

shrieks. For the first time since she'd left the office on Friday afternoon, she'd finally settled into something resembling a sitting position, her laptop—still closed—resting on the seat next to her.

On the drive out of the city, she'd promised herself and her husband that she was going to leave work behind for the weekend. The
past two months had been insane: a pressure cooker of projects new
(various monetization schemes involving creators, subscription,
and potential new forms of payment) and old (yet another revamp
of Twitter Blue, and the Blue Check that was now fundamentally
attached to the subscription service). This trip to Great Wolf Lodge
was meant to be a chance for her family to reconnect and have fun.
But no matter how physically far she was from Caracara—no matter
how many twelve-dollar hot dogs on soggy buns she consumed or
how many times she got knocked flat in the nearby wave pool—her
thoughts continued to circle back to the intense and progressively
more worrying atmosphere she'd left behind.

In the first few weeks after she'd met with Elon and told him the
company was spiraling out of control, she'd been optimistic that
he'd at least heard what she'd had to say, and had begun thinking
about ways to turn Twitter around. He had appeared to be fully
chastised by the events leading up to his trip to Qatar and the subsequent CEO poll; when he'd finally emerged from Caracara, he'd
been somewhat muted for most of the month of January, and had
seemed attuned to the needs of the company that Esther had laid
out. He'd made great efforts at rebuilding connections to the advertising community, had mostly avoided the sort of tweets that had
gotten him in trouble in the past, and hadn't engaged in any mass
firings, as far as she was aware.

But within the first two weeks of February—and especially in
the days around the Super Bowl—he'd gone back on the warpath.
Not only had he gone entirely Captain Bligh over his tweet losing

out in engagement against the president of the United States, but he'd gone on a mini, and very public, firing spree. A Twitter engineer, self-described as having six years of experience working on the platform for Android devices, publicly corrected, on Twitter, Elon's explanation for the platform's slow performance in "many countries." The resulting argument—tweet by tweet, over a period of hours—ended in Elon responding to a voyeuristic commenter with a succinct

He's fired.

When another Tweep attempted to defend the engineer's argument, she too found herself rapidly out of a job: *"lol just got fired for shitposting."* These two firings came on top of the firing, a few days earlier, of another engineer who had apparently committed a mortal sin by suggesting that Elon's engagement was going down because he just wasn't as popular a tweeter as he had been when he'd first taken over the company (though this was before the algorithm was juiced to give his tweets a 1,000x magnification).

The rapid firing of engineers over petty disagreements was concerning enough, but Esther had also witnessed Elon's paranoia ratcheting up in the days since—and in the past week, she felt his paranoia was at an all-time high. Elon had made no secret around the office that he believed that many of Twitter's employees were conspiring against him. Now he'd begun to set his sights on the company's internal Slack channels; perhaps he'd become convinced that if employees could talk to each other, unfettered, there might be some sort of an uprising—maybe even an act of internal sabotage to take the platform down.

On Wednesday, just three days before Esther found herself at Great Wolf, dodging inner tubes, Twitter's Slack had gone down for what the Tweeps were told was "routine maintenance." However, a Slack employee would tell Platformer "there is no such thing as 'routine maintenance.' That's bullshit." The only reason Esther could think of for Elon taking down Slack, in the same way he'd shut down journalists' accounts after the incident with X's car—was a fit of paranoia, maybe even rage.

Esther knew she wasn't alone in her feelings that the atmosphere at work was becoming more and more unstable; even what was left of Elon's inner circle seemed to be walking on eggshells. One incident stood out in particular. After a series of firings and resignations, including one top engineer who had been with Elon at Tesla—walking out the door after expounding, *I've never seen this Elon before, I can't in good conscience be in this anymore*—James Musk, Elon's cousin, had found himself in charge of all of Twitter's engineering. It did not appear James had anywhere near the requisite training, education, or experience for the job. One late night in the office, Esther had stumbled upon James hiding out in one of the headquarters' hermetically sealed, soundproof phone booths fighting back tears. The job, she thought, was becoming too much for him.

Esther had tried to reassure him: *Hey, you're his cousin, you're related to him, it will be okay!* James had responded that she didn't understand Elon: *Nobody is safe! Anyone can be cut at any time!*

At least James could see how insane the environment at Twitter was becoming. Steve Davis, on the other hand, appeared still fully on board, the leading acolyte in the cult of Elon, and more and more, Esther found herself at odds with the jittery businessman.

One such interaction had led to fireworks. Esther had been asked to find a way to add the crypto Dogecoin to Twitter's payment structure. Dogecoin was a form of digital currency that had been created as a joke, meant to mock the crypto industry, yet had become a popular "memecoin" after Elon had supported it on Twitter. Esther had demurred, writing up a document on why it would be foolish to add a form of payment as volatile and rife for manipulation as Doge to Twitter.

After she'd handed over her concerns, she'd found herself once again in Caracara. A heated exchange with a handful of the acolytes, including Davis, pushed her to speak her mind. She'd told them that Elon didn't need yes-men: he needed to be told the truth, he needed people with common sense to help guide him forward.

But her words fell on deaf ears. She feared that the people who were supposed to be keeping Elon safe, *because he was special,* were actually egging him on, pushing him forward, furthering the damage to his reputation. Maybe it was as simple as that: maybe he had surrounded himself with the wrong people.

In just the past few days, Esther had started to get the feeling that the wrong people were once again circling the wagons. Monday morning, she'd gone up to the tenth floor to find that Davis had added an external lock to Caracara, with no explanation. When she'd glanced inside, she'd seen a pair of giant whiteboards with every important remaining Tweep's name written on them, a sort of reverse spreadsheet, listing Twitter's employees from the most expensive to the least. Davis and James Musk and Jared and Jehn went in and out of the room, making notes and having hushed conversations—and the fact that they didn't call Esther in, didn't invite her to look over their org chart or make suggestions or kick anything around—was a major red flag.

She'd tried to put it out of her mind, and by the end of the week she'd pretty much succeeded. She'd been all smiles as she'd packed up the car for the trip to Great Wolf, making sure the kids had enough bathing suits and a cooler full of snacks for the hour-long drive.

It was only halfway into the trip that she'd turned to her husband and joked, "You know, there's a fifty percent chance I won't
have a job when we return to San Francisco."

They'd both laughed at the time; now, a day later, watching
waterlogged inner tubes bob past on the River Styx, she couldn't
stop herself from reaching for her laptop, flipping open the case, and
firing up the screen.

For a moment everything seemed normal, the glow from the
laptop flashing off her cheeks as she sighed at her own foolish
thoughts—and then, quite suddenly, the screen

Went

Black.

She stared at the laptop, and began hitting keys. Nothing. Her
laptop—her *work* laptop—had been *bricked*. Like so many Tweeps
before her, she'd been locked out of her email, locked out of Slack,
locked out of Twitter.

At first she felt confusion. Was that it? Had she really just been
fired? She'd heard of colleagues who had gone through similar
moments, only to find the lockout had been the result of a technical
glitch, or yet another outage. She even knew of an employee who
had found himself locked out of his account, but no matter who he
asked, he couldn't get a straight answer whether he was still
employed or not. Esther had begun to think of the colleague as a
Schrodinger's Tweep, both fired and employed at the same time.

But no, as she hit the space bar with her thumb, click-click—
nothing—she knew, deep down, that it was really over. Elon had
fired her.

Maybe it had been the email, and the follow-up conversation,
about Twitter spiraling down toward devastation. Maybe it had
been his growing paranoia, and the continuation of his anger, his

confusion, his dismay at the events leading up the CEO poll. Maybe it was just another sudden swipe of the blade, another effort to whittle down Twitter's bottom line.

With Elon, it probably wasn't personal, even though with Elon, it somehow always *seemed* so personal. And Esther knew, there were some ex-colleagues and Twitter acquaintances who would have a field day at her expense; she had, after all, risen while so many others had fallen—and even though she had done her best to work within the chaos of Twitter 2.0, her loyalty to Elon had left her fired on a beach chair at Great Wolf Lodge.

But she had no regrets. She'd tried to make a difference, and for a short time, she'd worked side by side with the world's richest man, trying to make Twitter better.

Even now, she didn't hate Elon; in truth, she felt bad for him. She would walk away from Twitter proud of her accomplishments—and with a very sweet parachute, since she would now be paid out (healthily) for Twitter's acquisition of her former start-up, something she doubted Elon had even taken into consideration. She had her memories, and more than that, she had her family, and her future.

Closing her laptop, she leaned back against the rickety beach chair. Closing her eyes, she pictured him—alone in that big glass conference room, at the center of that long, empty table. Just Elon and his phone.

In that moment, she didn't think of him as a billionaire, or as some sort of demanding, whimsical, sometimes tyrannical boss, or even as the genius behind Tesla and SpaceX.

She thought of Elon as she'd last seen him, as she'd so often seen him. Alone in Caracara, with his phone, at that table.

Maybe the saddest, loneliest man she'd ever met.

All of that money, all of that power, all of that brilliance, all of those dreams that she truly believed came from a good place, all of it—and still—

The saddest, loneliest man she'd ever met.

She took a breath, tasting the chlorine in the air.

Then she opened her eyes, because it was time to move on.

# April 20, 2023

**Eight thirty-three** in the morning and the thunderous countdown reverberated through the Starbase command center—FIVE FOUR THREE TWO ONE—and then the entire world started to tremble and there was a roar like a thousand suns exploding at once and suddenly Elon leapt out of his white-backed chair and onto his feet, the momentum carrying him forward toward the wide bay of picture windows and the phalanx of flat-screens suspended from the ceiling, and he barely stopped himself at the last moment from crashing right through the glass, his entire body hunched toward the spectacular event unfolding, in real time, IRL, right in front of his wild and wide eyes. A true precipice on the timeline of human history, a signpost in civilization's evolution, a DA VINCI–MONA LISA/EINSTEIN-RELATIVITY/NEWTON-APPLE/ PROMETHEUS-FIRE maybe even STEVE JOBS-iPHONE/ZUCKERBERG-FACEBOOK moment, a heart-pounding pulse-rocketing stomach-churning laser-beams-shooting-from-his-freaking-eyes moment, a once-in-a-thousand-years event, the simulation hitting on all cylinders event.

309

It was actually happening. T minus zero and the roar and the massive plumes of white smoke billowing outward from the Raptor 2 engines, the massive conflagration of yellow-white flame from the methane-hydrogen mix, the entire launchpad and half the tower engulfed in what could only be described as a tornado of heat and fire, and at the center, trembling and pulsing and goddamn throbbing, the biggest fucking rocket in the history of the world. Elon's four-hundred-foot-tall glittery stainless-steel Starship, sitting atop its heavy booster, and it was utterly spectacular, the most beautiful sight Elon had ever seen, the most beautiful thing anyone had ever seen, the most perfect thing that existed in life, the universe, and everything, and the whole fucking room shook and shook and shook.

And slowly, maybe a little too slowly, maybe with a slight tilt, the great rocket began to rise. Word swept through the room that three of the thirty-three Raptor 2 engines had been purposefully shut down because they weren't healthy enough for full thrust—but still thirty was enough—yes, the great rocket began to *rise.* Lifting up on the plumes of fire and smoke, scaling the tower foot by foot, gaining speed as it gained altitude, and then it was up, right at the top of the tower, its conic nose aiming at the slightly cloudy—but still aquamarine—Texas sky.

And Elon gasped, the entire room around him filled with engineers gasped, as the rocket cleared the top of the tower and pierced that aquamarine sky, swallowed by the infinite pixels of the simulation, and then Starship was rising even higher, and faster, and higher. For twenty-seven wonderful seconds, higher and faster and higher—until someone signaled that communication had been lost. Another thirty-five magical seconds—as word spread that something had knocked out the heat shields of four more of the Raptors.

Another twenty-three world-changing seconds—until the magnificent spaceship lost thrust control.

And then, as Elon watched through the windows and on the flat-screens, there was a brief pause, and the ship began to tumble. One, two, three loops, a spiral, that goddamn word *spiral,* and the decision was made, instant, automatic.

The explosion was sudden, a burst of fire and smoke, as the flight termination system finally kicked in. And just as sudden—the room around Elon erupted in applause. To an outside observer, it might have been a jarring sight; engineers applauding, celebrating, while behind them their exploding rocket lingered on the flat-screens and across the infinitely pixelated canvas of the aquamarine sky—but Elon knew better.

Starship had cleared the launchpad and the tower. The biggest rocket in history, the most powerful rocket ever built, the rocket that would one day carry man to Mars and make the human species interplanetary, had proven itself.

He dropped back into his seat, swept up in emotion. He knew his mother and other members of his family were watching from nearby, on a viewing site overlooking the launch tower. He knew thousands—millions—of others were watching as well, in person around the Boca Chica campus, online, and even on TV. But he also knew that the audience, as large as it was, was torturously out of scale with what had just been accomplished.

Fifty years ago, the entire world would have been watching—and celebrating right along with him. There would have been ticker-tape parades and fetes in Washington, DC, and Hollywood newsreels playing in every movie theater in the country. Yes, the rocket had exploded—or, as SpaceX would describe the controlled termination in a tweet a short time later, "*Starship experienced a rapid unscheduled disassembly.*" But the incident, though slightly disappointing, was hardly unexpected.

Elon himself had publicly cautioned, on a Twitter Spaces a few days earlier: "*we get far enough away from Launchpad before something goes wrong, then I think I would consider that to be a success.*" "*Just don't blow up the Launchpad,*" he'd added, and it appeared—though the launchpad was indeed damaged, the concrete cracked and buckled by the immense heat and waves of sound that had pummeled the flattened surface for a few seconds too long—that the pad hadn't (at least entirely) blown up.

But even despite what had happened to the pad, there was no way for Elon, or his engineers, to see the launch as anything other than a success. The rocket had gotten extremely close to stage separation, the phase when the Starship itself would separate from the heavy booster to continue its journey to orbit, and the launch was always intended to end in some level of destruction. In its first flight, Starship wasn't going to gently land back on the pad. At best it was going to crash down in water, to be recovered and pored over by Elon's engineers. There was no payload, no crew, and the whole point of the launch had been to gather information, and to prove that it could be done.

There was reason for raucous, worldwide celebration. Yet, Elon would soon find out, not everyone would share the sentiment. In fact, the world's media would have a very different reaction, as evidenced by the screaming headlines that would soon dominate mass media.

AP News would breathlessly report: "**SpaceX giant rocket explodes minutes after launch from Texas.**" CNBC would shout: "**Starship rocket launches in historic test but explodes mid-flight.**" The *New York Times* would tweet: "**SpaceX's Starship rocket launched but fell short of its most ambitious goals when it** exploded minutes into its flight." The *Washington Post* would exclaim: **"Four minutes till failure: Watch SpaceX's Starship come apart in flight."** And the BBC would report: **"Musk's SpaceX big rocket explodes on test flight."**

All the headlines would be factually correct, but there were facts, and then there was the Truth. No doubt Elon had expected a fair amount of criticism surrounding the test flight; he had, after all, rescheduled the flight for 4/20 after an aborted attempt—a date that raised eyebrows, given its association with marijuana; similarly, his price offering for Twitter had been 54.20, a value even Elon had stated had been more than the stock was worth, perhaps to reference the term for the drug.

Even so, the headlines seemed unfair. The enormity of what Elon had accomplished with Starbase, the Truth of what Starbase represented for mankind, should have overwhelmed the raw facts.

Fifty years ago, they would have been celebrating in the streets.

Even six months ago, they might very well have been cheering Elon on in newsrooms across the country and around the world.

Sitting back in his white chair as the engineers applauded, perhaps Elon's jaw tightened, his eyes narrowed.

This should have been his moment. This was, after all, the Elon the world wanted, the Elon the world had formerly, nearly universally, loved. The Elon of Tesla and SpaceX, of electric cars and interplanetary dreams. The genius who made rocket ships and dug tunnels beneath cities.

But he must have known, now, since Chappelle, since the night after the gas station parking lot off the 110, since the CEO poll, to much of the world, he wasn't *that* Elon anymore.

The same day that Starbase had pierced the sky for the very first time, Elon had ordered Twitter to officially end the legacy Blue Check system across the platform—taking away the previously

vaunted check from every celebrity, journalist, politician, and notable who hadn't yet ponied up "eight dollars" for the newly revamped
Twitter Blue. In one fell swoop, Elon "leveled the playing field"—
meaning that every tweet, whether it came from a scientist who had
spent his life in a laboratory, or a history professor with multiple
degrees, or a war journalist on the front lines of some conflagration,
or a movie star, or a grizzled newsman with fifty years at the *Times*,
or a billionaire—was indistinguishable from every other tweet,
from the late-night musings of a stoned college kid to the angry,
conspiracy-laden fever dreams of a YouTube junky on his fifth
Vodka Red Bull.

Perhaps Elon had believed that the notables, the celebrities, the
journalists, and the scientists would—reluctantly? enthusiastically?—
be willing to pay for the check they'd previously gotten for free, even
though it no longer meant they were special, even though it no
longer even meant they were verified? Or perhaps he simply didn't
give a damn; it was more important that Twitter had a level playing
field—no caste system, no special treatment (other than Elon
himself).

Whatever Elon thought would happen, the notables, the celebrities, the journalists, on the whole wanted nothing to do with the
newly devalued Blue Check. In a single, remarkable move, Elon had
managed to do something quite extraordinary: he had transformed
a digital product that, by his own admission, was once so highly
coveted that people were willing to pay tens of thousands of dollars
for it in an underground market, into something so repulsive to that
same customer base that they now refused to spend even eight dollars on it.

Worse, by the end of the day, as the Blue Check became something so unwanted, so ridiculed, that notables were making sport of
anyone who'd purchased one, Elon began handing them *back* to

celebrities and notables, for *free*. At first Elon doled them out selectively, to LeBron James, Stephen King, and William Shatner, the most vocal of the new Blue Check's detractors. But then word quickly spread that Elon's Twitter was giving them back to any celebrity whose account had over a million followers.

Just as suddenly as the level playing field had begun, it had ended; the legacy Blue Check system was back in place, as arbitrary and inequitable as ever, with the added indignity that now hundreds of thousands of accounts sported checks because they were paying for them, while a rarified circle of celebs, some handpicked by Elon himself, received them for free.

This wasn't the Elon of Tesla, of SpaceX, of electric cars and giant rockets. This was the Elon of Twitter. The Elon whose ideology might have seemed sound: a Level Playing Field, Free Speech, Humanity Reaching for the Stars—but whose efforts quickly became chaotic, manipulative, reactive.

He had bought Twitter because he believed that it had been infected with some sort of "woke virus," that free speech was in danger, that without an unfettered, barely moderated global town hall, humanity would not be able to take advantage of the window of enlightenment that had opened. It was only a brief moment when human civilization could become interplanetary, and protect itself from inevitable destruction. He had bought Twitter for the same reason he had just launched a massive rocket into the sky: *to save the world.*

But Twitter wasn't SpaceX, and the Twitter platform wasn't some rocket you could toy with, tinker with, maybe blow up. Twitter was built around *people.*

Elon had tinkered with, and eventually blown up, the Blue Check system out of some notion of equity—a means by which, he'd expressed, over and over, Twitter would become the ultimate source of Truth on the internet. Yet he had spent the past few months chasing notables and news organizations off the platform, devaluing journalists who'd spent their entire careers learning their craft. Just as Elon could never have launched a rocket built by "citizen engineers," the Twitter platform would never be an ultimate source of Truth without the participation of those who had spent their lives learning how to report the news.

Similarly, Twitter would never truly be a bastion of free speech without the sort of guardrails that allowed such speech to flourish. Without someone actively shining a light into the dark corners of the internet, Twitter itself might very well become the darkest corner *on* the internet.

Elon's goal with the platform had been the exact opposite: he'd wanted to turn Twitter into a bright light in the darkness. Instead he'd dipped the platform into chaos, and the blowback had tarnished his reputation, perhaps irrevocably.

He could no longer pretend to be oblivious to the harm his takeover of Twitter had done to his image, to the world's perception of his abilities and his character. Soon he would take steps to try to salve those self-inflicted wounds. On May 12, less than a month after the Starship launch, he'd announce that he would indeed finally acquiesce to the poll he'd sent to his followers five months before; he had found a new CEO to run Twitter: Linda Yaccarino, a seasoned advertising executive who would trade her position as chairman of global advertising at NBCUniversal to take the top Twitter job.

In Elon's words, Yaccarino would "focus primarily on business operations" while Elon would continue to lead "product design & new technology," but it seemed clear that Yaccarino's true role was to be the adult in the room—someone competent and respectable, who could perhaps make advertisers comfortable enough to return to the platform, while taking some of the spotlight off Elon, shielding him from more reputational damage. She was there to resurrect Elon's persona, in much the same way Sheryl Sandberg had been brought aboard Facebook to help turn wooden Mark Zuckerberg into a real flesh-and-blood boy.

Yaccarino would have her job cut out for her, trying to rein in the mercurial billionaire while rebuilding the bridges to the advertising community that Elon had burned. There was no telling how long she would actually last, but a new CEO would only be a first step toward fixing Elon's reputation. Even the addition of famed journalist Walter Isaacson's splashy and laudatory biography, filled with anecdotes about Elon's difficult childhood, work ethic, and unvarnished successes—announced within days of Yaccarino's hiring, as if part of a multipronged PR campaign—might not be enough.

The perception that Elon had broken Twitter, and that in turn, Twitter had broken Elon, was as compelling, and likely as durable, as any "woke virus" that had ever infected a social media platform. It would take more than a new CEO or a glowing biography to fix the damage. It was going to be up to Elon himself, through his words, and his actions.

The Truth, on its own, would always be dependent on subjective forces. Elon was seeing this happen for himself, in real time: the launch of a rocket could be the most important technological advance in recent history, or it could be a massive explosion filling the Texas sky. In reality, it was both: because as Elon knew, better than anyone, the simulation wasn't rendered in black and white; it was drawn with all the colors that made up light itself.

Sitting in his chair at SpaceX, watching the last tendrils of smoke spiraling down in that Texas sky, Elon now had a choice. *Which Elon was he going to be?*

## ACKNOWLEDGMENTS

**Enormous thanks** to Beau Flynn, an extraordinary producer and friend who nudged me in the direction of this story. I'd been obsessed with Elon and Twitter separately for years, but I don't think I'd have had the guts to dive into this complex tale if it hadn't been for Beau's urging. I am also indebted to my wonderful editor, Karyn Marcus, who helped make this one of the better writing experiences of my career, and to Ben Sevier, Colin Dickerman, and Karen Kosztolnyik for shepherding this book with care and brilliance. Enormous thanks also to my amazing agents, Eric Simonoff and Matt Snyder, for having faith that I could pull this off. Thanks also to Ian Dorset, for working round the clock at breakneck speed, Jimmy Franco, Janine Perez, and the entire team at Hachette for riding with me down this rabbit hole.

A project like this lives and dies by its sources. I was fortunate to have had the help and insight of many, most of whom need to remain anonymous. I am amazed and inspired by your stories. A special thanks to Ross Gerber, who once again taught me a lot about Tesla and finance.

Most important, and as always, thank you, Tonya, my secret weapon. And Asher, Arya, Bagel, Cream Cheese, my parents, and to the memory of Bugsy—you make it all worthwhile.

## CHAPTER TWO

*"I wanted my circumstances"*: Tom Randall, Josh Eidelson, Dana Hull, and John Lippert, "Hell for Elon Musk Is a Midsize Sedan," *Bloomberg Businessweek*, July 12, 2018.

## CHAPTER THREE

*behind the wheel of one of three other vehicles*: Harsh, "Car Collection of Ousted Indian-Origin Twitter CEO Parag Agrawal," *CarBlogIndia*, November 2022.

*As he'd stated in a podcast*: "EmTech Stage: Twitter's CTO on Misinformation," *EmTech MIT* podcast, Gideon Lichfield, produced by Jemma Strong and Emma Cillekens, *MIT Technology Review*, November 18, 2020.

## CHAPTER FOUR

*As he would later explain*: Informed Conference 2022, Knight Foundation, Kara Swisher and Yoel Roth, Session 10.

*Interestingly enough, Yoel*: Ibid.

## CHAPTER FIVE

*"My strong, intuitive sense"*: TedX conference, with Chris Anderson, April 14, 2022.

**CHAPTER SEVEN**

*A twenty-by-twenty prefab*: Brittany Chang and Tim Levin, "See inside the $50,000, prefab tiny house that Elon Musk uses as a guest house in Texas," Business Insider, August 5, 2022.

**CHAPTER NINE**

*The message was from Leslie Berland*: Zoe Schiffer, Casey Newton, and Alex Heath, "Extremely Hardcore," The Verge, January 17, 2023.

*Spiro was one of the top trial lawyers*: Dan Adler, "How Alex Spiro Became Elon Musk's (and Megan Thee Stallion's and Jay-Z's) Go-to-Lawyer," *Vanity Fair*, March 6, 2023.

**CHAPTER TEN**

*Jason Calacanis: "Back of the envelope"*: Elon Musk text exhibits, Exhibit H.

*Hardwood floors culled*: Mae Rice, "Inside Twitter's Fun and Functional San Francisco Headquarters," builtinSF, February 18, 2020.

*She wasn't sure if he was still in the building*: Kate Conger, Mike Isaac, Ryan Mac, and Tiffany Hsu, "Two Weeks of Chaos: Inside Elon Musk's Takeover of Twitter," *New York Times*, November 11, 2022.

*Twenty-five percent, possibly fifty*: Erin Woo, Kaya Yurieff, and Becky Peterson, "Inside Elon Musk's Wild First Week at Twitter," The Information, November 5, 2022.

*Sean Edgett, Twitter's lead legal counsel*: Zoe Schiffer, Casey Newton, and Alex Heath, "Extremely Hardcore," The Verge, January 17, 2023, https://www.theverge.com/23551060/elon-musk-twitter-takeover-layoffs-workplace-salute-emoji.

*Jessica was only familiar*: Conger, Isaac, Mac, and Hsu, "Two Weeks of Chaos."

*As would later be reported by the Verge*: Schiffer, Newton, and Heath, "Extremely Hardcore."

*"Elon puts rockets into space"*: Alex Heath, "Elon Musk is putting Twitter at risk of billions in fines, warns company lawyer," The Verge, November 10, 2022.

## CHAPTER ELEVEN

*In fact, he'd given Robert Kaiden*: Kate Conger, Mike Isaac, Ryan Mac, and Tiffany Hsu, "Two Weeks of Chaos: Inside Elon Musk's Takeover of Twitter," *New York Times*, November 11, 2022.

## CHAPTER THIRTEEN

*"Devil's Champion-Leather Armor Set"*: Brock Colyar, "It Was a Real Wormy Halloween This Year and at Heidi Klum's Party, We All Got Haunted by Elon Musk," The Cut, November 3, 2022.

*"EVERYONE who is ANYONE is here"*: Naledi Ushe and Elise Brisco, "Bathtubs of Blood, a Giant Worm, Elon Musk: What We Saw Inside Heidi Klum's Halloween Party," *USA Today*, 11/1/2022.

## CHAPTER FOURTEEN

*over three hundred fake accounts*: Dan Milmo, "Twitter Trolls Bombard Platform after Elon Musk Takeover," *Guardian*, October 30, 2022.

## CHAPTER FIFTEEN

*Yoel would tell Kara Swisher*: Informed Conference 2022, Knight Foundation, Kara Swisher and Yoel Roth, Session 10.

## CHAPTER SIXTEEN

*"Let me be crystal clear"*: Alex Heath, "Inside Elon Musk's First Meeting with Twitter Employees," The Verge, November 10, 2022.

## CHAPTER SEVENTEEN

*Dressed entirely in black*: Zoe Schiffer, Casey Newton, and Alex Heath, "Extremely Hardcore," The Verge, January 17, 2023, https://www.theverge.com/23551060/elon-musk-twitter-takeover-layoffs-workplace-salute-emoji.

*"This isn't a right-wing takeover of Twitter"*: Ibid.

## CHAPTER EIGHTEEN

*"I think one of the things that is tricky about Elon"*: Informed Conference 2022, Knight Foundation, Kara Swisher and Yoel Roth, Session 10.

## CHAPTER NINETEEN

*"Ladies and gentlemen"*: "Elon Musk Tries to Tweet Through It after Getting Booed at Dave Chappelle Show," Salon, December 12, 2022.

## CHAPTER TWENTY

*the billionaire had dissolved Yoel's Trust and Safety Council*: A. J. McDougall, "Twitter Dissolves Its Trust & Safety Council After Founding Members Resign," Daily Beast, December 12, 2022.

## CHAPTER TWENTY-ONE

*Somewhere between nine and ten p.m.*: Drew Harwell and Taylor Lorenz, "Musk Blamed a Twitter Account for an Alleged Stalker, Police See No Link," *Washington Post*, December 18, 2022.

*The truth was*: Jack Sweeney, "Elon Musk Wanted to Buy My ElonJet Twitter Account—I've Named My Price," *Newsweek*, November 3, 2022.

*"It's impossible to square"*: Rebecca Kern, "Musk Reinstates Majority of Suspended Journalist Accounts," *Politico*, December 17, 2022.

## CHAPTER TWENTY-THREE

*Nearby stood the CEO*: Pete Syme, "Elon Musk was photographed with the CEO of Qatar's sovereign wealth fund hours before asking followers if he should quit as Twitter boss," Business Insider, December 21, 2022.

*A few seats over from Jared*: Sanya Jain, "Elon Musk with Lakshmi Mittal in Viral Pic from FIFA World Cup Final," MoneyControl, December 20, 2022.

## CHAPTER TWENTY-FIVE

*but many of Twitter's big-name clients*: Nicole Farley, "Advertisers Slow to Return to Twitter despite Musk's Claims," Search Engine Land, April 14, 2023.

*Even more surprising, the message*: Zoe Schiffer and Casey Newton, "Yes, Elon Musk Created a Special System for Showing You All His Tweets First," The Verge, February 14, 2023.

## CHAPTER TWENTY-SIX

*However, a Slack employee*: Casey Newton and Zoe Schiffer, "New Cracks Emerge in Elon Musk's Twitter," Platformer, February 23, 2023.

*These two firings came on top of the firing*: Zoe Schiffer and Casey Newton, "Elon Musk Fires a top Twitter Engineer over His Declining View Count," Platformer, February 9, 2023.

# INDEX